ON THE GRID

Other Books by Scott Huler

A Little Bit Sideways: One Week Inside a Nascar Winston Cup Race Team

On Being Brown: What It Means to Be a Cleveland Browns Fan

Defining the Wind: The Beaufort Scale and How a 19th-Century Admiral Turned Science into Poetry

No Man's Lands: One Man's Odyssey Through The Odyssey

ON THE GRID

A Plot of Land,
an Average Neighborhood,
and the Systems That
Make Our World Work

SCOTT HULER

RODALE

First published in hardcover by Rodale Inc. in 2010
This paperback edition published in 2011

Book design by Christina Gaugler

The Library of Congress has cataloged the hardcover edition as follows:

Huler, Scott.
   On the grid : a plot of land, an average neighborhood, and the systems that make our world work / Scott Huler.
      p.   cm.
   Includes bibliographical references and index.
   ISBN-13 978–1–60529–647–0   hardcover
   ISBN-10 1–60529–647–3   hardcover
   1. Infrastructure (Economics)—United States.   I. Title.
HC110.C3.H85   2010
363.60973—dc22   2010007835

ISBN-13 978–1–60961–138–5   paperback

Distributed to the trade by Macmillan

2   4   6   8   10   9   7   5   3   1   paperback

We inspire and enable people to improve their lives and the world around them.
rodalebooks.com

For June

CONTENTS

INTRODUCTION

Raleigh versus the Garbage Disposal

To MODERN SUBURBANITES, DROUGHT CAN SEEM LIKE THE MOST SURREAL of weather events. All other severe weather—cold, wind, snow, rain—affects your life immediately and profoundly. If streets are flooded, you can't drive; in bitter cold, you stay indoors and run your heater all day; in a high wind you can expect power failures and days in the yard with a chain saw.

But in a drought, there's still water everywhere. Turn on your faucet, even if it hasn't rained for 2 months, and you get a nice cup of cool, drinkable water. Run the dishwasher and the dishes come out sparkling clean. Flush the toilet, run the clothes washer, take a shower, clean your spectacles with soap and hot water if they get dirty: Life goes on pretty much as before, back when it used to rain.

So when the people managing the water suddenly stop using words like "shortage" and "conservation" and start saying "mandatory water restrictions," you sit up and take notice. That happened to us in Raleigh, North Carolina, during a recent drought, when officials warned that our drinking water might run out. We noticed. We also ended up doing some rather odd things, but that's getting ahead of the story. First, Raleigh, and water.

IF YOU WANT TO SEE EXAMPLES OF virtually every demographic challenge facing the United States, come to Raleigh. As one corner of an explosively growing region called the Research Triangle, Raleigh functions as something of a national object lesson. All those people leaving the Northeast and Midwest for the Sun Belt? They're landing right here in Raleigh. All those miles of roads being built to forestall traffic jams? Raleigh is building them. Those strip shopping centers filled with big box retailers that function for a decade or so and then wither and die, replaced 5 miles farther out with the same center, only newer? That's Raleigh. New development going up without a clear sense of who's going to pay for the sewers, the roads, the schools—and whether there will be, say, enough water for the new folks to drink? Welcome to Raleigh.

It's hard to say exactly what Raleigh's got, but it's got something. Call that something quality of life, but don't try to define it. It might mean public schools where most kids aren't flashing gang signs, at least not yet; it might mean plenty of nice ball fields and museums; it might mean free parking, and plenty of it. At any rate, in recent years Raleigh (along with the entire Research Triangle area) has often been declared the best place to live in the United States: For instance, *Money* magazine ranked it number one in 1994 and cable network MSNBC said the same thing in 2008. The Wake County Web site provides a long list of such accolades. Virtually every list of best places to live, to work, to start a business, to find a mate, to be young, to retire, to use technology, to buy real estate— they all include Raleigh. *US News and World Report* even rated its airport among the 10 least miserable.

So people come. A sleepy southern state capital founded in 1792 whose population didn't reach 100,000 until the mid-1960s, Raleigh thereafter profited from the regional Research Triangle Park science and technology business campus, which has created 40,000 jobs over the last 50 years. Raleigh exploded in growth: Its population now approaches 400,000. In 2008 the Raleigh metropolitan area was the fastest-growing metropolitan area in the country, its population growing by 4.3 percent per year, a full half-percent faster than its closest rival, Austin, Texas. Wake County, Raleigh's home, is the second-fastest-growing county, by percentage, in the nation—it added almost 40,000 citizens in 2007, a growth rate of 4.9 percent, raising the county's total population above 800,000 people. Percentages aside, by numbers alone Wake was still the country's seventh-fastest-growing county. With more than 15,000 of those new residents in 2007, Raleigh itself was the country's 13th-fastest-growing city. What's been happening in America over the last half-century is Raleigh.

And it's not just people: Amid tangles of wires and roads and pipes and cables, Raleigh is not so much growing as metastasizing, flinging asphalt and aluminum in every direction like something from a science-fiction movie. Even if we don't notice it, that support structure—infrastructure—is everywhere and affects everything we do. Since 1950, Raleigh has grown in population by a factor of six, and through annexation it has grown in size from 11 square miles to 140. How many miles of new sewer pipe has Raleigh planted? How many miles of road have Raleigh and the state transportation department laid? How many cherry pickers have rumbled down how many streets to string how many miles of cable? And where have I been while all this has happened?

WELL, I'VE BEEN IN RALEIGH, WHERE I LIVE—happily enough, mind you—and I've been watching this mind-spinning expansion since 1992. And surely, the questions Raleigh and places like it raise for planners are vital: Whither public transportation? What of downtown? How long will our bridges hold up, our roads contain our traffic? Can we continue driving like this, using resources like this, buying like this? Everyone from Al Gore to Dick Cheney has an answer.

While those questions are vital, I'm more interested in minutiae. I keep wondering why the structure doesn't collapse—how the whole thing works as well as it does, which you have to admit is incredibly well. With those miles of electrical wires and sewer pipes, those new roads and cable lines and cell phone towers going up so fast you can't even keep track, why doesn't the system completely fail more often? Every time you flip a light switch, on come the lights; if the lights go out during a thunderstorm, you can expect to see a truck with a rotating yellow light on the top within a couple of hours. Want some cool, clear water? Just turn on the tap—there it is, 24-7-365, as much as you like. Hungry? You can drive on safe, passable roads for less than 5 miles to at least half a dozen markets, open 24 hours, that have not just everything you want but such an abundance of it that if you're alone in one of them late at night it can almost make you cry. At my television, computer, or telephone I can press a few buttons or keys and see anything, talk to anyone, on the planet.

And as for the waste all this living generates? Just flush your toilet, roll out the trash cans once a week, throw the plastic bottles in the recycling bin, and don't think another thing about it. You may sit in a traffic jam while a road is being widened or repaved, but that's probably about as inconvenient as your life will get if you live here. It's unbelievable—if you'd told someone at Raleigh's founding that scarcely 200 years later we'd be living this Jetsonian life, he'd have laughed at you.

Of course, most of us don't know anybody who knows how any of it works. It's background stuff—*infra* means "below," and a good bit of this "below-structure" actually runs below ground, out of sight, or above our heads in skinny little wires we don't notice anymore; what isn't out of sight remains out of mind—until it fails. When it does, most of us can do little but whimper, hoping somebody will come along and fix it, like Harry Tuttle, the dashing freelance heating engineer in the movie *Brazil*, who rappels in wearing a headlamp and a balaclava, magically connects a few wires or ducts, then leaps off with a salute and a glint in his eye. More likely, we fear we'll run into the plumbers from that movie, with or without a form 27B/6. If we think about infrastructure at all, we think of it as an impossible tangle of things we can't understand. The only other time we see infrastructure is when monsters destroy it—Godzilla tossing around elevated trains in Tokyo or the 50-foot woman straddling a freeway here in the United States. You just don't appreciate your electricity until the giant woman throws down the transmission tower.

AND THEN WE ALMOST RAN OUT OF WATER. During a recent drought, things started looking extremely scary. Our reservoir had diminished to about 30 percent of capacity—a few months' worth, and then we'd be out. After many months of denial we were finally letting our flowers die and wondering how life would feel if we ended up getting our water from emergency tanker trucks. Leaves shriveled; lawns browned; streams trickled and then vanished entirely. For a few months convenience stopped seeming so certain. We talked about restrictions and rationing and gallons per person per day. We turned off the shower while we soaped; we dry shaved; if it was yellow, we let it mellow.

And water was far from Raleigh's only problem.

Subdivisions were sprawling north of downtown and swallowing tiny nearby farm towns, transmogrifying them into suburbs, turning local streets into choked feeder roads. A decade-long foray into planning for a regional rail system finally collapsed in 2006, leaving an underfunded bus system as a Raleigh resident's only alternative to adding yet another car to those jammed streets and highways. Interstate 40, the main route connecting Raleigh to its sister city, Durham, 25 miles away, and to Research Triangle Park midway between them, had served more cars than it was designed for almost since the day it opened in 1988. Overuse had necessitated frequent onerous repaving projects, including one in 2007 that was costing the state $27 million to repave 10 miles it had just spent 2 years repaving. About a third of the state's highway bridges were considered deficient or obsolete. The construction of the buildings that would house, educate, and employ the tide of new residents was sending a steady stream of murky runoff tinged with the red clay of Piedmont soil into every local stream and river, joining with oil, antifreeze, and fertilizer to kill wildlife and destroy habitat.

By far the most important problem, of course, was that drought—the worst drought in Raleigh's recorded history. After several years of below-normal rainfall and sometimes none at all for weeks on end, by early 2008 Raleigh was parched. Falls Lake, an impoundment dammed in 1981 that supplies Raleigh's burgeoning population with water, was 10 feet below its normal depth—a significant diminution for a lake whose average depth is about 12 feet. The 15 billion gallons of water usually allocated for drinking water had been reduced to about 4.5 billion. Raleigh's supply of drinking water would be gone in only a few more months.

Crumbling roadways. Little public transportation. Questionable highway bridges. Strangling streams. And, of course, a real crisis: We were running out of water. Into the maelstrom of those staggering problems, Raleigh's city council strode boldly forward in March 2008 and took action.

It banned garbage disposals.

THAT'S NOT AS CRAZY AS IT SOUNDS. The city had in the previous 2 years faced 99 sewer overflows caused by grease clogs, including one that geysered up through the street with such force that it created a hole large enough to swallow a car. Backed-up sewage is a messy problem not only for home owners, but also for the creeks and streams it pollutes. The North Carolina Division of Water Quality was threatening to fine the city for backups of more than 1,000 gallons. And to be sure, the garbage disposal strongly encourages people to put down the sink not only grease, but also all kinds of waste the sewage system is not designed to handle: "Nothing more solid than toilet paper," one official told me when I asked about it later. "We're just going to have to fish it back out at the treatment plant. Do you really think that piece of carrot is going to biodegrade in the 18 hours it takes it to get to the treatment plant?" So it's a fair point: We probably ought to consider doing without garbage disposals. But people quibbled about the suddenness of the action.

In fact, the city went mad. Petitions were circulated, physically and electronically. People spouted in rage about a council that had waited months to ban car washing as the reservoir drained and then suddenly announced a complete ban on new garbage disposals (and a fine of $25,000 per day for scofflaws). The phrase "They can have my garbage disposal when they pry it from my cold, dead fingers" appeared on Web sites. After weeks of bitter and very public debate, the council, perhaps fearing open rebellion, backed down. Raleighans to this day can wash their leftovers down the magic hole and flip the switch.

And it eventually started raining, so people calmed down about water, too.

BUT THE QUESTIONS REMAINED. Consider all those systems that serve our lives of convenience. The garbage disposal affects four of them— each one negatively. Running water while it grinds? A waste of treated freshwater, which, as Raleigh recently learned, is neither free nor limitless. Same thing for the electricity used to run it: It's not much, but it's not necessary, either. Then there's the wastewater stream, which obviously would run smoother without grease and ground-up food waste.

Finally there's the diversion of that solid food waste, which in the best case could be composted and otherwise would at least be in the landfill, drawing the bacteria that help break down other waste faster. Add in the stormwater system and drainage streams that are fouled by the sewage overflows created by those grease clogs, and you're up to five central infrastructure systems negatively affected. You could say the garbage disposal is a lose-lose-lose-lose-lose proposition.

But you didn't need to wait for the garbage disposal debate if you wanted to hear about infrastructure. The March 29, 2008, City & State section of the Raleigh *News & Observer* had five stories on its front page, of which four dealt with infrastructure issues: one about the difficulty of crossing one of Raleigh's main streets without getting killed; one about impact fees that the city was considering levying on new development so it could afford the roads, pipes, and wires needed to support that new development; and two on solid waste (one about new trash trucks that require fewer employees but break down a lot, the other about a routine fire inspection in an industrial park that uncovered almost a million pounds of sodium hydrosulfite, which under the wrong circumstances could have endangered or killed everyone within a couple of heavily populated miles).

We're surrounded by wires and pipes and utility poles and earthen dams and pumping stations and cell phone towers that demand our attention, time after time, but only briefly. Mostly, we ignore them. As science historian James Burke said in the 1978 documentary television series *Connections,* "Never have so many understood so little about so much." Michael Barker, of the Council of State Planning Agencies, put it more succinctly in the 1981 debate-setting publication *America in Ruins:* "The public paid scant attention to public works. . . . The man in the street was quite content to leave the matter to government, so long as the government provided the street."

And then a line touches a tree in Ohio in 2003 and the entire Northeast goes dark. For 2 weeks every newsroom and cocktail party buzzes with people standing in circles nodding sagely, saying to one another, "Infrastructure! Infrastructure!" Articles and television specials come out about "the grid," whatever that is, but then something happens to

Donald Trump and the story trails off. Or Katrina comes and the levees fail and for a week we all shriek about dams and dikes and water management, but that's far away, and we're above sea level here, and the conversation rumbles into the distance like thunder, even though 6 months later gasoline prices are still through the roof. Or the bridge collapses in Minneapolis and the cars fall into the river, and the next day your local news shows film of a frowning engineer wearing a hard hat staring at a local highway overpass, arms folded, solemnly shaking his head. Then it's the playoffs or a sitcom finale and, like a baby when car keys jingle, we lose focus once again.

But the infrastructure doesn't lose focus for a minute. The pipes carry water to your faucet every time you turn it on; the wires pour current into your light sockets even in the middle of the night; the roads get us where we need to go. Cables pump signals into our houses; towers fling them through the air or zap them to satellites. I decided it was time to pay attention: I wanted to know how all this stuff works.

THE GOOD NEWS IS, IT WORKS SO WELL that we notice a failure within minutes, and if something does go wrong, we know about it and we complain and somebody fixes it. The bad news is, it may not work much longer. If you're just too cheerful, go to the Web site of the American Society of Civil Engineers and check the page about the Report Card for America's Infrastructure, where you'll find some scary factoids: 27 percent of the country's bridges are obsolete or deficient; the federal government funds less than 10 percent of our clean water needs; you can plan to spend 46 hours a year stuck in traffic—meaning actually motionless—helping to waste 5.7 billion gallons of gas.

And that's just the public works portion of our infrastructure—what about the electrical grid and what might fuel it (and what might happen if we all get electric cars), or the gas pipelines, or the cables, or the thousands of cell phone towers that have already popped up like mushrooms after a spring rain?

And then we elect a new president who talks about putting our effort and our money into revitalizing our infrastructure and sponsors an $850 billion stimulus package containing lots and lots of infrastructure stuff—and we all sort of nod our heads, except the thing is that most of us don't know exactly how any of this infrastructure works.

SO I DECIDED TO FIGURE THAT OUT. We all hear about enormous projects like Boston's Big Dig, which widened and buried the Central Artery highway to reconnect parts of the city torn asunder by highway bridges, and New York's Tunnel No. 3, the new aqueduct under construction since 1970 and not scheduled for completion until 2020. We may even be familiar with other big undertakings: The New Narrows Bridge in Tacoma, Washington, which replaced the overtaxed bridge that had itself replaced the Tacoma Narrows Bridge that famously oscillated and collapsed in a 1940 windstorm. The New Orleans levees. The Bay Bridge in California, whose deck collapsed in the 1989 earthquake but has now been earthquake-proofed—probably.

But that's all the high-profile stuff, the stuff you see on the news. That stuff relates to your neighborhood infrastructure in the same way the *Sports Illustrated* swimsuit issue relates to the women in your PTA. The special case is sexy and fascinating, but we do much better when we spend less time fantasizing about the special case and more time learning to appreciate what's right around us.

So that's where I started. I stood in my own backyard and looked around. There, on the back corner of the house, a bunch of wires came in and brought me electricity. If I started there and made my way back to the nuclear plant 20 miles away, what would I find along the way? Not 15 feet from the electrical wires a pipe popped up from the ground, bringing me natural gas for my heat. Where it came from, though, I had no earthly idea. Stormwater rolled off my yard in two directions and went . . . somewhere, by some mysterious means; what might happen if I waited for a rain and followed it? Same thing with the pipes that brought my freshwater and took away my wastewater. Where would tracing them take me? Who figured out how to bring water into houses, anyhow, and how to so effectively get rid of it when we're done with it? Who decides how big a reservoir needs to be to quench the city's thirst, and how do we make sure it's clean enough to actually drink? Who drank it before us, and who'll drink it next? My street has no sidewalk on my side. How did that happen and, come to think of it, how did we decide to make the street its current width?

The American Society of Civil Engineers estimated in 2008 that the United States needed to invest $2.2 trillion over the next 5 years to save America's infrastructure, an unimaginable number to fix what seemed like unimaginably mysterious systems—and a number that, by the time you read this, will surely be laughably dated. Billions of dollars, trillions of dollars—frankly, none of this reaches me. But those electrical wires that come to my house? That gas pipe? The guy who drives the truck that takes away my trash once a week? If I wanted to understand all this infrastructure talk, my own yard seemed like the place to start.

So I started asking questions.

CHAPTER 1

THE LAY OF THE LAND

A surveyor's total station looks something like a movie camera. A rotating lens set in a tough yellow metal housing sits about head high atop a firm, heavy tripod. It measures exact distances by bouncing an infrared signal off a reflector on a pole; it also measures angles to an accuracy of a second or so (less than $\frac{1}{1,000,000}$ of a circle). A total station showed up at my house one day in the company of Sherrill Styers, a cheerful, slow-moving surveyor in a broad-brimmed hat, T-shirt, and pants held up by suspenders. I'd invited him over because I figured the place to begin understanding how infrastructure got to my property was on my property itself—the ground *infra* which all those *structures* lay. Surveying occupies itself with knowing exactly where you are, in all three dimensions. Sewer pipes need to be pitched at just the right slope; a backhoe swipe in the wrong spot can darken dozens of homes and disconnect hundreds of people from the Internet; almost any infrastructure project involves right of way, and nobody wants the city to have an inch more than it deserves. You have to know exactly where you are.

"People don't realize that when they see new roads going in," Styers said. "Before the bulldozers know where to cut or fill, they need surveyors to tell them where and how much." Styers talked as he set up to find my property's corners. He first used a metal detector to find what my deed calls an "existing iron pipe" at the front corner of my yard and dug a little hole to expose the metal bar. Then he set up the station above it, using spirit levels and hairline sights in the machine to orient directly above the center of that old iron bar, sunk there probably 90 years before.

While I held the reflector, he took sightings to the corner of my house, the other property corner along the street, and the back corners of my property. Surveying, he explained, is trigonometry: You take extreme care to measure the length of a line, then you take sightings to a distant point from each end, measuring angles. "Then you've gotten your angle-side-angle," Styers said. "You can use the law of sines to calculate, and that's your distance." You use the calculated lengths as the bases of further triangles, in order to measure more angles and calculate more lengths.

Styers practices what he calls cadastral surveying, but is also called metes and bounds surveying: The surveyor starts at one corner monument and describes a trip around the property border, giving measurements (metes) from one landmark to another (bounds). Those landmarks tend to be monuments left by other surveyors: An old survey of my yard starts "at an existing iron pipe" and also mentions "an axle," which, like the pipe, was still right where it was supposed to be, a solid iron rod sticking a good foot out of the ground. "That looks like it could be from...a buggy, maybe," Styers said, opining that in 1918, when my property was platted, cars were taking over and buggy axles may have been losing value. Then he decided it might have been from a Model T. Either way, he liked it—it wasn't going anywhere, and it told you in no uncertain terms that you were at the corner of my backyard. Good, solid surveyor values.

A modern total station measures distances itself, though if the surveyor can't sight directly along a line (if, say, a tree is in the way), he or she has to use the same triangulation method surveyors have been using for centuries. Some stations even use Global Positioning System (GPS), but, as Styers comments almost dismissively, "your GPS equipment doesn't work too well beneath tree canopy." Google Earth can swoop in on your house, those latitude and longitude tickers spinning dramatically along, state and county borders of pale yellow and blue appearing and disappearing until you get that final view from the sky, shockingly clear, of T-shirts stopped midflap on your clothesline; that's very nice. But if you run into trouble with your neighbor about whose fence is on whose land, the courts will want to know about the piece of iron pipe some surveyor sank to mark your property corner 100 years ago, not what a GPS device says. "There are a lot of precedents set in court," another surveyor told me. "I'll give you an example: If your deed says you have a boundary of 200 feet, and it's from the oak tree to the maple tree, and when you measure it it turns out to be only 190 feet, it's still gonna be the oak tree and the maple tree. Regardless of what technology you use."

Or more simply: "What you *buy* is represented by your deed," Styers told me, peering along my property line at a privet hedge inconveniently growing directly on the boundary. "What you *own* is what a surveyor took a transit and a chain and went out there and sunk monuments in your property corners." Transit? Chain? Monuments? There's so much to learn.

START WITH A SURVEYOR JOKE: What does a surveyor say upon seeing Mount Rushmore? Answer: "Well, there's three surveyors, but who's that other guy?" That other guy is Teddy Roosevelt, the only one of the big four who never made his living surveying. The point being that surveying used to be a great way to get your life started: All you needed was a chain (a chain was $\frac{1}{80th}$ of a mile: 66 feet long, 100 links per chain, made of metal), a compass and transit (or some other instrument for accurately measuring angles between objects; the total station is the modern version), and a strong back. After that it was all hiking and trigonometry, and you could make a fine living in a growing country by pacing and setting the boundaries of the land constantly being bought, sold, settled, and connected. In fact, it was one of the true growth industries in a new nation whose greatest resource was almost limitless land.

Talk to a real estate agent or developer for a while and sooner or later he or she will say, "They're not making any more land." But that cliché has become true only in the last century or so. Until then, though new land wasn't being created, new land was constantly being explored, mapped, and usually, in recent centuries, seized from its occupants and made available to European settlers. In fact, the United States was from the outset, and in many ways continues to be to this day, fundamentally a great big land development scheme. "After the Revolutionary War, the United States was poor in everything but land, so real estate development became the chief source of entrepreneurship," Witold Rybczynski wrote in *Last Harvest*. This applies to Raleigh as much as anywhere, and perhaps a good deal more so, as I learned when I went looking for the history of that little quarter acre on which my particular node on the infrastructure grid stands.

RALEIGH'S STATE CAPITOL SITS AT THE TOP OF A SLIGHT RISE in the terrain, surrounded by a gridwork of streets, largely because an enterprising settler named Joel Lane appears to have gotten some commissioners from the brand-new state of North Carolina drunk enough to buy his property. It's a long story, plausibly true, and beloved by Raleighans. After the Revolution, legislators of the new state needed to plant their capital somewhere that would offend neither the coastal cities in the east nor the Appalachian settlers in the west. The great middle of the state was largely unsettled; Wake County, in 1792, still lacked a town of any description. The local Tuscarora Indians never had a settlement here, and even the European farmers working their way west seem to have found little here of interest: Of the 1,000 acres Lane eventually sold to the state, three-quarters were virgin forest.

With six sites under consideration, including several on the Neuse River, the commissioners remained deadlocked until they spent a night at the home of Lane, who allegedly served them a mixture of bourbon, sugar, and cherries called Cherry Bounce. The next morning the commissioners voted to buy Lane's 1,000 acres, which were several miles from the Neuse. Raleighans like to point out that their town sits where no town ought to be and that land development schemes can thus be said to be in Raleigh's DNA.

A surveyor laid out the town, basing the design on William Penn's for Philadelphia, with five squares arranged like the five-spot side on a die. The central square would hold the statehouse, the other four other state buildings or parkland. The main streets leading away from the middle of the center square along the chief compass points were designed to be 99 feet wide—exactly 1½ surveyor's chains—for easy construction; all other streets were 66 feet wide—a single chain—which was even easier.

At that point my lot, on a ridge a couple of miles north of town, was likely oak-hickory forest, a naturalist has told me. But actually, the history of my lot starts long before that. Past is prologue: You have to look underneath, down to the bedrock. All those New York City skyscrapers rest secure because they're on the solid granite base of the island of Manhattan; those Oakland bridges fell down during the Loma Prieta earthquake because of the Jell-O soil they were built on; New Orleans floods because it's below sea level, and its continuing sinkage profoundly stresses those fragile levees. As geologist Kenny Gay told me in explaining what's beneath my lot in Raleigh, "Every little hill has reason and meaning. It's not random. Geology is a fundamental science, because everything else is derived from the geology."

About 500 million years ago, the ancient ocean Iapetus, situated between the proto–North American, European, and African landmasses, began closing up. The resulting squeeze did more than create the mountain range that eventually became the Appalachians. More important for my quarter of an acre, it took the sediments that had built up on the floor of that ocean and metamorphosed them into gneiss, a sparkling, gray, striated bedrock. The dirt on my lot turns out to be from a soil series called Cecil, the famous southern red clay. "The gneiss, when it decomposes, creates that classic sticky, red, stain-everything clay," Gay said. Granite, on the other hand, which forms the bedrock east of Raleigh, decomposes into a much sandier soil. Feldspars, common in granite, turn into a small-grained clay that the wind blows away, leaving behind a nice, sandy soil composed of quartz. It's great for growing cotton and tobacco, and you can still easily find both of those crops growing not 10 miles east of my house.

It's different to the west. "Not much wants to grow in that," Gay tells me. "So people plant grass—grass is one of the only things that grows." In fact, the red-clay land west of Raleigh was considered so valueless that for years it lay empty. When the Research Triangle Park developers showed up, they finally found something that would grow there: buildings. This was nothing Joel Lane hadn't known a couple of hundred years before. My lot was finally platted after World War I, when Raleigh still had fewer than 25,000 people, and the neighborhood was built mostly after World War II, at which point Raleigh annexed the neighborhood, sticky red clay or no. And new development remains a constant, turning the red clay of Wake County to civilization at the rate of close to 30 acres a day. I went out to see how the surveyors tell the bulldozers where to go.

RON VANDERHOOF TURNS HIS RED PICKUP off Yates Store Road and we begin driving backward in time. To be sure, along Yates Store we had drifted from finished houses to houses on dirt lots to empty lots, even passing one odd vista where paved streets wound among nothing but a forest of new Victorian-style streetlights, firm and thin like saplings in an orchard. But turn onto the unlabeled streets of phase three of the Amberly development (Amberly Three), and layers rapidly peel away. The pickup slows to a crawl as we leave asphalt and begin driving on gravel: subgrade, in the language of contractors.

The subgrade is unpaved but nonetheless bordered by concrete curb—there are machines now that squeeze out that concrete curb like toothpaste from a tube. Everywhere you look, the bones of the infrastructure stick out of the ground: metal boxes that protect connections to the electrical system; capped cylinders full of wires to connect telephone and cable lines; PVC pipes that reach down into the earth, grasping for sewer or water pipes. Drive a little farther and the subgrade vanishes, the road turning to red clay. Only the corners have curbs, and here and there a manhole cover is planted in the dirt; the storm and sanitary sewer lines are laid before the road is. And everywhere, waving from tall stakes in the ground, are gay little tape flags of bright red, blue, lime green—different subcontractors marking the spots where different elements of infrastructure will go.

If you want your water meter at the corner of a lot, not under the driveway, you'd better know exactly where you're digging. Same thing for hookups to the storm drain or sewer system: The difference between water moving in the right direction and the wrong direction is the difference between a basement and a swimming pool. Vanderhoof points out two stakes by a pile of 5-foot-diameter concrete pipe segments: the site of a future sewer manhole. The two stakes mark a straight line perpendicular to the center line of the road. "Each stake is marked with the distance to the center line," Vanderhoof explains—one is 25 feet, the other 35 feet—so workers have two measurements to make sure they find the right spot to start digging. It's a neat technique: simple, exact, and redundant. Vanderhoof smiles. He works for C. C. Mangum, the contractor preparing the site for the hundreds of houses that will be built there. His company grades the land, lays the roads, and buries the pipes and wires. Mangum is an infrastructure company, Vanderhoof is an infrastructure guy, and exactness is where he lives: He is Mangum's chief surveyor. So when he says 25 feet to the center line of the road, he means 25 feet, not 24 feet, $11^{15}/_{16}$ inches.

But the stakes are not really what we have driven out here to see; in fact, we came to see the opposite. We drive even farther, to the end of the road, where bulldozers and graders trundle over fresh earth, gears grinding and signals beeping, and Vanderhoof points out what we do not see.

"You don't see a single stake." He waves an arm to indicate the entire section, a dozen acres at least. "See? All this right here—this was done with GPS. We've built some jobs where the only survey stakes we used were for sanitary and storm sewers—all the rest was GPS." That is, instead of driving bulldozers along earth marked with surveyors' stakes—and occasionally knocking them over, then having to wait while a surveyor drives out to the site, sets up equipment, and resets stakes—the bulldozer drivers take their orders from the sky. "Before, when we used to mass grade a site like this, we'd have to go out there and grid it, and we'd stake it. Then they'd go out there and level, and then we'd have to go out and stake again. Now, with GPS, we don't do any grid staking whatever."

Vanderhoof points out a 10-foot vertical pole on the blade of a bull-dozer, with a receiver on the top about the size of a dinner plate. This is a GPS receiver, which gets information from GPS satellites and compares it to a plan loaded into a machine on the bulldozer's dashboard (which is also in communication with a base station on the site sending wireless updates). He hoists himself up onto the track of the yellow bulldozer and ushers me into the driver's seat so I can see the guidance machine, about the size of a pocket DVD player, which offers several screen views, very much like a computerized driving game.

"Like a video game," Vanderhoof agrees. "Just a little bumpier." He shows me a bird's-eye view, with contour lines, and a side view that shows the dozer as a simple yellow line drawing with the grade of the land in green. The best view—and the one he says a driver is most likely to use when doing street grading—is the simple windshield view, which he flicks up. A red ruler runs along the sides, showing that the machine is now sitting 4.5 feet above its final grade. "Red means cut," he says, "so you know you got some digging to do."

Actually, not me. But by the time the driver has done several rough grading passes, Vanderhoof says, I almost could: At that point, all the driver does is steer. "Once he gets close to grade, there's an automatic switch. Then it adjusts the blade by itself." The bulldozer, shaping the earth according to the designs of engineers and surveyors and planners, orients itself to satellites thousands of miles away and does the final, inch-by-inch grading itself. "We have an alarm that will flash on the screen if you are getting out of tolerance. I think we have it set at $\frac{2}{10}$ of a foot"—that is, less than 3 inches. If that's not enough, there's a system called Millimeter GPS made by a company called Topcon. "We can measure to the nearest millimeter today," he says, then grins and admits, "Actually, our forefathers could too." On a computer, Vanderhoof demonstrates the plans for Amberly Three in a TIN (triangulated irregular network) model, in which the computer does to a two-dimensional drawing what surveyors do to the earth: It represents dimensions—the slope of a culvert, the plane of a street—with triangles, ending up with a representation that looks something like a crystallized stick-figure version of the site, with different elements expressed in red, blue, and purple. "These are called 3-D face lines," he says, blanking out a layer. "That was a sewer line I just turned off."

Vanderhoof can tilt the file, zoom and pan, view it in almost any way he likes. But the value of the file is not what he can see, but what the Topcon FC-200 can see. The FC-200 is a yellow machine that I also saw mounted on the GPS-equipped bulldozer, and it takes its direction from a base station mounted on a 30-foot pole at the site. The base station can broadcast 1,500 feet, so multiple dozers can be working all over the site at once.

Although a bulldozer driver can manipulate his screen view to choose the line he needs to follow and just follow it, he's still got to check and make sure his blade is calibrated, because a few millimeters of wear on the blade would change everything: "We'll set up benchmarks for the dozer operators to check into; there's a place on the screen they can adjust for wear." The file has to be localized to the site, as well. "If you just go with strict GPS coming out of the sky, it may or may not be on the same coordinate system the engineer used—more and more surveyors are using the State Plane [Coordinate] System," which translates coordinates into a state-specific system.

Older surveys, Vanderhoof points out, used simpler landmarks. Coordinate "Beginning at a pine…thence…North 30 degrees west 400 poles to a pine, thence west 200 poles to a Red Oak…thence to the first station," reads a survey completed in August 1778 that I found in the North Carolina State Archives when I went looking for the original grant to the piece of land that now contains my house. Such a cadastral survey is used less as a way of globally understanding landscape than of resolving property disputes. Viewing the earth as an enormous jigsaw puzzle, cadastral surveying is used to make sure each piece of property fits with the ones bordering it. Even the US Bureau of Land Management notes on its Web site that cadastral surveys certainly use scientific methods and precise measurements, but, like Vanderhoof and Styers, it points out that cadastral surveys "are based upon law and not upon science."

BUT SCIENCE IS NEVER FAR AWAY. There's a tiny diner close to my house that I used to walk to for breakfast. On the way, I passed a 3-inch metal disk sunk into the concrete sidewalk: REDSKINS, it says, and N.C. GEODETIC SURVEY HORIZONTAL CONTROL 1988, all stamped into the medallion around a little triangle with a dot at the exact center about the size of a pen point. I always wondered what this meant.

I got my answers from Gary Thompson, director of the North Carolina Geodetic Survey. Similar monuments of brass and steel line his windowsills the way cacti do in other offices. More than 1.5 million of those disks dot the American landscape—they're the global equivalents of the pipe and axle in my yard.

Geodesy is the science of understanding the size and shape of the earth. For centuries geodesists have been making increasingly accurate measurements of the earth. They take into consideration elements that affect measurement, such as the difference between a spherical reality and its representation on a flat map, but also such variables as changes in the earth's magnetic field and fluctuations in gravitation as a result of variations in the mass and density of the earth. The disks are the marks they leave as reference points when they've taken measurements. Each of the little circular brass monuments has either a cross or one of those triangles in the middle for accuracy (surveyors would consider the 3-inch brass disk itself laughably inaccurate) as well as a name and a date. Some identify themselves as horizontal controls, others as vertical benchmarks, but all share that simple metal-disk design.

These monuments are part of an enterprise that started in 1807, when Thomas Jefferson convinced the US Congress to earmark $50,000 to establish the nation's first scientific department, the Survey of the Coast. Trade was essential to the growth of the new nation, and since accurate sea charts would improve in the meantime shipping, Jefferson committed the federal government to provide the information for those charts. Surveying techniques have improved in the meantime, but the goals of the federal surveyors have never changed: to map the country as it grows, and to make its information available to whoever needed it. "We're not a regulatory agency," Thompson told me. "We're a service agency."

The first survey monument was placed in New Jersey in 1817. It was called WEASEL, probably after local fauna; monuments are commonly named after some local landmark, though nobody has been able to explain the REDSKINS of my local monument. North Carolina got its first monument in 1848, when surveyors laid down the Bodie Island Baseline on Bodie Island in the Outer Banks, one of several triangulation starting points along the coast from New York to Louisiana. With excruciating care, surveyors used metal rods (four to the chain) to measure a line 6.7367 miles long, then started triangulating their way inland, noting existing landmarks and leaving new ones such as piled stones, notched trees, or stone blocks.

North Carolina had been the subject of surveys long before the US government got involved. The first book about the region, *A New Voyage to Carolina,* published in 1701, was written by John Lawson, a surveyor sent by the owners of the eight original land grants to the state issued by King Charles II of England. Lawson's book described a land thickly populated by Indians, mostly Tuscarora. Lawson didn't take the kind of detailed survey that would enable us to follow the transfer of specific pieces of land—he did little more than take latitude readings from star sightings—but his book paints a picture of central North Carolina when Europeans arrived, describing clear, rocky rivers, long trading paths, rolling countryside, and, at least initially, cooperative natives.

The eight absentee landowners who had employed Lawson didn't make good use of the information he sent back, and their organizing and granting land to settlers was catastrophic: They never visited their holdings, the same land was sometimes granted to several people, surveys were not always taken, and few records were kept. The system became such a mess that in 1729, they sold much of the land back to the English king.

So it's no surprise that clear surveys were a requirement of the new nation, or that with so much land, surveying kept so many notables busy. In fact, even before Jefferson started the Survey of the Coast, the Land Ordinance of 1785 undertook to lay a square grid on the territory west of the original colonies that had been won in the Revolutionary War. The system was simple: The entire continent was divided along due north-south and east-west boundaries into townships of 6 miles square, each of which was further divided into 36 sections measuring 1 square mile, or 640 acres (surveyors were to be paid $2 a surveyed mile, "including the wages of chain carriers, markers, and every other expense attending the same"). A quarter section would be 160 acres, and the more manageable quarter quarter, thus, 40 acres: "The back 40"? "Forty acres and a mule"? All such terms originated with the Land Ordinance of 1785. In any case, if you wonder why all the square states out west are square, that's why.

A measure of that same logical organization was brought to all states with the adoption of the State Plane Coordinate System in the 1930s by the Survey of the Coast's successor, the US Coast and Geodetic Survey. It breaks some larger states into zones (North Carolina is a single zone; Texas has four), with the goal of providing for each zone an accurate map that accurately expresses, like a Mercator projection, a curved land surface on a flat map—accurate, that is, to within 1 part in 10,000. Each state zone has its own system, and surveyors use that system on any project entirely within that zone, though not on projects that cross state lines. The starting point for each state plane is placed south of the state's southernmost point and west of its westernmost point, so all points on State Plane Coordinate surveys are expressed as north and east of that point—REDSKINS, for example, is 747999.58 feet north and 2111450.92 feet east of the North Carolina starting point in western Georgia.

BUT OF COURSE WHAT HAS ROCKETED SURVEYING into the future is GPS. Surveyors have been looking to the skies to fix positions on earth since the dawn of time, so it's fitting that the most accurate system ever developed for finding your position involved placing our own objects in the skies.

GPS was created in the 1960s, when the US Navy wanted a way to keep track of its submarines and submarine-based missiles. Funding issues nearly killed it in Congress, but in 1983, when Korean Air Lines Flight 007 strayed into Soviet airspace and was shot down, President Ronald Reagan pledged to make GPS operational and the technology available to civilians, reasoning that with access to nascent GPS technology, KAL 007 never would have lost its way. "We started using [GPS] here in 1988," Thompson says, when there were only eight satellites and his receivers had a 3-hour window per day to get positions. By 1993, the US Air Force had put up the 24th satellite, providing the almost unimaginable service of, as a US government Web site puts it, "accurate location and time information for an unlimited number of people in all weather, day and night, anywhere in the world." As long as you're not under a tree.

"All those satellites are is more of those monuments," Thompson says, "except they're moving." Each satellite broadcasts a signal more or less constantly, identifying itself, the time it broadcast the signal, and its position. The GPS receiver calculates its position by comparing the time it takes four of those signals to reach it.

"But the time delay is the least accurate way to measure," Thompson says. "We as surveyors use a different technique." Surveying-quality GPS receivers don't focus on the time information in the signal—instead they decode information in the signal wave. They correct for conditions in the ionosphere and the troposphere—the highest and lowest layers, respectively, of the earth's atmosphere—and for how much water is in the atmosphere. Such Continuously Operating Reference Stations (CORSs) are placed throughout the country, each one sampling satellite signals every 30 seconds or less (of the 65 in North Carolina, all but 2 sample every second). On his desktop computer, Thompson brings up the Web site of a station near Asheville, which includes photographs both from and of the receiver. This receiver looks like a small paper plate on a post mounted on a state Department of Transportation building.

The average dashboard GPS is something of a blunt instrument—it's interested in which intersection you're approaching and doesn't need to be much more accurate than that. But with some software manipulation of that phase-shift data, Thompson says, "we take a tool that people use to navigate to keep 'em on the main road and we can measure up to 2 millimeters."

Surveyors aren't the only ones finding GPS remarkably useful. Thompson smiles. "Scientists that measure plate movement use these systems now." Then he brings up a screen of the Real Time Kinematic (RTK) network, which shows what he calls "active GPS base stations"—stations that constantly keep in touch both with the GPS satellites and also with local machines. Green triangles flash and jitter across his screen, each one representing an active system—it could be one of those bulldozers; it could be a farmer's tractor (a computer maps the yield of a field, so the GPS-connected tractor automatically drops extra fertilizer where yield is low); in a mountain state it could be a snowplow (they use active systems to stay on the road). He shrugs—there's a new application every day.

Thompson and his counterparts in geodetic survey departments nationwide are still setting monuments, both physical and electronic, in places where there's likely to be new development, where a county develops a new flood map, or where the geodesists haven't been for a while. "Where are the surveyors going to be working?" he asks. That's where they go. And together all those data points, the more than 1.5 million monuments and the information about them, all the discrete points of horizontal and vertical data, going back in some cases as far as the original 1817 surveys, have coalesced into what is called the National Spatial Reference System—what David Doyle of the National Geodetic Survey (NGS) has called "arguably the most sophisticated surveying data base in the world."

And those data are available, for free, to whoever needs it. "Other agencies use our data all the time—especially the Department of Transportation," Thompson says. And above all, he notes, "This is the foundation for all these GIS systems."

Oh yes, geographic information systems—if GPS is the infrastructure of the infrastructure, GIS is its graphic designer. A GIS takes the survey data that organizations like Thompson's provide and mixes them with data provided by others, like streets departments, water and sewer departments, utility companies—and those data themselves are commonly based on the geodetic survey data.

Lenny Wallace, GIS technician for the Raleigh Information Technology department generates maps for city and county departments and members of the public, flashing layers of geographic information on and off his computer screen with the touch of a key: streets, fire hydrants, building footprints, sewer lines, utility poles, traffic lights. It's breathtaking and rather lovely: You can obtain a map of your neighborhood showing, say, valves in the water system, plus traffic lights, plus water meters—whatever you want, colored and labeled however you want it. It's magnificent, but it can seem like just more computer magic. What's the point?

"The point," says Colleen Sharpe, GIS manager for the city of Raleigh, "is the information attached to it." That is, it's fine to be able to plot fire hydrants. But if you tie that map to a database showing when each one was installed, last exercised, last painted, last used by the fire department, reported broken, scheduled for replacement—then you've got information that might do you some good, whether to plan the day of a crew turning hydrants on and off or to requisition parts for aging hydrants. "You're trying to give yourself the answers to questions you're going to ask in the future," a GIS person in the Public Utilities Department told me later.

"The first example of a GIS," Sharpe quotes an old teacher, "was the map drawn by the doctor in London of the cholera outbreak." "The doctor" is infrastructure hero John Snow, who, during an 1854 cholera outbreak in a London neighborhood, drew a map showing houses that had cholera cases as black squares and public water pumps as black dots. The black squares clustered around a single dot established that the outbreak was centered on one pump, providing the first clear evidence that cholera was transmitted by contaminated water. "All GIS is," says Sharpe, "is taking data and maps and trying to make sense of it. It's nice to have dots and lines and polygons. But it's the power of the information behind it that *tells* you something."

Thompson's geodetic surveys are crucial to Raleigh's GIS. "The monuments that Gary lays out there are the basis for the mapping that we do," Sharpe says. Every year, Raleigh pays for planes to crisscross the city, taking digital orthographic photos that show buildings from directly above. A house would be shown only as a rectangle of roof, a manhole as a little circle, and so forth. "Surveyors [went out] last week to put big white panels in the shape of a V, pointing at monuments," she explains. Then, after the planes have taken their orthographic photographs with the white Vs in place, the digital images are matched to their exact coordinates in Thompson's geodetic survey maps. When through plan review or observation Raleigh's GIS department learns of a new object on the street—"our threshold is 10 feet by 10 feet"—Sharpe sends employees out to locate it and they add it to the map. When a new subdivision is built or a house gets a new porch, the finished survey makes it back to her office and into the data. And every year there are new orthographic photos, so the data never go out of date.

"And that is the basis of all our mapping."

It's staggeringly accurate. If you bring up the planimetric layer on one of Lenny Wallace's maps—that's the orthographic view, showing only the horizontal outlines of features, such as the rectangle of that house—and gray it to 30 or 40 percent so you can see through it, the representations of buildings fit perfectly over photographs of buildings. "Our horizontal accuracy for spot elevations is within plus or minus 6 inches," Sharpe says. "We hear from surveyors all the time about how accurate our stuff is."

Every city department takes advantage of GIS. Sharpe mentions the Stormwater Management Division as one example: "All $15 million of their budget is based on our mapping—their fee is based on what's pervious and impervious," and that information, based on the orthographic photos, is available for each piece of property in the city. During the drought, Sharpe's maps showed water use failing to diminish in certain neighborhoods despite repeated warnings. It turned out these were Hispanic neighborhoods, and the city solved the problem by issuing Spanish-language warnings. The GIS system tells when a pipe has been replaced, a road resurfaced, a hydrant painted—and based on that, departments determine what to maintain, pave, paint.

North Carolina, like most states, operates cooperative centers called ULOCO—utility locators, or "call before you dig" lines. Before any street digging or repair is begun, Raleigh's ULOCO center contacts each utility, which consults its GIS and sends someone out to spray paint its locations on the surface. The American Public Works Association has adopted a color code: Blue shows where water lines are; green traces sewers and drains; red marks buried electrical conduits; orange shows communications cables. Yellow is for gas, and purple is for reclaimed water, irrigation, and the like. White lines show the proposed excavation, ensuring that each utility representative knows where to check, and temporary surveying marks are drawn in pink. All this explains the multicolor hieroglyphics you sometimes see surrounding manholes or cracks in the road.

Like Thompson, Sharpe emphasizes that the information is all free to the public. When the city originally tried to charge for data, she successfully lobbied the other way: Apart from the fact that the data help drive the development that keeps the region churning, she was falling behind in her own work because her employees spent too much time gatekeeping. With data available on the Web for citizens and for downloading by to engineers, surveyors, and developers, she keeps her staff busy making and updating maps.

Sharpe never loses track of the difference between a map and reality. She loves the complaints she gets when a surveyor finds one of her maps off by a few inches. Her maps aren't supposed to be a substitute for even a survey, much less for reality. She smiles and shakes her head. "The only way to *know* what is on the earth is to go out there and look at it."

THERE'S SO MUCH INFORMATION OUT THERE—not just on but literally out there, zinging its way through the atmosphere at enormous sampling rates. From satellites; from CORS stations shouting, "Talk to me! Talk to me! I'm here! I'm here!" every second, like a bird in a perennial dawn; from personal GPS systems keeping track of you as you walk across a parking lot from your car to the restaurant at lunchtime and from RTK units talking to multiple machines sculpting the earth at a frantic pace. And it's certainly nice to know that my house is at latitude 35 degrees, 48 minutes, 22.14 seconds north and longitude 78 degrees, 37 minutes, 53.75 seconds west (if you prefer degree-decimal coordinates, that's N35.80615, W78.631597; if you prefer the North Carolina State Plane Coordinate System numbers, it's north 228154.783 meters, east 642896.111 meters), but to be honest, all those numbers do is raise questions. They're nice and exact, but…is that the front of the house or the back? What if I take two steps to the left?

Maybe I just fell under Sherrill Styers's spell, but as amazing as GPS and RTK are, I ended up finding something deeply satisfying about that axle in my backyard, which raises no such questions. It's a big, solid piece of iron sticking out of the ground, and it's been there for almost a century. The surveyor who first staked out my lot put it there, and every surveyor since who's needed to map my lot has stopped by to check it out. It stays where it belongs and admits of no interpretation: There it is, and there it stays. It overtly admits what the surveyors know and the courts uphold: This is real out here. This is actual land, real estate, not just numbers: It physically exists, and after all your satellites and your information and your calculations, as Colleen Sharpe told me, you still have to stand on a piece of land if you want to really know what's there.

When information overload takes charge—when I lose track of a complex concept, when a computer crashes, when some Internet site thousands of miles away boggles my mind—I go out to visit that axle. It stands gracefully, rusting near the grave of one of our cats, a tangle of old torn wire fence, and a couple of maples that survived my last assault with a chain saw to keep the jungle back. It wears a nice pink ribbon, courtesy of Sherrill Styers, and it seems almost to stand sentinel over the yard. It's at pretty much the high point of the yard, which slopes very gently downward in two directions, to the south and the west. Sometimes I go there when it rains and stand beneath the maples, watching as the water saturates the ground and then streams downhill. It takes thousands of dollars' worth of equipment for a surveyor to keep track of that axle, and millions of dollars' worth of equipment to keep track of all its tribe all over the world, forever and constantly plotted on X, Y, and Z axes. But the rain is free, and it seems to know where to go.

CHAPTER 2

THE PIG AND THE CRAB

Unshorting the Circuit in the Hydrologic Cycle

THE MOST ASTONISHING THING Robert Kirkpatrick pointed out when he visited my house is something I had not noticed in 16 years of living on my street: There are no storm drains. I'm embarrassed not to have noticed this, but it's what Kirkpatrick sees—he's a stormwater guy, and his job is noticing where water flows in the city.

Wearing a neatly trimmed beard and a blue work shirt with a Raleigh Stormwater Division raindrop logo on the breast, Kirkpatrick seemed the model of the cheerful civic engineer. Sitting at my dining room table and flipping through maps of my house and neighborhood, Kirkpatrick showed me where a drop of rainwater that fell on my lot would go. To meet the requirements of the Clean Water Act, the city has been undertaking a complete inventory of its stormwater system and putting the information on the Internet. With the help of this online data, Kirkpatrick taught me some fundamental facts about stormwater and its infrastructure.

First, he pointed out that the city doesn't construct storm sewers: Developers do that, taking steps to manage the water of their finished property as they build, whether through underground pipes, surface swales, or channels leading water to natural ditches and streams, all according to constantly changing Raleigh plans and codes. The main rule, which goes back through English common law all the way to Roman law, is that anybody downhill from you is responsible for the water that flows onto their property—as long as you don't increase the volume or intensity of the water. (The Roman laws of the Twelve Tables, from the 5th century BC, mention that you're on the hook if your stormwater does damage to your neighbor because you somehow diverted it.) That is, since pretty much the dawn of civilization, rule one about stormwater is: "Your problem, buddy."

IN AREAS THAT ARE NOT INDUSTRIALLY DEVELOPED, it's mostly nobody's problem. Stormwater is part of what water managers call the hydrologic cycle: Water from the ocean, rivers, and lakes evaporates into the air, where it collects in clouds, then falls as rain and either is absorbed and eventually exhaled by plant life (in a process called evapotranspiration) or percolates into the ground (in a process called infiltration) to charge streams or fill deep underground aquifers. In undeveloped areas, roughly half of the rainwater infiltrates (one-quarter stays shallow and becomes groundwater, and one-quarter continues down into aquifers); another 40 percent is absorbed and evaporated in evapotranspiration. Only about 10 percent runs off on the surface, finding its way into the natural gullies and creeks (whose base flows are fed by infiltrated groundwater) that small-scale development leave alone. From there it makes its way into larger creeks, then into rivers and streams, and on to the ocean. Where streets are unpaved, water either soaks directly into the streets or is diverted into roadside ditches, from where it follows the same path as other surface water, to gullies and creeks and on to the ocean.

As places urbanize, though, they create impervious surfaces: buildings, compacted soils, walkways, roads, and parking lots. And impervious surfaces change everything. Retired US Geological Survey (USGS) hydrologist Ralph Heath of Raleigh gave me a brief lesson in hydrology, and of all the materials he presented to me none was more startling than a table showing how much water the ground can absorb. The table discussed the properties of the sandy loam soil of the Cecil series, a common soil type in the North Carolina Piedmont that happens to be the type of soil in my yard.

In undisturbed forest, 12.4 inches of rain per hour can fall before you get runoff. That is, if the worst hurricane Raleigh has ever experienced

(Hurricane Fran, in 1996, dropped 10 inches of rain over 12 hours or so) dumped all its rain in an hour, the land in an undisturbed forest wouldn't even puddle. (And that's not all absorption by the land, mind you—a good portion is absorbed by trees and never hits the ground; plenty more is absorbed by the foot or so of leaf litter that covers the ground in undisturbed forest.) But if you turn that forest into farmland for a while, then let the forest in reclaim it—which describes every inch of Raleigh that is currently forested—then the compacted soil can absorb only 1.9 inches per hour, a sixth of its natural rate. The best lawn in town, with the least-compacted soil, might absorb half an inch of rain in an hour, diminished to about $\frac{1}{24}$th of its original rate. Which means an awful lot of the water on a rainy day doesn't percolate into the soil—it runs off. And then there are the impervious surfaces that make up 18 percent of Raleigh's land, according to Raleigh planning documents: These absorb exactly nothing, running off every drop.

Knowing how bad impervious surfaces are for water absorption, I expected Kirkpatrick to be pleased by my gravel driveway. "Sorry," he said, smiling: Raleigh's surface surveys classify gravel driveways, atop hard-packed red clay, as impervious. He pointed out that half of my gravel had collected in a pile at the base of the driveway, where rainwater had washed it before continuing its journey along the gutter of my street. Of course, runoff is essential: Kris Bass, an extension associate in the department of biological and agricultural engineering at North Carolina State University, points out that of the infrastructure needed to support a human community, the first priority is drainage. Before worrying about roads or a communications, even before doing anything more complex with drinking water than going to the river with a bucket, you have the job of making your life livable—keeping your feet dry, and your bed, and your stuff. Food, clothing, and shelter are your basic needs, and shelter means keeping the rain off. Wet ground rots food, dismantles structures, impedes movement, breeds disease. "Ever since the beginning," Bass said, "every engineered structure, be it a castle or a road or some sort of a building, is based on its interaction with water." Or as another stormwater engineer I spoke with said, "You ought to title this chapter 'Never Buy a House at the Bottom of a

Hill.'" Actually, several stormwater experts told me that.

Some years ago, when a plumber abandoned his post during our bathroom addition, our contractor resisted completing the installation of the shower. The plumbing and the fiberglass walls had been installed, but not the door, and our contractor didn't want to take responsibility for any part of the construction that involved water. So I asked his assistant for hints as I prepared to install the glass walls and door myself. He told me to remember that water always wants to go down, and that you have to learn to work with it: "You have to learn to think like water."

So as I looked at the roots of Raleigh's infrastructure, I tried to think like water.

THAT FLOW OF WATER DOWN MY DRIVEWAY AND DOWN MY STREET perfectly symbolizes the problems with stormwater. The automobile requires smooth surfaces—paved streets and parking lots. A suburb with quarter-acre lots, like mine, averages nearly 40 percent impervious surfaces; the shopping centers all of us suburbanites drive to average more than 90 percent. Standing water on those surfaces makes them unusable, to say nothing of breeding insects and other vermin. So we run that water off into what stormwater-management types call the curb-and-gutter system, which both solves the problem and instantly creates a new one. It solves the problem by channeling water into pipes below the streets, keeping the streets clear for traffic. Unfortunately, it does this so effectively that the gathered water shoots from their outfalls as if from firehoses, turning natural drainage ditches into torrential flood streams that are scoured deeper with every rainstorm. That is, traditional curb-and-gutter development takes stormwaters that would have been absorbed into the ground and become part of the local groundwater (taking anywhere from months to centuries to make its way to the ocean) and shoots it into streams where it makes its way to the ocean within weeks.

And we're talking about a lot of water. An average rainy day might drop half an inch on Raleigh's 140 square miles, which equals 163 million cubic feet of water, or 1.2 billion gallons. That's almost the same amount of water that goes over Niagara Falls in an hour. And instead of percolating into the soil, most of that water now shoots down gutters, cascades into catch basins, jets from outfalls into defenseless creek basins, and races to the ocean. Kris Bass calls it "a short circuit in the hydrologic cycle"—and just as a short circuit prevents electricity from doing the work it's supposed to do (light a light, run a toaster), the hydrological short circuit prevents stormwater from doing its job of recharging streams, watering vegetation, and filling aquifers. I have heard the modern suburb called a machine for turning rainwater into garbage.

My first lesson about the hydrologic cycle came from Kirkpatrick, who surveyed my backyard and explained sheet flow, which is the way the water makes its way across my muddy backyard when it rains and the soil becomes saturated—it doesn't find a channel, it just flows as a sort of film. Then he introduced me to my neighborhood swale, the lowish, grassy route the water follows behind my neighbors' houses as it makes its way down to Georgetown Road, where it hits a gutter and turns left, downhill, joining the flow from the front of the houses—and also the flow from my front yard, which has gone down my driveway and street and turned downhill into that Georgetown gutter. At the bottom of a hill it finally hits a storm catch basin, through which it drains into a 15-inch pipe to cross beneath the street, then joins a series of 30- and 36-inch pipes that run underground for a half-mile or so into the Pigeon House Branch, a filthy, silty, ruined stream that comes from downtown, then coils around Capital Boulevard, an ugly divided highway between lines of warehouses that is Raleigh's gateway to the north. I don't know that I had genuinely expected some atmospheric underground tableau out of *Les Misérables* or *The Phantom of the Opera*, but a half-mile of buried pipes dumping water into an eroded ravine filled with floating 20-ounce soda bottles, sagging grocery bags flapping on every snag, didn't seem like my definition of infrastructure.

WELCOME TO THE STORMWATER UNIVERSE. Kirkpatrick's first map, showing his surveys, did not represent *the* Raleigh stormwater system: There isn't just one. There are about 20—you or I would probably call them watersheds, but the map calls them drainage basins. A basin boundary is the line where a drop of water on one side would trickle into one basin and a drop of water on the other side would trickle into the other. My house sits at the very top of the Pigeon House Branch drainage basin. If you stand at the very northeast corner of my lot, its highest point, you might find a spot where water will run down the hill across the street and directly into the Crabtree Creek, another of Raleigh's 20 basins; from everywhere else on my property, it goes into the Pigeon House, which drains about 4½ square miles, then itself eventually pours into the Crabtree. The Crabtree, along with its tributaries, drains about 140 square miles; it makes its way to the Neuse River, a few miles east of downtown Raleigh, which is our main watershed (newer storm drains are stamped with a picture of a fish and the directive "No Dumping! Drains to Neuse River!"). The Neuse drains 6,235 square miles of North Carolina before emptying into the Pamlico Sound and the Atlantic.

The stormwater system doesn't run anything like the water or sanitary sewer systems, where at some point, beginning or end, there is an enormous centralized facility for managing the massive volume of water. Stormwater management is distributed: The goal is to take something that's spread out, like rain, and get it out of the way without concentrating it any more than you absolutely must.

So it has always been. According to sewer historian Jon Schladweiler, the earliest storm drains we know of were created in a place called Mohenjo Daro, a city of some 30,000 people in the Indus River valley, in modern Pakistan, more than 4,000 years ago. "They had a problem," Schladweiler says. "When storms came, water wasn't draining out of town very well." In the standing water, the soil composing their earthen buildings dissolved, so every couple of generations they'd have to rebuild the city atop the wreckage of the collapsed last version: "The English translation [of Mohenjo Daro] is 'city of the dead' or 'mound of the dead," Schladweiler says. By 2500 BC, "they came up with the idea of rectangular channels, open on top, lined on three sides with cut stone or masonry" that ran along the streets. Of course, Schladweiler notes, "On day one, that facility was a storm sewer, but on day two it was a combined system," washing away the human waste that people threw into the streets as well. The people of Mohenjo Daro soon began running channels from their houses directly to the street drains (channels ran from kitchens, bathing rooms, and indoor latrines), and before long they covered the sluices with flat stones. The world had its first enclosed combined sewer system.

But hardly the last. All roads may lead to Rome, but what got Rome started was what led away from it. The Forum, one of the greatest public meeting places in the history of the world, is set in the low area surrounded by Rome's seven hills. The ancient historian Livy tells us that sometime in the early 6th century BC, the Etruscan king Lucius Tarquinius Priscus started to drain the swampy place that indigenous Etruscan tribes used for occasional meetings. Tarquinius probably just channelized the creek that ran there, helping to keep its flow within its banks and to make its way to the Tiber, but that's what got things started. A century or two later the creek was covered, and by the first century BC, when the geographer Strabo described the resulting tunnel, he said it was wide enough to drive a haywagon through. Meet the Cloaca Maxima: the great big sewer. It's still there—the enormous brick arch of its outlet stands on the east bank of the Tiber, just south of the Ponte Palatino.

THE OUTLET OF MY NEIGHBORHOOD'S STORM SEWER at the Pigeon House Branch is nowhere near as charming, though it does emerge near a low bridge where a main road crosses the Pigeon House. The creek pools beneath the road, and with long grasses growing around it, after a rain sluices it out somewhat, the pool can be rather pleasant. Most days, though, not so much: From the postapocalyptic kudzu-covered slope between some train tracks and warehouses, a 30-inch concrete pipe empties into sluggish feeder stream that seems to barely move. Deep pools of opaque, greenish blue water join the clearer Pigeon House as it trickles over some bare rocks—probably the gneiss that lies below most of western Raleigh. Flecks of feldspar glint in the sun as the water burbles along little channels it has worn. Because sanitary sewer lines use gravity to do most of their work, ductile iron pipes from those lines naturally crisscross stormwater drainages—they're both just trying to find the most effective way down. Here along the Pigeon House, one of those iron pipes makes an effective little dam, creating the wide pool just downstream from the granite, the water gently cascading over the pipe before it goes under the road.

This brings up an important advantage Raleigh has in its stormwater infrastructure over many older and larger cities. Traditional stormwater management—from Mohenjo Daro and Rome through Paris and London to New York and Philadelphia—routes stormwater and sewage into the same vast underground culverts. This made perfect sense before people understood the link between sewage and disease, starting in the mid–19th century. Until then, management of both stormwater and sewage followed a simple plan: Get it out of here fast and send it somewhere far away. Because the sewers needed to be large enough to handle the volume of water from a daylong rainstorm as well as the regular, steady flow of sewage, this led to those enormous *Phantom of the Opera* sewers.

By the time Raleigh was big enough to be installing sewers and building stormwater pipes in the late 19th century, city governments had figured out not only that large, combined sewer systems were expensive and required a lot of cleaning and maintenance, but also that separate systems enabled cities to more easily manage the final destination of sanitary sewage. So in the late 19th century Raleigh, just like Buffalo, San Diego, Omaha, and other cities, created a separate sewage system. To handle stormwater, instead of building a vast underground network of man-made caverns, Raleigh mostly did nothing more than leave its natural drainage ways open. The State Capitol is built atop a small hill at the borders of three of those drainage basins—Pigeon House Branch, Walnut Creek, and Rocky Branch—so water flows away from it on all sides. The original square mile of downtown has been served from the start by those drainages.

Even the people in the city stormwater department couldn't tell me when they had first channeled the water into underground pipes; the first city planning maps, made in 1922, already show a mile or so of storm drainage pipes. The best guess of project engineer Mark Senior was "somewhere around when cars showed up. Until then, everybody built on high ground and farmed the low ground, and everything was copacetic. Then land got to be worth more and someone figured out, 'I can put the creek in a pipe and build right on top of it.'"

Which started all the trouble.

ONE OF RALEIGH'S TREASURED "REVENGE OF THE ENVIRONMENT" TALES involves the Crabtree Valley Mall, plonked right down in the floodplain of Crabtree Creek, whose average flow of about 50 cubic feet per second can leap nearly to 10,000 during heavy rainstorms. When the creek rises up and floods the mall, which it does every now and then—most recently in 2006—Raleighans (though presumably not merchants) enjoy the irony of the namesake creek reclaiming its turf. What people don't remember is that creeks have been doing that since Raleigh has been building shopping centers. My own little Pigeon House creek, upstream from me, tells a tale.

Cameron Village, Raleigh's first shopping center and one of the first in the Southeast, opened in 1949. It had dozens of stores and nice, big parking lots, which had been built directly on top of the trickling source of the Pigeon House Branch. The stream had simply been piped and buried and then, joined by runoff from the shopping center, it now emerged a few hundred yards downstream.

Things immediately went downhill for the Pigeon House. By March 1949, before the center had even officially opened, a story in the *News and Observer* described the Pigeon House downstream from the center as "rambunctious" and discussed plans for "reforming" it; water from the cleared land was causing flash flooding after every rain. John F. Danielson of the public works committee had a simple solution: They could dredge the creek to make it deeper, and they could take out some of the curves. In addition, they had already planned to build walls to channelize it. Mr. Danielson probably went to bed happy that night—he had solved a problem.

Stormwater engineers now spend almost all their time unsolving it—or anyhow solving the new problems caused by solutions like that. Stream restructuring—straightening, deepening, and channelizing to move the water out as quickly as possible—is the partner of the curb-

and-gutter development model in destroying natural waterways, according to Kris Bass of North Carolina State. Those pipes, designed to take the water as fast as possible from the streets to the streams, bring much more energy to the stream than nature prepared it for, so the water scours out the bed of the stream: "We have made these pipes that are like rifles or double-barreled shotguns, shooting into our rivers, and we have turned the rivers into these perfectly straight raceways."

A river's usual channel, hydrologists say, is expected to carry the water of only, say, a 1- or 2-year storm—a storm small enough that you'll see one that size every couple years. The bigger 5-year, 10-year, 50-year storms? The river is supposed to overflow its banks and expand into its floodplain. Then that extra water slowly infiltrates the surrounding earth, evaporates, and recedes back into the channel, fertilizing the banks as it goes. That's natural, and in the absence of large-scale development, that's what a river does.

Then come malls and shopping centers in the floodplain, plus those curbs and gutters, increasing the flow—and the energy of the flow—into the streams, at the exact same time that land is growing more valuable, causing people to start building closer to riverbanks. Along most of the length of the Pigeon House, parking lots back right up to the steep banks. More impervious surfaces means greater runoff, more pollution, and more energy being sent into streams; channelized and straightened streams means faster flow, at least at first, and so faster buildup at dams and clog points; and development in flood plains means there's no place for that backed-up water to go except into those neighborhoods. What happens in local creeks is just a smaller example of what happens in giant rivers: Channelize the Mississippi and what do you get? A good outcome for the people along the channel, but worse flooding downstream. Then more development and channelization upstream eventually lead to flooding no matter what you do. As long as you let the river, large or small, behave like a river—overflow its banks every couple of years into its natural floodplain—things are just fine. "It wasn't a problem," Senior said about Raleigh's little drainage creeks, "until they built stuff in the floodplain." Words to live by.

The groundbreaking federal Clean Water Act of 1972 wasn't much concerned with stormwater, targeting instead what engineers call point sources of pollution: sewage treatment plant outflows and industrial sources. Now more than half of water pollution comes from nonpoint sources, especially runoff. In 1987 Congress updated the act to address nonpoint-source pollution like stormwater—and it even redefined the collected stormwater that jetted from the outflows of urban storm drains as point-source pollutants, raising the standards for its cleanliness. Since 1987, engineers have been working to undo a large part of a century of stormwater management.

WHEN I FOLLOWED THE PIGEON HOUSE DOWNSTREAM from that roadside pool, I got an object lesson in why Congress had to expand the Clean Water Act so it applied to stormwater. It was a tour of watercourse torture techniques.

Once the Pigeon House crosses the road, the course narrows to go through a small half-pipe culvert beneath a railroad bridge, so the stream swells into a pool about 20 feet across. For a good 6 feet up the steep banks, the kudzu was covered with silt, showing how high the water had risen during the last rain. Soda bottles, Styrofoam cups, and plastic bags were strewn everywhere; a shopping cart was mostly submerged in the main part of the pool. Just the same, I saw shadows of palm-size fish: The Pigeon House even here was not dead. A stand of bamboo forced me away from the stream up onto the railroad embankment, after which I picked my way along beneath a highway bridge, where mattresses, graffiti, and bags of clothing gave evidence of homeless residents. Down a slope, between a couple of warehouses, and I was back in a gully lined with riprap, rejoining the mighty Pigeon House as it followed Capital Boulevard—that is, as the boulevard followed the creek, a vale between two ridges. With its sides sometimes channelized with riprap, sometimes simply left to collapse, and spindly birches leaning across the stream as their banks gave way beneath them, the Pigeon House still tried to maintain a degree of dignity as a river, though parking lots and the lanes of the highway were never more than 15 feet or so from its banks. Between the clean-looking

Milner Inn and the less-clean-looking Foxy Lady strip club I found a little log bridge crossing the Pigeon House's 20-foot width—from there, with the sun filtering through the leaves of the trees on its crumbling banks, the little creek felt almost like an amenity; certainly, a pleasant place for a motel guest to enjoy a cup of coffee. The water below fairly swarmed with those little fish; on another visit I actually saw a heron there.

Just the same, the Pigeon House was fighting a losing battle. Capital Boulevard came within feet of it on one side, and parking lots did the same on the other. At the Flea Market Mall, on the eastern side of the vale as it starts to rise, a parking lot big enough for hundreds of cars tilts toward the creek. The asphalt ends directly at the bank, where the water simply shoots out of pipes directly into the creek, eroding the banks and bearing a full burden of brake dust and motor oil and antifreeze. By the time I had followed the creek for 2 miles, I had stopped calling it the Pigeon House: Just as Raleighans regularly shorten the name of Crabtree Creek, Raleigh's main northern drainage, which accepts the waters of the Pigeon House, to the Crab, I looked at the banks of the Pigeon House and shortened it to the Pig.

And those were the nice miles. The Pig makes a hard right away from Capital Boulevard, thence running behind a line of stores, its banks "stabilized" by boulders, hunks of curb-and-gutter, pieces of asphalt, sections of mortared brick wall—construction debris, which was, I was later told, bargain riprap, back in the day. Tires, HVAC vents, and coin-operated newspaper boxes spread out on the flat banks; antifreeze jugs and those omnipresent juice, water, and soda bottles nestled among the roots of the trees that hung over the water in various stage of slow-motion collapse.

Shortly before the Pig reaches the Crabtree in a swampy park, it receives water from a final pipe, a 30-inch outfall that drains a last few sloping neighborhood acres of runoff rich in pet waste, fertilizer, and fluids dripped from Dumpsters and cars. The water from that pipe, with no riprap in sight, has dug a narrow trench for itself a good 10 feet deep that winds to meet the Pig within 100 feet of its junction with the Crab, slightly clearer water joining water that is slightly browner. From there, unless the water level is extremely low, you can follow the Crabtree in a kayak to where it joins the Neuse River a few miles downstream. The two join at a lovely park called Anderson Point, and standing on the point where the rivers join even carries a sense of moment: Here's the Neuse, our major river, such as it is, a few miles east of downtown; here's the city's stormwater runoff, coming to meet it (Walnut Creek, which drains the southern part of Raleigh, joins in less than a mile farther downstream). Together, the three don't quite make 500 cubic feet per second, 1 percent of Niagara Falls, but they never run dry, and you could drop in a canoe there and reach the ocean.

And that's how my stormwater gets where it's going, combined with chemicals and grit from roads, pet waste, and silty runoff from construction sites, and often separated from asphalt by not even a strip of grass, much less the floodplain the stream needs.

"THAT'S BASICALLY WHY I HAVE A JOB," Kris Bass told me of the 1987 Clean Water Act update. The updated act authorized the Environmental Protection Agency to implement National Pollutant Discharge Elimination System (NPDES) regulations, which by the mid-1990s had filtered their way through state and county offices to the city of Raleigh, and in 2003 the Stormwater Management Division was a part of Raleigh Public Works. (It gets its money by assessing taxes according to property owners' percentages of impermeable surfaces, estimates based on the GIS maps made by Colleen Sharpe.) The federal regulations require larger cities not only to document their stormwater systems and find ways to adhere to the new guidelines, but also to educate their citizens on current best-management practices for stormwater. "We use this as a sort of education project," Bass said as he walked me along a manicured trail beside the meandering, pleasantly forested Rocky Branch, a stream in south Raleigh that he and his colleagues have almost completely restored. "This just used to be a grand canyon," he said—it had been dug out, straightened, and channelized, left by development as an arrow-straight ditch between two straggly little rows of trees. "We came in and filled the ravine back in, put in stormwater wetlands, and kind of started over."

Starting over starts long before the stream. The most important new approach to stormwater management involves making a complete about-face from traditional practices. Instead of getting the water to go somewhere else, engineers now do everything they can to keep the water where it is. Bass points out a garden area in front of a new building on the North Carolina State University research campus near the Rocky Branch. It looks like a shallow garden with spindly, weedy-looking plants surrounded by sandy mulch, but it has a lot more going on. "This is a bioretention area," he says. Pipes from the building and surrounding pavement bring water into the area, where it ponds up to about a foot deep. The leggy vegetation is wetland plants that flourish under those conditions. Beneath the plants is a layer of sand that filters the water as it trickles into the earth; 4 feet down, there's a drain that eventually channels away the water that makes it down that far. The water drains away over a few days, before it can breed mosquitoes, and the pond is designed to absorb 1½ inches of rain—well above Raleigh's ordinary rainfall. Even if a storm brings more rain, the pond cleans what stormwater engineers call the "first flush"—the first flow of water carrying the bulk of the chemical and waste buildup from roofs and streets. And if water overtops the pond, that water is the last water into the pond and thus the cleanest. "Water that comes out of here is exceptionally clean," Bass says. Probably clean enough to go into the Rocky Branch, but it doesn't—it goes through the buried drain to a manufactured wetland of about 20 yards by 10 yards in front of the building, with areas for water to pool for the long term, surrounded by more wetland plants. Water in the wetland water remains for much longer periods, allowing it to infiltrate the soil. The plants absorb some of the pollutants; the pools provide habitat for fish, wildlife, and birds. The whole arrangement manages stormwater as a resource rather than sluicing it away as a nuisance.

A good 50 yards away, the Rocky Branch flows, like the Pigeon House, like most Raleigh streams, in a trickle meandering through a broad channel 10 or 12 feet below grade—the result of the extra erosion caused by years of high-energy stormwater flow. "Now, that's the size the stream wants to be," Bass says, "but the streambed should be up here," where we're standing. That is, the stream ought to be at about ground level, so when flow increases during a rainstorm it widens out, slowing down and releasing energy; instead steep banks bound the water, keeping the energy high and causing more erosion in an endless cycle. He notes that the Rocky Branch also suffers because a sewer line follows the same route (naturally, since the sewer line flow is powered by gravity). To keep tree roots from infiltrating the sewer pipes, trees are cleared out from the sewage right-of-way—removing yet another stormwater buffer. Current Raleigh development rules require a 50-foot riparian buffer for the Neuse River and its tributaries, but most of the development along these creeks took place long ago. These streams are candidates for rehabilitation, not protection.

And they're getting it. Bass and his colleagues—and a burgeoning phalanx of trained consultants now helping with both new construction and restoration—take straightened creeks and reinstate what they call meanders, which improve habitat and remove energy, slowing flow rate and reducing erosion. They use the root systems of removed trees to stabilize banks (and provide welcome habitat for fish). They build crossvanes, weirs, and other so-called check dams to encourage the natural process of stream pooling, which, again, provides fish and animal habitat, slows and removes energy from the stream flow, and enables plants to grow, helping to clean the water; at the bottom of the pools are bacteria that consume the matter that settles out.

THE TRANSFORMATION IS ALMOST MAGICAL. From a simple mechanical process of nuisance removal—get it out of here and forget about it—the stormwater infrastructure has become a biological process of resource management. And don't forget that it's a social process, too, says water quality engineer Amy Hathaway, who walked me around a similar pool recently constructed in a park near my house, on an unnamed drainage that flows into the Pigeon House. An upper pond ("our technical term for that is 'forebay'") detains water and allows sediment to drop out; from there it drains to a marsh before it heads to the Pigeon House, though near the final drain a deep pool remains wet at all times, whereas the marshy areas temporarily fill only after a rain. A tiny trickle of a creek connects the two ponds when the weather is dry. Wisps of newly planted vegetation were establishing themselves in the still-muddy banks, though a pair of ducks appeared perfectly satisfied with the park wetlands already.

The neighbors were harder to convince.

"This is a constructed wetland," Hathaway said, "but for the public we've been calling it a water garden." That is, when presented with a leap forward in stormwater management that would protect rivers, recharge groundwater, and also provide a lovely pool and wildlife habitat in an otherwise abandoned portion of a park, people at community meetings heard "wetlands" and protested, imagining the mosquitos and alliga-tors of the Florida Everglades. "Snakes, mosquitoes, rats," Hathaway says, smiling. "Anything bad you can connect with a swamp." So Hathaway learned to say "water garden," which people embrace as an amenity. Where she and her colleagues have designed bioretention areas for parking lots, she has learned to call them "rain gardens," with the same positive result.

Raleigh is encouraging low-impact development that focuses on retaining water on-site, whether through rain gardens and retention ponds to encourage infiltration, cisterns to encourage reuse, or grass roadside swales to pool water rather than sluicing it into gutters. Permeable pavements—porous asphalts and concretes that allow rain to pool, then penetrate, and pavers with holes that encourage infiltration—are now being used. When storm drains are still built, it is usually to fill retention ponds located at the lowest point of new development, and only then does any stormwater continue on to creeks.

And this is happening nationwide. The Green Streets program in Portland, Oregon, not only plants rain gardens between sidewalks and curbs—lowering them below street level for added capacity—but even extends them into the street, exchanging paved roadway for soil, runoff for retention. It encourages green roofs (roofs covered with soil and vegetation), which not only retain water but also filter it. (The Portland Bureau of Environmental Services also claims that green roofs save money: A 40,000-square-foot green roof on say, a big box store, saves $60,000 in storm drain improvements and prevents nearly a ton of particulate stormwater pollution per year.)

Philadelphia plans to spend $10 billion for four enormous underground cisterns to catch combined sewage overflows during rainstorms (as well as the pumps to empty them), but local engineer Howard Neukrug would like to spend that money instead on retention projects that will keep the stormwater from entering the combined sewer system in the first place. "We talk about the triple bottom line," he says, referring to not just economics but ecological and social costs and benefits. Neukrug calls the cisterns "tunnels to nowhere: Nobody drives through them, nobody has picnics near them; they provide no benefit to the world other than catching sewage during rainstorms." Creating ponds and wetlands isn't cheaper, he says, but "there are so many additional benefits that it's ridiculous not to do it." Raleigh and other cities are also doing what is called "daylighting"—digging up streams that have been consigned to culverts or pipes and returning them to their more natural states, with attendant benefits when the vegetation that grows along new banks helps filter water on its way to the creeks and provides renewed animal habitat.

And freshwater is a scarce and most vital resource, so we don't want to send all that stormwater downstream. Long Island, New York, started practicing stormwater retention in 1930, both to save money on stormwater management and to recharge its aquifer, its only source of freshwater. The 4,000 basins in use by 1990 helped almost half of its annual rainfall infiltrate rather than run off. Thus each of the million or so people living in the area can comfortably withdraw the 100 gallons per day it's been estimated that Americans use, since nature puts an average of 240 gallons per person back into the ground each day.

These improvements address more than just the volume and energy of the water. Whereas people like Kirkpatrick and Senior focus on quantity, Hathaway concerns herself more with water quality. The city tests its creeks to determine the health of its drainages and streams, checking for chemical pollution and what it calls benthic invertebrates, breaking the critters down into three categories: tolerant (things like crayfish that can live almost anywhere), midrange, and sensitive. The city has a long way to go. "Everything we've found in the Pigeon House is in the tolerant category," Hathaway says. Sensitive creatures tend to be larval forms of bugs such as dragonflies and mayflies. "If you find a stone fly larva, that creek is really clean. There's only one or two places in Raleigh you can find those."

DEFINITELY NOT IN THE PIGEON HOUSE. Still, the Pigeon House was my creek, and though I'd followed my water from my house to the Pig and downstream from there, I yearned for a certain subterranean romance I hadn't found. So I went down to the Pig one last time and headed upstream. Think of Burton and Speke searching for the source of the Nile, only a shorter trip and with considerably fewer hostile natives.

Less than a mile upstream from my house, the Pig is at its most corralled, running alongside yards where the city of Raleigh keeps its garbage trucks and maintains its other vehicles. Those yards had been paved to the very edge of the bank, though here and there Amy Hathaway's restoration work had replaced the last 10 feet or so of pavement with a berm, pooling water and sending it through ponds and sand filters. Just a bit farther upstream, nearer to downtown, the Pigeon House vanishes, then emerges from a 7-foot concrete culvert beneath a bridge. It flows for a while through a lovely 10-foot-deep stone culvert along what used to be the concourse of Devereaux Meadows, an old minor-league ballpark; rusting fixtures for old drinking fountains still poke from concrete abutments supporting the steep slope up to the train tracks. Just further upstream the Pigeon House disappears under a street.

I was thrilled. From Rome's Cloaca Maxima to the Grand Égout of Paris (built in 1370 and eventually evolving into Paris's famous sewer system), creepy tunnels containing secret flows have formed the backdrop for atmospheric literary events of the highest magnitude. At last—my *Phantom of the Opera* moment awaited me somewhere upstream in that culvert.

So I prepared. I got my closest-to-waterproof hiking boots and put plastic grocery bags inside; I bought an LED headlamp; I packed a knapsack with an extra flashlight, a camera, and a notepad. I put on a baseball hat for a modicum of cushion against any low-bridge moments. Then I chose a dry day and went inside.

The first few steps required me to clamber beneath water mains; since these are only a few feet underground, stormwater regularly crosses their paths. Within a couple of minutes I had left behind the glowing opening of the culvert and, sloshing my way upstream through 2 inches or so of consistent flow, I was alone in the dark, listening to the echoey rush of the water. A center support wall separated the rectangular concrete culvert into two parallel paths, though cutouts kept the sides connected.

Not long after the light from my headlamp became the only light I could see, a loud rush announced the inflow from a 60-inch concrete pipe carrying the flow from the east side of downtown. Mark Senior of the city of Raleigh had told me that if I wandered up that pipe I would come to a place where a culvert was built directly atop bedrock—he thought I'd like to see it. The pipe's steady flow of water echoed like a tub faucet running at full open in a tile bathroom, and it probably had just about that much flow. So I headed up the pipe.

I hadn't gone on for 5 minutes when I found just what Senior had described: I emerged from the pipe into a low rectangular culvert 4 feet tall or so, the sides built of stacked and mortared boulders, my headlamp illuminating the stream on the bottom as it wore itself a groove in an outcropping of gneiss. I found a flat spot to sit and listen. The splashy flow felt natural: Down here underground, channelized and piped and bounded to be sure, this tiny tributary of the Pigeon House Branch was doing nothing more than acting like water, going downhill.

Back in the main culvert, I continued upstream beneath buildings and streets. For once, the stormwater system looked like I had imagined it would: Here and there pipes large and small entered, sometimes simply into the side of the culvert, at other times at junction boxes beneath manholes. Occasionally a tiny trickle of water dripped, but mostly the pipes were dry. At manholes I found I received an adequate cell phone signal, so I called a friend to keep him apprised of my whereabouts—if he stopped hearing from me he was to notify the police. Before long I emerged at a low downtown intersection under a railroad bridge, then plunged right back into another culvert. I was nearing Glenwood Avenue, and I remembered a notation I had seen for this area on the 90-year-old planning map hanging in the Stormwater Management Division lobby: "brick culvert."

My headlamp glittering in the trickle of water, I kept sloshing forward until—yes, a lovely brick tunnel arched over my head; below, under a foot or more of water held back by a large stone weir, was a flagstone base. I couldn't tell whether the weir had been put up purposely or was just a stone tumbled there by the water, but either way it pooled the water behind it. The setting, if hardly romantic (and far from large enough to serve as a secret lair, much less to give me room to practice the violin) was almost lovely. As the water trickled over the stone and dropped out of the brick archway into the next section of tunnel, it pushed grit away, clearing a space for itself. Underground, culverted for a century, the Pigeon House was still behaving like a river, trying to do the things that Kris Bass was helping it to do aboveground: Create pools, meander, make its way to the sea.

FOR THE PIG IS MORE THAN A DRAINAGE DITCH. Raleigh has a system of greenway trails following other drainages, turning the necessity of riparian buffer zones into the virtue of walking and biking trails. I couldn't help thinking that as stream restoration efforts continue, the Pig, winding as it does along Raleigh's main northern gateway, could be the centerpiece of the greenway system without losing a bit of its efficacy as stormwater infrastructure.

But that was in the future. Now I emerged from the tunnel, continuing upstream along an open concrete streamway behind a brand-new apartment building that backed directly onto the culvert. Pieces of two-by-four and dropped nails littered the floor of the stream. Then, after another half-block under the street, the Pigeon House Branch came out between the backyards of houses, arrow straight between the attractive stone walls hemming it in: These were the very walls built by the city in 1949, when the shopping center at the source of the Pig started flooding it, making it "rambunctious." Now it was nothing more than a trickle. I made my way between the houses, listening to the barking dogs and seeing their waste in the stream next to clippings from people's gardens. A little farther up I emerged in a park, where, finally, the Pigeon House Branch looked like it must have before all the engineers got involved: just a creek.

A USGS stream meter at the park later allowed me to retrieve online the value of the flow I was wading through: It was about $\frac{4}{100\text{th}}$ of a cubic foot (about a third of a gallon) per second, which is about 20 percent below its mean value over the last 12 years. But that was just the headwaters of the Pigeon House, which joins two other main branches and absorbs countless tiny tributaries; in addition, it wasn't raining and we'd just been in a drought.

So you have to pay attention.

To pay that final piece of attention, I followed the creek up through an extension of the park, seeing where riprap and weirs had been used, again, to slow the creek down. At last I got to the outlet of the enormous 60-inch pipe that channeled the stream from beneath the shopping center. A steady trickle of clear water emerged, sparkling in the late-day sun. Of course it was clean: This water was, fundamentally, springwater, though it sprang into a concrete pipe. I still had the headlamp, so I even continued upstream for a while, but once you've been in bedrock culverts and underground brick archways, a concrete pipe loses its charm. I looked up through the holes in the last manhole I reached and saw the side of an unmarked white van.

So I emerged, climbed up to the parking lot, found the van, and then followed the manhole covers uphill to the top of a ridge, where I sat on a bench in a little playground park. Of course, the top of a ridge—I was looking for the edge of a watershed, which is a ridge by definition, but it still seemed amazing. It's the type of geograph ical detail that somehow, driving around town in my car, I had missed—just as I had never noticed the lack of storm drains on my street. Then I lifted my head—and next to the park was a water tower. This also made perfect sense: A water tower stores water and provides pressure for the surrounding houses, so you wouldn't put it in a valley, you'd put it on a ridge.

I remembered the last piece of wisdom stormwater engineer Robert Kirkpatrick had imparted. We were talking about Tropical Storm Hanna, which had recently hit Raleigh. A tropical storm is always a big event in Raleigh, so the television meteorologists had indulged themselves with their usual warnings and horror stories. But Kirkpatrick had known that Hanna was a relatively fast-moving storm, so its heavy rains wouldn't stick around long enough to flood, or if they did, the flooding would be minimal and extremely brief. (My son and I drove around to road crossings the morning after Hanna hit, as the rain stopped: After 5 inches of rain, the worst flooding we saw was a spot where Crabtree Creek had overtopped its lowest bridge for about an hour before receding.) And though Hanna had come with 40-plus-mph winds, it hadn't caused much tree damage and didn't knock down a single building or sign. We were a region emerging from a drought, but weatherpeople talked about dodging a bullet. "No, wait a minute," Kirkpatrick said, "we *wanted* that bullet. Hanna was almost like a perfect storm for us. The intensity was perfect, the speed was perfect, the time of day was perfect, it peaked out at 2, 3 a.m., the next day was a Saturday." It refilled the reservoirs, flushed out the creeks, and maybe even infiltrated the ground a bit without so much as disrupting a rush hour.

"Think of stormwater in reverse mode," Kirkpatrick said. "Turn on your tap and what you get is actually stormwater."

Of course it is. And the usual method for gathering drinking water is the simplest method of stormwater detention: the dam. We had hundreds of dams forming little flood control lakes around Raleigh, and I had questions about those. More important, we had a great big dam a few miles north that turned the Neuse River into Falls Lake, 42.8 billion gallons of flood control, fish and wildlife habitat, Neuse River water quality control, recreational space—and the drinking water for Raleigh and most of Wake County.

That sounded like the next place to go.

CHAPTER 3

A CHESS GAME
YOU NEVER WIN

Cleaning and Distributing Water—and Saving Fish

THE FAUCET IN OUR DOWNSTAIRS BATHROOM WAS DRIPPING. Not much—it dripped once every 10 seconds or so; if we left a bucket underneath, we barely had a cup of water overnight. But if you add it up, that's 173 gallons per year. During a full-blown drought, when you've reached the point of reusing bathwater to flush the toilet, you don't feel good about 173 wasted gallons. Fortunately, the leak stopped on its own before we had to spend $100 on a plumber. On the water itself we saved another, say, 58 cents per year.

Yes, good, clean, fresh water pours out of the tap at 3 gallons for a penny. When I checked my water bill to figure this out, I was stunned. A sixth of the world's population can't even get clean water, and I get a gallon for less than I pay for a single paper clip—and if I want the paper clip, I have to go to the store, but the water comes to me. I drink it, cook with it, wash my babies with it, all without giving it a moment's thought. The pipes aren't the only thing hidden about water. I started digging.

THE STORMWATER GUYS HAD TAUGHT ME that stormwater is also water supply: It comes down as rain and somebody does the job of gathering it up for me. My water starts as evaporation from the oceans—probably the Gulf of Mexico, given North Carolina's weather patterns. It condenses into clouds and rains down in the upper Neuse River basin, making its way into our reservoir either quickly as surface flow or slowly as groundwater. The people who do the gathering are the Army Corps of Engineers. They keep my water where they want it with the Falls Dam, a 1,900-foot-long, 92-foot-high earthen dam that holds about 43 billion gallons of water in a 12,400-acre reservoir called Falls Lake, opened in 1983. A ranger named Dana Matics let me tag along as she dangled a sounding instrument called a piezometer into the narrow PVC tube of a monitoring well beside the dam.

"Eighty-five," she muttered, measuring the depth before she hit water. "Probably . . . eighty-seven, so there's water down there."

Matics explained that Falls is a zoned-earth dam, which means it has different zones that keep the water in place: grout and concrete at the wide base, virtually impermeable clay holding back water on the upstream side (protected against wave motion by riprap), and silty, clayey sand on the downstream side, with a permeable draining layer running through the center of the dam and a gravel filter above the grout at the bottom. Upstream, you want the dam to be impermeable, to keep the reservoir where it is; downstream, you want rain to percolate through; otherwise it runs off and erodes the dam. The Hoover Dam uses the compression of its concrete arch along with its enormous weight to hold back the water; other dams support their structure with buttresses or barriers of steel or wood. But an earth dam is simpler: It's a big pile of earth (or rock), waterproof upstream and extremely wide at the base.

The Army Corps of Engineers monitors each of the dam's 35 wells at least once per month, with much more thorough maintenance checks of the whole dam annually. Every 5 years it actually shuts down the dam and personnel take a walk through the conduit that channels water through the dam out to the Neuse River. That conduit, built of poured-in-place concrete pipe, is big enough to drive a truck through, Matics said, but she's never been in there. "Most of us actually end up on fish duty," looking for creatures left high and dry when the river suddenly stops flowing. "With nets and waders. It's pretty comical. Saving fish."

Which underscores the tremendous complexity of a multipurpose dam. Saving fish downstream is as much a part of its function as retaining water for drinking upstream, to say nothing of providing flood protection, recreation, and wildlife habitat.

RALEIGH HAS FALLS LAKE because the Neuse River used to flood terribly—floods in the early 20th century raged south of Raleigh at a staggering 35,000 cubic feet per second. The Flood Control Act of 1965, passed in response to Hurricane Betsy, which caused Lake Pontchartrain to flood New Orleans, gave the Army Corps of Engineers the responsibility to redesign the levees meant to protect New Orleans and introduce improved flood control dams throughout the nation. By 1965, the Neuse presented more than just a flooding problem—it also presented an attractive water source for Raleigh, which had doubled in population between 1940 and 1960 and was continuing to grow rapidly. Land purchase for the new reservoir started in 1969, the corps started filling the lake in 1981, and by 1983 it was full.

A recent assessment by the corps rated the dam "High Priority (conditionally unsafe)," on a scale from "Normal (safe)" to "Urgent and compelling (unsafe)." This frustrates Matics. The dam was found to be in excellent shape, but it received the rating because if it should burst, people downstream would be flooded. Rating a dam unsafe because if it burst people downstream would get wet seems a bit like rating an airplane unsafe because if it crashed people would die. In a post-9/11 world, emergency plans rule. (The rating program started in 2005; fearing terrorism, the corps will not release the map of the expected postfailure inundation.) But the dam is safe: When asked what he would do if he lived downstream from it, the corps operations manager at Falls Lake told a newspaper reporter: "Absolutely nothing."

Matics showed me the intake—the concrete tower just in front of the dam that controls the flow of water through the conduit—though security prevented her from taking me inside. We walked out on the long bridge that stretches from the dam top to the top of the intake. The tower intake has four main steel-plate gates, in two pairs of two at the bottom of the lake. Each pair consists of a service gate, raised and lowered to control water flow, and an emergency gate, just in front of it, that can slam shut if something goes wrong. Each 19- by 8-foot emergency gate provides redundancy for its service gate, and the second pair provides redundancy for the first, the beginning of a theme of redundancy found everywhere in the management of water. Each pair leads into its own chamber, the two chambers leading to that same 18-foot conduit taking the Neuse under the dam and releasing it. During the summer the water quality at the bottom of the lake is poor, so to maintain the health of the Neuse, they operate 8- by 8-foot water quality gates in the middle of the tower rather than at the bottom.

There's one more gate, too—the piggyback gate, a tiny, 1- by 1-foot gate within the service gate that is operated by hand crank, used when the lake is releasing extremely small amounts of water. The day of our visit followed a week of heavy rains, so the dam was releasing 1,000 cubic feet per second (cfs), which rushed out of the conduit downstream to the evident delight of several kayakers. "A more normal release for us in winter is about 100 cfs," Matics said. "In summer, more like 250." To keep the lake steady after thunderstorms and to protect the quality of the Neuse, the dam is obligated to release at least 100 cfs in summer and 60 cfs in winter. During the drought, Matics said, "we were operating just on that piggyback gate, partly open."

But the lake was nice and full when Matics and I walked the dam, Matics keeping one eye busy checking for cracks in the roadway or wiggles in the guardrail that might alert her to any settling and the other eye on families enjoying picnic areas. Some children were using cardboard boxes to grass-sled down the downstream slope, and she asked them to cut it out. It's a dam—you don't want to erode the surface. Just visible from the dam was one more concrete structure, a little platform, like a cross between a diving platform and a bridge abutment, rising a few feet above the surface of the lake about half a mile upstream. This is the intake for the Raleigh water treatment plant.

Raleigh gulps as much as 50 million gallons of water per day, which require the intake to suck out 80 cubic feet per second. Letters to the editor of the local newspaper during the drought demonstrated how little residents understood about the lake's multiple purposes. Raleigh residents uniformly wanted the gates shut tight, every drop saved for drinking water, whereas people downstream lobbied for continued releases—the opposite of what happens during a busy hurricane season, when locals want the sluices wide open to keep the lake low enough to absorb a potential 5-inch dump of rain, whereas downstream residents prefer the lake to hold everything back to prevent flooding. The corps has a simple rule: It aims to keep the lake surface at 251½ feet above sea level and that's that. If the water rises any higher, it kills trees and loses the capacity to absorb floodwaters; conversely, no matter how low it gets they never slam the door. During heavy rain, the corps holds the water until the crest of the rising river reaches Kinston, 5 days downstream, then releases water on the back end of the surge. And it releases water even in drought times—for the communities who eventually drink the water downstream, and for those fish.

FOUR 2,000-HORSEPOWER PUMPS—two working, two backups—haul the water from the reservoir intake. Each can pump up to 40 million gallons per day, and they hoist water about 3 miles through one 54-inch pipe and one 36-inch pipe to two enormous holding reservoirs of 70 million gallons apiece that flank the E.M. Johnson Water Treatment Plant. From there, gravity takes charge as the water works its way through the plant. Behind a rolling security gate, the unprepossessing plant looks something like a redbrick warehouse. The only decorations in the low, dim, echoing lobby are a couple of murals showing schematics: On one wall is Raleigh's now-abandoned first treatment plant, built in 1940, with pipes running from four different reservoirs south of town. The opposite wall shows the present plant, though since it was built in 1967, long before the dam, it shows how the pumps brought water from the Neuse River.

In the lobby I met Ken Best, the plant facility manager, who gave me a quick rundown of the treatment plant. It can treat up to 86 million gallons per day (mgd), though the city system (including the systems of several nearby towns that Raleigh has absorbed in recent years) averages around 50 mgd. The Raleigh system contains about 2,000 miles of pipe, some 27 pumping stations, and 25 elevated storage tanks (which just means they're aboveground, not necessarily water towers). The combined capacity of all those storage tanks is about 36 million gallons, plus another million or so in the pipes themselves. Toss in the finished water in the plant's 17 million gallons of clear wells, and Raleigh has a full day's supply of water in tanks.

RALEIGH MADE ITS FIRST ATTEMPT at a municipal water system in 1818, using a water wheel to pump water from a creek through wooden pipes to a water tower at the center of town and thence to a nearby reservoir piping water to the rest of the city. It completely failed—the pump didn't work well, and the pipes and tanks leaked—and was abandoned within a couple of years. Since Raleigh was then a city of only about 1,000 people occupying ⅔ of a square mile, it wasn't such a hardship for people to use wells and streams. By the late 1800s, Raleigh had grown to some 10,000 people and nearly 2 square miles; there were hand pumps along the streets (nine on the central Capitol Square alone). Still, people worried about water quality and, in Raleigh as all over the world, about firefighting.

In 1886 Raleighans hired a consultant, chose a creek south of the city, and built steam pumps to pull water through two 14-inch wooden mains to a 1.8 million-gallon reservoir. Sandpits gave the raw water a first cleaning, and charcoal and gravel filters cleaned it again before it entered the reservoir. Two pumps could move 2 mgd to a 100,000-gallon water tower standing just south of the state capitol. When the system started up in 1887, it powered six fire hoses for most of an hour, each shooting water 120 feet into the air. By 1892 Raleigh had 20 miles of water mains; by 1910 it had 55. Demand increased enough that the creek's flow couldn't guarantee the water supply, so the city built connected reservoirs in 1912 and 1914 that totaled about 1.5 billion gallons. But Raleigh kept growing.

The stone-and-brick water tower still stands, by the way, though the tank is gone. Like Philadelphia's columned Greek revival waterworks or Chicago's famed Water Tower, Raleigh's downtown watertower denoted civic progress and advertised the safety and modernity of the city. It must have worked: By 1934 Raleigh was already listed by *Forbes* magazine as one of the 10 best cities in the country for business.

Whether that first-ever top-10 list for Raleigh helped or not, the city kept growing. Private water companies commonly ran pipes only where wealthy customers could pay. (Typhoid rates in the South around 1900 ran twice as high among African Americans, whom the water companies didn't care to serve, as for Caucasians, whom they did.) But in the first part of the 20th century, municipal governments nationwide, including Raleigh's, began to take over functions like water service. By 1939 Raleigh reached the limit of those original 2 mgd pumps and used Works Progress Administration funding and city bonds to raise the $700,000 it needed to build a new plant. The E.B. Bain Water Plant could pump 10 mgd (and could expand to double that). The builders put it up without interrupting the flowing water supply.

That expansion capacity helped, as did two more new reservoirs in 1952 and 1956 that totaled about 3 billion gallons, but it was a losing game. The future was north—and in 1967 the E.M. Johnson plant opened, working in tandem with the Bain plant. In 1987 the city shifted all treatment to the Johnson plant; though it still uses the Bain reservoir, the plant itself sits empty, an Art Deco masterpiece moldering behind chain-link fence. (Lake Benson, the reservoir built in 1952, came to the city's unlikely aid in the drought of 2007, providing 25 cubic feet of water per second to the Neuse River through never-used sewer pipes from an unfinished development, allowing Falls Lake to curtail its minuscule releases.) On the Bain reservoir's shores the city's third-ever treatment plant now rises, ready to add 20 mgd to Raleigh's capacity.

KEN BEST LED ME OUT THE BACK DOOR OF THE PLANT and we were surrounded by acres of gray concrete basins of very still water—it looked like a factory for dreary swimming pools. A single 48-inch pipe runs from each of the two 70-million-gallon reservoirs of what plant operators call raw water that flank the plant. During the several days that water spends in those reservoirs, leaves and other suspended particles settle out. The pipes lead first to treatment with ozone. Extremely reactive, ozone bonds with herbicide and pesticide residues and precipitates metals and pollutants, which can then be filtered out; it also pokes holes in the cell walls of bacteria and viruses. The water then receives coagulants to help precipitate other organic matter as the water enters what Best calls the "flash" mix: a good stirring in two tanks to thoroughly mix the chemicals. The water then flows into the flocculation basins among which we stood, a long, double line of 60 concrete pools, each about 20 feet square. There, very slow mixers called walking beams—they look like the scales of justice, patiently tilting right, left, right, left, one per pool, lined up on long central axes 30 pools long—gently encouraged the formation of the precipitate, called floc ("flocculent" means "like wool;" the floc is a kind of fluffy mass that the chemicals precipitate out).

The treated water then flows into five vast settlement basins—each is 15 feet deep, holds 1.5 million gallons, and is bigger than two Olympic swimming pools—where traveling bridges called monorakes circulate around the basins as the water slowly moves through. When the water enters the tank it's brown; soon enough there's a narrow clear layer above something that looks like a snow globe full of brown snow; and by about halfway through all the water is nearly clear. The mud the monorakes scrape off the bottom into valves is eventually treated on-site and sold as soil treatment.

From there Best led me to what most people think of as the natural element of water treatment: 22 filters, each the size of about three flocculation tanks. The settled water descends through 24 inches of anthracite coal and 12 inches of sand to catch any remaining dirt and floc. Water coming through the filter must meet standards for turbidity (a measurement of the opacity of liquids due to invisible suspended solids); the anthracite lasts for decades. A little chlorine and ammonia is added both before and after filtration, and fluoride is also added afterward.

People first started filtering water through sand, in 9th-century Venice, to improve taste and smell. Paisley, Scotland, is widely cited as the first city to filter its public water supply, in 1804. In 1854, British physician John Snow made his map of cholera cases in London (Colleen Sharpe of the Raleigh information technology department cited it as the world's first GIS map) and showed that they were clustered around the

Broad Street water pump, thus making a breakthrough in the understanding of the waterborne disease process. By removing the handle of the pump, which prevented people from drinking from it, he ended the epidemic (it was later discovered that the pump's water was contaminated with sewage). Understanding that water contained disease vectors caused people to turn to chlorine, which had been discovered in 1774. It was first used to treat municipal water in England in 1897, and it turned out to have almost miraculous properties. Continuous chlorination was instituted in Belgium in 1902 and in Jersey City in 1908. In 1908, 25 Americans out of 100,000 died of typhoid; 40 years later, none did, and cholera, dysentery, and hepatitis A followed similar patterns. Citizens resisted what they called "doping the water," but the treatment's obvious success eventually won out.

Raleigh's water is slightly acidic, so tanks add sodium hydroxide at several points during the process to raise pH levels, preventing the water from corroding any pipes—if you see green around your faucet's mouth, that's dissolved copper from your pipes, and you probably have slightly acidic water. (In cities where the water strays toward basic, the water is treated by adding dilute hydrochloric or sulfuric acid.) Raleigh's filtered, pH-balanced water goes to two clear wells—one holds 12 million gallons, the other 5. Its slow flow through the clear wells gives the chlorine disinfectant time to do its job, after which the water is called finished water and can be pumped out into those 2,000 miles of pipes, pumps, and water towers. Look at different treatment plants and you'll find different technologies—osmosis filters instead of charcoal beds, say, or the use of UV light instead of some chemical processes—but basically there you have it: sedimentation, filtration, treatment, and then out to the pipes.

There are exceptions, but not many. New York City runs its water in from reservoirs hundreds of miles away; the water is so clean that it isn't filtered at all, though it still gets some chemical treatment. San Francisco's water comes from Yosemite National Park, 160 miles away, and gets only simple chlorine purification. Many other cities, especially large ones on the east and west coasts, have to duct their water in from afar, but most public water systems (about 86 percent of Americans get their water from some kind of public system) are not much different from Raleigh's: local water supply, treatment plant, distribution pipes. (Even New York's water gets clean by running through a multiple-reservoir system that functions exactly like a series of sedimentation basins; the same is true of the water that came to the ancient Romans through their aqueducts.) The EPA requires constant testing, both within the plant and in the field; an entire staff of people goes out all day and does nothing but gather samples from throughout the system, bringing them back to the plant, where white-coated lab technicians test for treatment by-products as well as for the usual bugs (cryptosporidium, giardia), algae blooms (which cause taste and odor problems), inorganics such as lead and copper, and the pharmaceuticals and personal care products that people dump in their toilets and that aren't caught by the sewage plants upstream.

It could all be considered absolutely dull—millions of gallons of water doing nothing, sitting in tanks and pools, barely seeming to flow. Walking among the concrete basins, I never felt a sense of the natural life of the water, but neither did I really absorb the miracle of the technology that makes all that water safe to drink. Best took me through pump rooms, where enormous elbows of blue-painted pipe connected tanks and filters, and the 50 mgd and 22 mgd pumps (two of each—redundancy again) that push the water out into the system create a roar that renders conversation almost impossible. But even the vibration of all that moving water failed to provide the thrill I had hoped for from the water plant.

Then we went to the control room.

BEST OPENED A HALF-GLASS DOOR into a room that looked like a cross between a high school chemistry lab and a factory supervisor's office. Picture windows opened out onto the concrete grid of filter and sedimentation basins; along one wall 11 labeled faucets ran constantly: "raw," "pretreated," "settled," and so on, all the way to "finished," sampled from the 48- and 54-inch pipes leaving the plant, all ready for sampling and testing at any moment. A Hach 2100N Turbidimeter to measure suspended particles sat by one wall, looking like a small gray printer; a periodic chart of the elements hung from another.

But the action was on the other side of the room, where three or four guys stood around in front of a bank of computers: the SCADA system, which stands for supervisory control and data acquisition. The system automatically manages the flow through the plant and the distribution system, measuring flow and pressure rates, adjusting chemical feeds, turning pumps on and off throughout the hundreds of square miles the system serves. The guys were plant operators, watching the SCADA system and making decisions about where water needs to go.

Water usage spikes first thing in the morning and at dinnertime, but the plant doesn't want to throttle up and down to respond to those fluctuations; the 500- and 2,000-horsepower pumps that push the water out into the system (and the smaller pumps that keep it moving through the plant and the system) are either on or off, so the plant has to keep water moving in chunks of millions of gallons per day. The answer lies in storage tanks. Operations supervisor Mike Hughes, a tall, sleepy-eyed guy with a shock of tousled black hair, explained that the system constantly adjusts to the changing demands of its customers. "I guess I'll start at the beginning of the day. At night nobody is using much water, so we've got certain tanks in the system that we kind of pump down." Most water towers have only a single pipe, with water building up in the tower when the local pumping station provides more than the system is using in that area and drawing down when it's the other way around. The entire distribution system is divided into pressure zones, designated by the altitude of the water level at the top of each zone's water tower when it's full: From 655, where the tall Leesville tank stands in the hilly northwest of the city, to 495 downtown, fed by large storage tanks right on the ground, there are eight pressure zones and a total of 25 pumping stations. The zones are separate, but connected through zone separation valves that share water if a main drops pressure in one zone. Pressure runs between 50 and 80 pounds per square inch: If it's lower, water won't get to the upper floors of buildings; if it's higher, it starts popping the connections off washing machines. "If there's a weak spot in the plumbing," Best said, "that's how you'll find it."

Each water tower holds about a million gallons. Two of the three main downtown tanks, Bain and North Hills, are much larger—one holding 8 million gallons, the other 6.4 million—and so have the special job of evening out the daily flow. "A tank like Bain, we've got an out-tube here," Hughes said, "so at night we'll pump into it, but during the day we close the valve there, so we only pump out of it. Then if we pump down 5 or 6 or 7 or 8 feet, when nighttime rolls around and nobody's using water, we have a place to put that water." This works just the same way as the water towers above buildings in large cities—small pumps fill them up during the night, and then they drain during the day, catching up the next night. The tanks store the extra water needed to respond to spikes in demand, and pumps refill them during the lulls.

Moving water around the system follows much the same principle: To keep the water turning over in water towers, operators will turn off pumps to different segments of the system, causing tank water levels to drop as customers use water; when the tank level gets low enough (operators like the water level within each tank to drop and rise by 8 feet or more each day), they pump water back in. Hot days cause chlorine to break down and by-products to build up faster, so operators try to turn over tanks faster then. "It's like a big chess game," plant superintendent John Garland said, "that you never win."

I asked when it gets most difficult to manage water—does the plant face, say, that famous Super Bowl halftime spike when everybody supposedly flushes toilets? Hughes shook his head, smiling. The Super Bowl question reminded Hughes of the day the new RBC Center, Raleigh's sports arena, checked its pressure by flushing every toilet at the same time: The system absorbed the shock just fine. But it does get crazy. Consider Thanksgiving. Raleigh, a place people move to from other places, also has 31,000 students at North Carolina State University, which means that on Thanksgiving the customer base drops by 15 percent or more. None of those students are flushing toilets, drinking water, or washing clothes, and a water plant that likes to run at 40 mgd suddenly faces a demand of 32 mgd or less. The problem isn't so much the pumps or the water towers—the problem is quality.

"Everything's automatic around here," Hughes said, speaking of the various delivery systems that pump treatment chemicals into the water. "Everything's flow-basing off another number and a dosage, so if it's usually running at 300 gallons per hour and now we're doing 40 gallons per hour, you run into problems." A pump working at the bottom of its range might put in, say, too little chlorine. That's automatically measured and noticed farther along in the plant, so the SCADA system tells the pump to speed up, at which point it puts in too much, which will also quickly be caught—but the chemical pump will grind up and down like a little kid oversteering on a bicycle, which is good for neither the pump nor the water quality.

Hughes sees the opposite, too. During a drought, customers are restricted to a single day or two of lawn watering per week. "Come June, with no water restrictions, when everyone's sprinklers are on? You're running 75 mgd. When you do have restrictions, you can only water Tuesdays and Wednesdays." People set automatic sprinkler systems accordingly and then demand spikes at 12:01 a.m. Tuesday, running through Wednesday night, "until at midnight suddenly you drop from 75 mgd to 45 mgd. You get 30 mgd swings, which is . . . wild." Wild or not, between the 17 million gallons of water in clear wells at the plant, the 14 million gallons in storage tanks, and the 22 million gallons in water towers, the guys operating the plant keep the water moving and haven't had any of the tanks overflow so far.

FROM THE PLANT, I WANTED TO FOLLOW THE ROUTE WATER takes to my house. The problem was, nobody knows it. I had assumed, of course, that my water would follow a path something like the opposite of my stormwater—that is, instead of from my yard, to bigger and bigger pipes and then streams and eventually to the ocean, my freshwater would go from a big pipe at the plant through smaller and smaller pipes until it came to my house. But it's not that simple. "It's more like the roads," Dale Crisp, the Raleigh Public Utilities Department director, told me early on. "If they dig up the street north of your house, you still get home—you just go a different way." But nobody can predict exactly how you'll go.

Friends at the Raleigh GIS department pulled up a map showing Raleigh's water lines. These largely follow the street plans, though you can see the occasional large pipe heading cross-country, shooting on its own directly toward a water tower or pump station—the express. Since the map assigns colors to pipes by both size and material (ductile iron, cast iron, PVC, asbestos, concrete, and other variations, including "unknown"), and since pipe sizes range from 2-inch to 54-inch, often in half-inch increments, the pipes showed up in so many colors that even when magnified, the map looked like multicolored spaghetti. We tried starting from the plant and from my house, but at both ends we quickly came to junctures, splits, loops. My water could follow an almost infinite number of routes. Which is, of course, the point—that's why my water gets to me no matter where the city digs up a water main to repair or replace it. Still, I wanted to do that trace.

Ken Best reached out to the engineering firm that does modeling for the distribution system: They calibrate their model by briefly turning off the fluoridation system, then introducing fluoride at various points to see where it goes. Within days they zipped back a picture showing a diagram of the water system with a red line from the pump to my house. So I can tell you that on its way to my house, water leaves the plant in a 48-inch ductile iron pipe and quickly splits off into a 36-inch ductile iron pipe, heading south along a main street, which instead of feeding the neighborhood buildings heads directly to the North Hills storage tank and pumping station (though it occasionally changes to PVC and then back to iron, likely as a result of repairs or routine maintenance).

From there the pipe continues another couple of miles south (the diagram says the water has been in the pipes for about 12 hours at this point) until it splits in two, one 12-inch pipe continuing down the main street and another veering onto a slightly smaller street. The engineering diagram said my water follows the main street, takes a left to follow a park, and then, among half a dozen other options, turns off into an 8-inch PVC pipe that climbs the hill to the main street nearest my house. At this point it joins an 8-inch ductile iron pipe headed my way, then takes a right into an 8-inch pipe of unknown material that lies beneath my street, and finally turns off into a 1-inch pipe that leads to my meter and from there into my house. According to Google Maps it's 9.8 miles, and it takes about 33 hours, depending on who's watering their lawns and who's out of town.

IT DIDN'T USED TO BE SO HARD TO KEEP TRACK. Remember the city of Mohenjo Daro, which invented stormwater drainage some 4,500 years ago? Not long after, also in the Middle East, an infrastructure improvement arrived: terra-cotta pipes, including T- and angle joints (they're first seen in Babylon and on Crete). By early in the 1st millennium BC, Persians were digging *qanats,* water tunnels many kilometers in length along very gentle downhill slopes to populated areas; the vertical tunnels used to remove dirt and aerate the qanats can be called the first manholes. The ancient Greeks developed aqueducts to bring water from springs to cities. The one at Samos, designed by Eupalinus, featured a tunnel constructed by two teams that began digging on opposite sides of a hill and met in the middle; the 5th-century BC historian Herodotus called this aqueduct one of Greece's greatest achievements. Greek water rules stated that people living within four stadia (about half a mile) of a fountain had the right to draw water there; beyond that, they had to dig their own wells (though if they dug deep enough without finding water they gained limited rights to other wells or springs).

The Romans turned aqueducts into works of art, described in tremendous detail by the Roman architect Vitruvius and, especially, the 1st-century water curator Frontinus. Frontinus tells us that Appius Claudius, the blind architect who designed the Appian Way, built the first aqueduct in 312 BC; it was mostly underground. By the time the Romans were done they had 14 aqueducts, the longest 59 miles long, all filling Rome with freshwater from the surrounding mountains. Periodic sedimentation basins slowed the flow and allowed impurities to settle, and where aqueducts approached each other they connected, allowing managers to divert flow and perform maintenance. They contained both siphons (dips in the pipes where they crossed valleys, using the momentum of the drop to push water back up the other side) and the famous arched bridges. The channels were lined with brick or stone and cement, and when they reached Rome they entered *castella*—large cisterns very much like modern storage tanks or water towers that were set on high ground to provide pressure to distribution pipes. Estimates for the amount of water flowing into Rome daily vary from 200 gallons per person per day to more than 1,000, but Romans undoubtedly had all the water they needed, and it was clean and safe. Hundreds of slaves worked on nothing else but the aqueducts, organized into five classes not unlike those in a current public works department: pipe workers; storage tank workers; inspectors, who also supervised the other workers; pavers, who put the streets back in order after subterranean pipes were fixed; and masonry workers, who managed the brick-and stonework.

When the empire crumbled, so did the aqueducts—and people mostly returned to springs or wells. By the 13th century, Henry III granted London water companies the right to bring water in from nearby Tyburn through lead pipes, from which it was channeled to cisterns available to all. In the 1500s, engineers in Germany and Britain began using pumps to drain mines, and it wasn't long before pumps (usually simple Archimedes' screws, which had been around since the 3rd century BC, but sometimes horse-powered wheels) were moving water into cities via cast-iron pipes. In 1581, entrepreneur Peter Maurice used waterwheels driven by the tidal flow of the Thames to power pumps on London Bridge that could shoot a jet of water over the top of a nearby steeple, enabling him to bring water into town. Pump and distribution systems spread throughout Europe.

And America, of course. Though most colonial Americans got their water from wells and streams, as settlements grew, people had to cast farther afield for uncontaminated water. Using pipes to distribute it only made sense. Boston laid wooden pipes—logs with their centers bored out—as early as 1652, and Winston-Salem, North Carolina, had a city-wide log pipe distribution system by 1776. (By 1850, instead of logs, most water mains were made of wooden staves bound by iron bands.) Wooden pipes didn't stand up well to modern pumps and now are mostly gone; workers at the Raleigh public works warehouse showed me the last one they had dug up in Raleigh not long before. The first cast-iron water pipes in the United States were laid in Philadelphia not long after the beginning of the 19th century.

Philadelphia's water system, in fact, was the model of the modern system. Philadelphians built it in 1799 after epidemics of yellow fever (they mistakenly believed it was waterborne) convinced them their wells were contaminated and they desired clean water to drink and to wash their filthy streets. They built two coal-fired steam engines to pump water through a 6-foot brick tunnel to two tanks at the city's center square, from whence it would be distributed through log water mains. The system started functioning in 1801—and soon shut down. The steam engines blew up, the log pipes leaked, the coal was expensive, and the system couldn't keep up with the population. So they dammed the Schuylkill River to power waterwheels, their gears housed in lovely classical revival buildings (now a museum), and pumped water to a nearby reservoir on a high point in the city. The system added pumps and pipes as the population grew, until a typhoid epidemic closed it down in the 1890s, after which new pumping plants with sand filtration beds replaced it.

Pumps, filtration, distribution: Since then we've tinkered, but today's water systems are just cleaner and sturdier versions of what came a century before.

SEVERAL PEOPLE HAD MENTIONED FIREFIGHTING as a central factor in water management, so it was no surprise that when Andy Brogden, Raleigh's water distribution superintendent, took me for a drive, one of the first things he told me about was hydrants. "The city of Raleigh has just a touch over 20,000 hydrants," he said. "And we have 10 people to maintain them." That's to keep them in repair, paint them, and "exercise" them—open and shut their these valves regularly to insure that they work when they're needed. (I later chatted with a couple of guys exercising a hydrant who estimated that the true count is closer to 30,000: "We keep finding more that aren't on the GIS.") Until recently the 28 local fire departments maintained their own hydrants, but "things kept getting lost in transition" between the schedules set by the city and the operations performed by the firefighters.

Brogden shared a piece of water trivia: In the early days of distribution, fire departments gained valuable time by simply drilling a hole in the nearest wooden water main instead of using the standard bucket brigade; one historian estimated that the time to fill a standard engine with water went from 15 minutes to 90 seconds. Then, when they were done, the firefighters simply plugged the hole with a piece of wood, like tapping a bung in a keg. "And you still hear a lot of people call hydrants that," he says. "Fireplugs."

Brogden started in water distribution "on the bottom, in the hole on a shovel," and he's had to stay smart to move up. "Years ago people went to work in public works because they had no skill. How much skill does it take to work a shovel? They had the choice of working on a water line or hanging off the back of a garbage truck." Now, beyond the classification of service worker, or laborer, every position on his crews is certified by the state, requiring growing levels of education, experience, and testing. "You get backflow and cross-connection certification," Brogden says. "Tests on pipe materials, disinfectants, trenching, regulations, math: If you want a 6-inch pipe a mile long to turn over twice, what's the flow rate?" And that's not even the advanced level.

Brogden walked me through his warehouse and surrounding yard, showing off pipes and joints, gaskets and flanges, connections and valves. The 2,000 miles of pipes he manages contain more than 50,000 valves: gate valves, which house an iron sheet that drops across a pipe; mechanical valves; tapping valves; air-release valves; pressure valves; and—"Hey, don't we have an old double-disk valve out here somewhere? Yeah—that big 30 is a double disk." (There are only six people on the valve maintenance team; hydrants need more workers because they have to be painted.) Saddles that clamp onto a pipe to seal a leak come in every size for every type of pipe. There are O-rings for hydrants (they all have the same thread; there's a plan to eventually adopt a national thread so that all hydrants will have the same connections), copper tubing for connections to meters, and the meters themselves.

Distribution maintenance is, to Brogden, good, honest work. "Everyone in this division has left a child's birthday party, or a spouse's party, or a basketball game" to go to work, he says. Around the clock, there is always at least one crew member on call. "These guys are not out playing in the mud. You are responsible for public health for almost half a million people. These people take that responsibility willingly." The distribution crew contains the valve and hydrant workers plus four corrective maintenance dig crews. Brogden also runs a mapping unit and eight locators, who do nothing but paint lines on the streets where someone is preparing to dig, showing where the water and sewer lines are.

He sent me out to watch a crew install a gate valve on a 12-inch main, which they did without turning off the main. It was an amazing process, something between a military drill, a ballet, and the picture you hold in your mind of 10 guys standing around a hole while two guys work. You've got the two-person valve crew in the hole, plus a laborer to run for tools; you've got track hoe and dump truck drivers, someone to manage the safety of the site, someone to supervise the work itself, maybe one or two people to manage traffic. Since this was a busy street and a high-profile project, a couple of other supervisors stopped in over the course of the afternoon. It wasn't uncommon for someone standing around the hole to shout down a suggestion that helped solve a problem—a bunched chain on the milling machine crank, an untightened lug. Brogden teaches his guys to look busy when TV cameras show up, but he says the facts are otherwise: They may not look it, but all those guys standing around looking in a hole are plenty busy, and the two or three guys inside horsing pieces of cast-iron pipe around need their help. It never looked easy for a moment, and everybody busted a sweat.

And that's every day. The supervisor on-site estimated the value of the valve at $5,000 and the milling machine at $50,000. Brogden says that in 2008 his department made 1,918 repairs, more than 5 a day, 11 of which were classified as main breaks. ("If it's below 6 inches we don't consider that a break—that's just a leak.") Breaks and leaks tend to occur when the temperature swings, so spring and fall are busy times. The average cost per work order was $3,000—a total of about $6 million just to repair problems, not including preventive maintenance, exercising valves and hydrants, and cleaning pipes. Brogden is proud of the average response time of 2 hours and the repair time of less than 6 hours. "The only time customers see us," he says, "is when they're gonna be late for work because we've got a backhoe sitting in the middle of the road. The unfortunate thing about our job is that as long as we're doing a good job, nobody notices."

THE CITY BRINGS WATER TO PEOPLE "by any means necessary," Brogden says without a trace of irony. Plant superintendent Garland told me that once or twice a day he looks out the window at the sedimentation basins and marvels that he's in charge of an enormous machine that is fundamental to the daily lives of half a million people: "It's pretty amazing that this thing runs," he says, "and it has to run forever." Best says, "I really don't think about it like that. There's just so much to do trying to keep the place running"—the new pipe running north, all the work on the new plant, constant work on the current plant—to say nothing of what comes from absorbing several small-town water systems. "We've spent the last 5 years trying to track down a lot of water problems we inherited," he says. And the system needs upgrading: Just to keep up with technology, Best says, would require an improvement budget of $20 million a year above and beyond maintenance and operating costs. Here Garland agrees, saying something that people up and down the line say about water: "It's too cheap."

They're right. When water was first pumped into cities, people tended to pay a flat fee for connection—it wasn't until the 1920s or later that people began paying metered rates for water. We seem to have retained a sense of entitlement about water, as Raleigh officials learned when they had to virtually wrestle people's garden hoses out of their hands during the worst of the drought; they continue to encounter that sense of entitlement as they try to implement tiered pricing to further encourage conservation. You'll pay more per cubic foot if you use more than a set amount, though the price still won't go much higher than the third of a cent per gallon we currently pay. Just the same, customers complain: The city encouraged conservation, and the result of that conservation, since the water utility pays its own way out of its revenues, is a price hike.

But water is still too cheap. When Raleighans consume the 100 gallons per person per day at home that the EPA says is the American average, our monthly water bills are under $32 per person. At that rate, not many homeowners will bother to get all dirty fixing household leaks (drippy faucets, running toilets, torn hoses), which the EPA estimates account for more than a trillion lost gallons per year in the United States. Nor will many showers be shortened or lawns allowed to go brown. Mine did, though—in my family we don't water, we flush only when necessary, and we use low-flow showerheads. Those are our only sacrifices, and we found that with no hardship at all, our four-person family gets along on 93 gallons per day. Even so, domestic usage is a small part of the water picture: Water for irrigation and livestock constitutes 41 percent of US water usage, and water used by thermoelectric power plants another 39 percent; total domestic and commercial use of water in the United States amounts to barely 12 percent of the total (such uses as mining and aquaculture make up the remaining 8 percent). For Americans to begin using less than the 400-plus billion gallons per day they use now, an awful lot about the way we eat and use energy will have to change.

Little about current water use sparks universal agreement, but one thing does: We've got to rethink our bathrooms. According to the EPA, of that 100 gallons of water per person per day that Americans use at home, the shower, bath, and washing machine cover about half. Washing dishes and getting water from the tap to wash or drink covers another 15 percent. Which leaves more than a third of our water consumed by either flushing toilets or letting water trickle away as toilets or faucets leak. Historians estimate that before widespread water distribution systems, an average person used between 3 and 5 gallons of water per day. We average 20 to 30 times that now—and we flush a third of it down the toilet. Water processors and administrators, public health professionals, and of course wastewater and waste treatment professionals all seem to agree: We've got to rethink our sewage.

That seemed like the next thing to look into.

CHAPTER 4

WHAT A RIVER WOULD DO

How Sewage Treatment Turns Out to Be a Somewhat
Less Nasty Business Than You Probably Thought

The guy running the snake down our sewer looks matter-of-fact. Our sewage has been backing up. Right next to the pipe connecting our house to the sewer line running down our street stands a 70-year-old willow oak, and I worry the tree's roots have found their way, during the droughty past year, into our line. He shrugs: Maybe it's tree roots, maybe it's a collapsed pipe, maybe it's a yo-yo. The snake went in only a dozen feet or so and found a clog, and now the little claw at the end is spinning. Once he pulls it out we'll know better what's going on. I leave him to his business, though I cast an annoyed glance at the oak. Sewer pipes fit together simply, with a bell joint, and tiny root hairs find their way to the nutrient-rich flow, then grow larger, eventually growing large enough to shatter the vitreous clay pipe that forms so many service lines or dislodge a joint if the pipes are cast iron. Nobody knows what our pipes, 70 years old, are made of, but I fear we're about to find out.

Fifteen minutes later he's winding the snake back up, writing a bill, and exonerating the oak.

"Do you have a baby?" he asks. We do.

"Do you use those flushable wipes?" We do.

"Don't," he says. The entire paper industry in recent years has worked to develop more and more flushable items: baby wipes, moist adult wipes, antibacterial bathroom scrubbers, diaper liners, diapers. He shakes his head: If it doesn't come apart in your hands, don't flush it. All it has to do is hold its form for an hour or so and it can find a place to catch: a joint, a root, a pimple on the inside of the pipe, one of the little mounds of rust buildup called tubercules. Then, like a snag in a river, it starts catching other stuff and you've got yourself a situation, either for you or for your whole neighborhood. We're like a nation of 1-year-olds, throwing everything in the toilet. "Toilet paper and what comes out of you," he says. "That's what should go in the toilet." Take the goldfish outside and bury it; otherwise the best case is it's just going to get caught in a screen at the treatment plant. It won't biodegrade on the way down, and it might cause trouble. And let's not even bring up those garbage disposals—we had had another guy out 6 months before and he excavated enough of a neatly processed carrot that with sufficient patience we could have reconstructed it. The sewer, person after person tells me, is for sewage.

Your favorite pop culture reference to sewage may involve Art Carney, in character as Ed Norton, singing, "Together we stand, with shovel in hand, to keep things rolling along." Or maybe it's one of those scenes from *Phantom of the Opera* or *Les Mis,* with all kinds of French high drama occurring amid the atmospheric flow. I prefer Carl Spackler in *Caddyshack,* cackling while creating plastic explosive animals against a backdrop of sacks of the common golf-course fertilizer Milorganite. You scarcely notice it, but I'll decode that: Milorganite is short for MILwaukee ORGAnic NITrogEn, a soil treatment produced by the city of Milwaukee's wastewater treatment plant since 1925 and now used on lawns all over the country. It's the end result of their sewage treatment, and they ship thousands of tons of it each year.

The point isn't so much that what happens to our sewage reaches into every crevice of our culture. The point is that once you're managing it instead of wishing it away, sewage turns out to be a pretty good thing.

In the North Carolina State Archives in Raleigh, just hanging around atop some cabinets lies an extra set of 4-foot-square planning maps made in 1922—the first planning documents in Raleigh's history. They make great idle-time study: "Locations of Fires in Buildings: One of a Series of Preliminary Zoning Studies," says one. Another shows the water distribution system, a 16-inch and a 14-inch line coming from the pumping station down by Walnut Creek to the city water tower; another shows hard-surface paving; a fourth demonstrates "Barriers to Street Extensions and Residential and Commercial Growth."

By far my favorite is "Sewer Mains and Laterals," with thick, colored-pencil stripes in brown, blue, and yellow showing the locations of different sizes of underground sewer pipes—starting from 6-inch diameters in neighborhoods like mine to the largest mains back then, 24 inches. What I love about the map is the outfalls—at Crabtree Creek north of town and Walnut Creek to the south (safely downstream from the pump that brings drinking water to the city), the colored-pencil stripes simply stop. That's where the sewage goes: into the river.

Those days seem almost absurdly quaint now, but they're not so bygone after all. In 1940, in some of the largest cities in the United States—Boston, Pittsburgh, Cincinnati, St. Louis, Kansas City—every drop of whatever you flushed down the toilet was dumped untreated into a nearby harbor, river, or lake. New York City in 1940 treated approximately one quarter of its sewage, and it reached 100 percent only in 1986. Until then, had you visited your Aunt Louise on the Upper West Side, all your business would have flowed directly into the Hudson.

Historians estimate that before indoor plumbing became widespread, the average person used less than 5 gallons of water per day; nowadays a good round (and low) estimate of American at-home water consumption is 100 gallons per day, per person. Some of that gets sprinkled on lawns and a bit washes cars and pets, but overall we use that water either for cleaning ourselves and our dishes and clothes, in which cases it ends up going down the drain, or for drinking, in which cases it ends up going down the toilet. Every day each one of us turns 100 gallons or so of water into sewage. That's a lot of sewage, requiring a lot of treatment—and very little of it is poop.

At least now we do treat it. Though people have been piping sewage for thousands of years, actual sewage treatment is barely a century old. People had to figure out first that human waste was not just noisome but actually unhealthy and then *how* it was unhealthy before they could begin figuring out what to do with it. Once they did, they got busy in a hurry; you can all but drink most of the water that comes out of Western treatment plants, and most of the biosolids removed during the process are used to fertilize crops and treat soil. The system is not flawless—biosolids sometimes contaminate water; grease clogs cause sewage spills or system failures; heavy metals, pharmaceuticals, and personal care products build up in biosolids—but overall it works splendidly.

PERHAPS THE FIRST WRITTEN SANITATION INSTRUCTIONS come from the Bible, which, written by and for a nomadic people, takes a small-is-beautiful approach: Deuteronomy urges you to dig a hole and "cover that which cometh from thee." By about 3000 BC, inhabitants of the Orkney Islands had invented toilets: Existing stone hut walls from that period have little niches with holes that drained to underground channels. The sewer historian Jon Schladweiler says that by a thousand years later, civilizations throughout the ancient Mediterranean and Middle East were using pipes to transmit both stormwater and human wastewater away from homes and cities and, usually, into waterways. By about 1500 BC the Cretan palace of Knossos had an actual flush toilet—a seat, a pan, and a slave to pour water to sluice what disposable-diaper companies call "the insult" to a drain in the floor. Cretan techniques for channeling water and wastewater spread throughout Greece, and by the 5th century BC, Athenians were piping wastewater and stormwater to a reservoir outside of town and using it to irrigate crops.

The Romans improved on even that: After considering Rome's many accomplishments, Pliny the Elder called the sewers "the greatest accomplishment of all." (The word "sewer" comes from the Latin *exaquare*, "to carry away water.") The constant flow of water coming into the city from the aqueducts supplied public fountains and baths, and Romans figured out that public bathwater ought to be changed a couple of times a day. "They built public latrine buildings immediately adjacent to the baths," Schladweiler says, and flushed the latrines by routing the used bathwater under them. The majority of human waste, though, was simply thrown into the streets; aqueduct water was used to wash the streets and sweep that waste into the drains. Because Roman sewers lacked ventilation, the only egress for sewer gas was those same drains and latrines. On the plus side, Romans also invented portable toilets, setting urns by the side of the road near the entrances to the city (vendors would rent you what Schladweiler calls "a modesty cape"). Further, the 1st-century emperor Vespasian had workers collect the contents of urinals, which he then taxed and sold to fullers, tradesmen who cleaned and dyed the Romans' clothing—they had figured out that the ammonia in urine had cleaning powers.

After the fall of the empire, Romans kept throwing filth in the streets, but nobody was washing them. In Rome many sewer pipes fell into disrepair. Everywhere else people got along without them as they always had: at best using latrines (unlined pits) or cesspits (pits lined with perforated masonry that let liquids drain away into the soil while solids piled up for eventual removal) and at worst throwing their waste into the streets and leaving it there. In the 13th century the French king Philip II paved the streets of Paris to reduce the stench, with the result that afterward the waste sat on the stones instead of percolating into the soil. In the 14th century, one of his successors, Philip VI, ordered Parisians to sweep in front of their houses and take the refuse to a dump; crews of sanitation workers were organized to clean up whatever was left. In a return to the technology of the Roman Empire, in 1370 Paris opened a series of drainage canals that also carried waste—the biggest was lined with masonry and called the Grand Égout, or Great Drain.

As cities grew, stormwater ditches and canals took on characteristics assumed by the modern sewer as people more and more commonly threw or sluiced in human and animal waste. Though elements of the Romans' ancient sewers remained beneath Rome, London, and Paris, they were still basically storm drains. In growing cities people dug cesspits beneath their houses, occasionally hiring gangs of workers to remove the contents and either dump it outside of town or reuse it as fertilizer. But the pits weren't cleaned often and the leaching liquids saturated the surrounding soil, so during the Middle Ages Europe remained largely a poop-in-the-streets world, with the predictable effects on public health.

By the 16th century one British royal castle had to post signs reminding people not to "foul the staircases, corridors, or closets with urine or other filth." When the palace of Versailles opened in the 17th century, it had lovely splashing fountains but no bathrooms or sewers.

The world changed in 1842, when the city of Hamburg, after suffering a terrible fire, decided to lay sewer pipes while rebuilding. The new pipes vented through house drains and had a mechanism for flushing using tidewater. The system was efficient, didn't stink, and became a worldwide model. (Before the introduction of these sewers, typhoid, transmitted through water tainted by sewage, caused 48½ of every 1,000 deaths in Hamburg; after the sewers came into use the number dropped by half.) Immediately thereafter the Parisians began turning their 14th-century sewer system into a wonder of the world, building hundreds of miles of huge brick tunnels to carry away stormwater and everything else Parisians cared to sluice inside.

When early American cities such as Boston and Philadelphia began paving their streets with cobblestones in the 17th century, gutters—and even some underground sewers—were included among the improvements. Private citizens built Boston's first systems, designed, like the Cloaca Maxima and the Grand Égout, to drain cellars and swamps. Bostonians soon grew weary of the constant repairs those wooden sewer lines required and undertook a sort of public-private partnership by issuing construction permits for sewers; everyone who wished to connect a drain had to share in the cost, and the contracts stipulated requirements about pavement reconstruction. Philadelphia had a system of culverts and some underground sewers by 1750, and New York City started putting a few sewers underground later in the century. Human waste, though, remained mostly a personal matter of cesspits and privies.

SEWERS REALLY TOOK OFF in 1854, with John Snow's discovery that the London cholera epidemic was caused by sewage-tainted drinking water. With advances in microbiology, people began to understand that human waste carried disease in the form of microbes, and increasingly they wanted to protect themselves from their sewage. What's more, the introduction of reliable water service in the 19th century and the spread of the modern flush toilet (the British Public Health Act of 1848, which required every home to have some kind of sanitary arrangement, listed "water closet" as one of the alternatives to an ash pit or privy) vastly increased the amount of wastewater households generated. Cesspits and privies that had already created offensive nuisances now produced vast, vile-smelling seepages, overwhelmed by the new volume of water. And it wasn't just toilets, either—connections draining sinks and tubs began overwhelming sewer pipes, too; in 1844 Boston tried to slow the tide, literally, by passing a law requiring a doctor's order for every bath.

As cities grew in size and density during the Industrial Revolution, they all had to build more, and better, sewers. The cholera epidemic wasn't motivation enough for London, but the "Great Stink" of 1858, when the Thames smelled so bad that Parliament considered relocating, got the city government's attention; it built new sewers in the 1850s and '60s to carry waste downstream from central London. Brooklyn introduced sewers in 1857, and Chicago not long after. Boston, still largely building sewers privately, had about 100 miles of sewers in 1869; by 1885 that had expanded to 226 miles, and new houses were expected to connect to the system both for pump and washbasin waste and for the human waste now going into flush toilets instead of privies.

Every city had its own problems and its own characteristics. Some of Boston's sewers had outfalls dammed by the tide 12 hours of every 24; others, built by unscrupulous contractors in land reclamation projects like the Back Bay, sagged and lost their downhill slope, causing settling, clogs, and backups. Sylvan Seattle had pipes made of wooden staves— and faced a tide problem so severe that at certain times of day toilets became foul geysers; eventually the city simply rebuilt itself higher than its sewer pipes. In Chicago, the outfalls of the sewers made such a mess of Lake Michigan that during large rainstorms the plume of tainted water flowed all the way out to the intake for the water system. In response, engineers built a series of canals and reversed the flow of the Chicago River, turning it from a drainage into Lake Michigan into a flow from Lake Michigan toward the Mississippi. They also moved the intake farther out into the lake.

All these "solutions" merely moved the problem. As one historian said in describing Boston's covering a brook filled with sewage and routing it to the Charles River rather than directly into Boston Harbor, this "somewhat lessened the nuisance caused by it, or at least transferred it to another locality." Older cities on the coasts built combined systems channeling both sewage and stormwater, whereas newer and smaller cities built separate systems—both storm drains and systems of much smaller pipes that handled only sewage—thus preventing sewage overflows in storms. Lennox, Massachusetts, built the first such system in 1875, and Memphis built one in 1880. Since then, that's what everybody has built.

RALEIGH LAID ITS FIRST SEWER PIPES in 1890. Fayetteville Street, Raleigh's main road, wasn't paved until 1886, at exactly the same time the first water pipes were being laid; where water pipes go, sewer pipes soon follow. The privies of Raleigh's population of barely 10,000 almost certainly had not yet polluted the soil enough to foul its wells, and the new sewer pipes, running north to Crabtree Creek and south to Walnut Creek, would not have discharged more than the streams could absorb. (A stream running at about 6 cubic feet per second can absorb the waste of about 1,000 people, so to support 10,000 people the two creeks together would have had to flow at around 60 cfs. Currently, on a dry day in a dry month, they flow at about 75 cfs.) Now, with 2,300 miles of pipes all heading roughly southeast to Raleigh's wastewater treatment plant, the sewer collection system turns out to be the only infrastructure stream that follows that natural tree pattern that I'd expected to find everywhere. The leaves are houses, connected by 4-inch service lines to 6- or 8-inch mains that run mostly beneath streets, and then to 18-, 24-, or 30-inch collectors that start out along streets but head downhill to creek basins, leading to larger and larger pipes and finally to the plant. I sat down with a friendly GIS expert to check it out.

The GIS map easily showed me the path of my own wastewater: the

4-inch lateral in my yard—the same pipe that "flushable" wipe clogged—runs into an 8-inch main, which heads downhill along my street until it crosses the Pigeon House Branch, down by the pool I like to sit by. It runs along the Pigeon House until it joins a 24-inch PVC east of town (the path is following rivers by then, not roads), and thereafter joins larger and larger pipes—some made of PVC, some of reinforced concrete, some of ductile iron. Eventually this stream hits the dual 72-inch reinforced concrete pipes that head directly to the sewer plant, though those sometimes separate into three or four pipes, for ease of maintenance. It's simple and, especially after the spaghetti tangle of the water lines, rather satisfying. It's much like the stormwater system, if every ravine in every drainage basin remained piped and they all came together in one place before entering the Neuse.

To find out what happens in these pipes, I talked to Raleigh's dean of pipage, sewer collection superintendent Hunter "Gene" Stanley. "We're not like New York City," Stanley says right off. "Some of those you can drive a truck through." New York has a combined sewer system that has to be prepared to move the billions of gallons of water that a major storm could dump on the city, not just the comparative trickle of sewage the city generates daily. Combined systems manage overflows with relatively simple mechanical junctions called regulators: basically weir dams in pipes or junction boxes. A weir is nothing more than a low barrier for steering water. When flow is routine, the dam routes it through pipes to the treatment plant; during large rain events, the flow of mixed stormwater and wastewater rises high, overtops the weirs, and flows directly through outfalls to rivers or lakes. Such an event is called a CSO, or combined sewage overflow. New York dumps about 40 billion gallons of CSOs into its rivers and harbors every year.

But before you draw too much comfort from Raleigh's system having to convey only sewage (the plant treats about 45 million gallons per day that are generated by the 400,000 or so customers connected to the system; it's rated for 60 million gallons, and it's being expanded to 75), consider this: The increase in flow caused by nothing more than rainfall and street flow coming in through manhole vents in low-lying areas can nearly double the flow to the treatment plant. Really? "Oh yeah, oh yeah,"

Stanley says. "A thousand gallons a day [per manhole] if it rains all day." Add in leaky joints, cracks, and holes made by thirsty tree roots, and you can have significant water infiltration during rainstorms. Though catching and correcting the breaks and overflows are an unavoidable part of his job, Stanley stays focused on preventive maintenance.

Stanley grew up in rural North Carolina and has called his preventive maintenance management "an ol' country boy work system"—he copies pages from the map book of his system and gives them to his crews. When the crew has flushed and inspected every line on the map, it comes back. The department logs its maintenance in feet per day, and it likes to reach 300,000 feet per month if it can, meaning that every pipe in the system gets a look-see once every few years. GIS keeps the maps updated, of course, but Stanley's system has been working since they were using nothing more than blueprints and as-built surveys; finding that what's an 8-inch pipe on the map is really a 6-inch is just part of keeping on top of things. That's why you carry different-size saw blades in your truck.

Stanley says a sewer is a simple thing: The pipe needs to drop about half a foot per 100 feet of length, a slope of 0.5 percent, which is fast enough to keep everything moving, but not so fast that the liquid races away from the solids. Bigger pipes—30 inches or larger—can slope even less. But they all must flow downhill, powered by gravity, which is why sewer pipes so commonly crisscross the stormwater drainages: Raleigh Public Utilities Department director Dale Crisp calls all the sewers that run in a particular drainage a "sewershed," which for a while became my favorite new word.

Of course, if wastewater pipes followed only natural gullies, the mains would eventually have to parallel the river, and for many reasons, from aesthetics to the catastrophic results of a spill, nobody wants that. The system generally moves downhill, but pipes sometimes need to cross rises. So the city has more than 100 lift stations, where the contents of pipes are pumped to join other flows or where wastewater from low-lying areas collects in sumps. When the water gets high enough, it trips a float valve and a pump clicks on and lifts it up a hill—kind of like your toilet, only this float valve starts the flush instead of stopping it. I visited one lift station, a 10- by 20-foot rectangle of electrical boxes that look like a central air-conditioning system behind chain-link fences between two houses, controlling an underground sump; even when it's pumping, if you were more than 10 feet away you wouldn't hear it. The station has a backup pump and a generator to power it, plus a little antenna to send information back and forth to the supervisory control and data acquisition (SCADA) system at the treatment plant; that's plenty of equipment, but just the same, if you weren't looking for it you wouldn't know it was there. A much larger station sits on the trunk line, giving a lift to pretty much all of Raleigh's waste on its way to the plant. It's underneath a highway on-ramp, and though some people suggested I could find it by following my nose, it didn't smell when I went out to visit it.

Stanley hands over a laudatory profile of Raleigh's sewer maintenance department in a recent issue of *Municipal Sewer and Water* magazine, then hands me off to Robert Smith, a sewer monitoring supervisor and asks him to show me around.

FIRST THINGS FIRST: We walk the yard, checking out trucks. Sewer guys basically do three things: They perform maintenance, they respond to crises, and they "TV" pipes, sending tiny little vehicles with cameras on them up the pipes to check both their condition as part of general maintenance and whether the crews who claim to have recently maintained them have actually done so.

Smith shows off the department's various trucks. Rodder trucks have a spool of linked rods, a sort of long chain that the workers feed into a manhole and then rotate, just like someone cleaning roots or a clog out of your drain at home. Some rodders have cutting blades or spiral grabbing implements to clear roots or debris. Flushing trucks carry enormous water tanks to feed high-pressure hoses with spinning heads on the end: Workers feed the hose into the system, usually past the next manhole, and then turn on a pump. Water pressure starts the head spinning, spraying water at thousands of pounds of pressure per square inch back toward the truck as the truck pulls back the hose, scouring the pipes along the way. Standard now is the combination truck, which carries tanks of water for flushing and a garbage-truck-size tank for postflush water, which the truck vacuums up with a huge tube that hangs from a derrick over the cab like an elephant's trunk. The driver eventually empties that tank onto a pad in the parking area, Smith explains; water drains off into the sewer system and the cleaned-out debris—tampons, bricks, gravel, roots, supposedly flushable materials—gets loaded into a dump truck once a week and sent to the landfill. Smith marshals those vacuum trucks when Raleigh has a sewage overflow, too. Another truck he calls a blockbuster has a water hammer—a pipe that uses water to rhythmically pound and break up large blockages. Finally, he shows me a sort of souped-up golf cart that provides access to the many parts of the system that, because they follow ravines rather than roads, are not easily reached by regular trucks.

But we're standing in a parking lot while people are out in the field, rodding sewers. "Hey," he says. "You wanna shoot the line?" You bet.

OUR FIRST STOP is a highway off-ramp, where two flush trucks and a pickup are parked behind orange cones. Several men wearing hard hats, green mesh vests, and rubber-palmed gloves manage a hose coming off a spool on the back of one of the trucks and running to a manhole 20 feet down a steep ravine. A hundred yards away, two guys stand at another manhole looking out for the spinning head of the water jet, which Smith says is called a Warthog. Once it's past, the guys still at the truck turn on the jet and the spool to start reeling it back in. Over the roar of the truck engine Smith explains that on the way out the head sprays as a sort of presoak; "on the way back, it's like a broom." Water-jet cleaning like this is standard for clearing roots, grit, and, especially, grease: "We run into some lines [where] you think, Where in the world did all this grease come from? It looks like you sprayed foam on that pipe." Because the bell-and-spigot joints in sewer pipes provide places for tiny tree roots to enter, and because trees got very thirsty during the drought, crews commonly run a saw through the line after cleaning just to make sure they've got everything. Where the vacuum trucks can't reach a manhole, the crew flushes debris downstream to one the truck can reach.

That's sewer flushing, and the sanitation department does it all day long. Ever since the Hamburg sewers first captured tidal water and then released it all at once to flush out debris, the basic idea hasn't changed much: You use water to flush, you use rods or hooks to attack clogs, and, as Ed Norton sang, you keep things rolling along.

Smith packs us back in his pickup and we drive to a parking lot and a box truck with a picture of a fish on it. The three guys in the truck are going to TV a pipe: Mike is preparing the camera and the screens in the back of the truck while Wayne and someone who introduces himself only as "the Rev" open the manhole, popping the cover off easily with a metal hook. Wayne and the Rev then retrieve the camera from the truck. With six tiny rubber wheels and an inquisitive single eye, it looks a bit like the Mars rover vehicle, only tiny and dangling at the end of a wire. When they come back to the manhole Wayne and the Rev are shocked to find it suddenly filled with sewage. This kind of backup indicates a block in the 6-inch pipe at the bottom of the manhole, though it drains away as fast as it backed up.

A few moments of observation shows two things: The backup comes and goes rhythmically, meaning there's a pump station upstream that sends a pulse of wastewater every couple of minutes, and the blockage is a bunch of pieces of some solid substance that nobody can identify. Out come spoons—hooked, perforated shovels on the end of 12-foot handles. Wayne, Robert Smith, and Eddie, another supervisor who has arrived, take turns scooping, pushing things back and forth between rushes from the pump and pulling them out with an awkward hand-over-hand motion that keeps the gunk barely balanced on the edge of the spoon unless you knock the handle against an overhanging tree branch. It's like using an iced-tea spoon to fish olive pits out of a bleach jug at the back of a cupboard. "And people think it's Ty-D-Bol that keeps their bathrooms clean," Wayne says.

The stuff turns out to be congealed grease, and pieces of it are sufficiently solid—and sufficiently far up the 6-inch pipe—that they block the progress of the camera every time the Rev dangles it down there and tries to get it running. The vacuum nozzle can clear the manhole but can't pull grease out of the pipe and it resists everything else they've got, so the crew finally gives up on TV-ing that pipe for the day, until they can clean the pipe—possibly by using a bucket truck (which feeds a cable past the debris and drags a bucket from one manhole to the next, pulling before it the kind of grit and large debris flushing just doesn't get) or possibly by sending someone down there in the hope that a simple scoop into the pipe will clear the debris. (Sending someone down a manhole, though it's only about 8 feet deep, requires confined spaces training, extra supervision, and ventilation equipment—sewer gas contains methane and hydrogen sulfide, and it has killed workers as recently as 2008.)

Smith shows me video footage from another TV-ing expedition that shows long traverses down shiny pipes half full of dull gray water. The color makes sense—much more of it comes from your washing machine and shower than from your toilet. "First thing people say is 'Eew,'" Smith says; "they think I'm walking around in feces." But even the wastewater filling up the manhole that day smelled more like runoff than poop.

Though most blockages are caused by grease or roots, the talk naturally turns to memorable clogs, and I hear about mops, golf clubs, firewood, riprap, and even a refrigerator that have had to be pulled out of manholes. Once a carpet remnant created a block so nasty it took most of a day to clear out. If you're on call and someone calls in a spill, especially one where the overflow is making its way toward a waterway, then it's show-time. "You go running after it like it's a Russian spy," Wayne says. "You chase the spill, pulling hose, four, five, six miles." First the crew finds the end of the spill in the waterway—where the water is still clean—and sets up a block using hay bales, which both dam the flow and filter any water that might trickle through. A pump immediately starts channeling the polluted water into the nearest downstream manhole. And while a crew works on clearing the clog itself, other crews chase the spill, hosing down the sides and bottom of the stream. You can tell when untreated wastewater has hit a stream, Smith says, by the powdery-looking buildup it leaves: "It looks like gray dust in the water," coating the rocks and sticks. The hoses clear the scum off the bottom and stir up the mud. "That muddy water acts like a glue to that stuff—it piggybacks on the mud." Then you pump it out at the end of the spill. "After we go through, that creek looks like nothing ever hit it. It's pretty neat."

ONE DAY I pulled over on a main highway to watch a sewer crew fix a leaky pipe using what's called cured-in-place pipe: A long liner impregnated with resin is pushed into a pipe by water, then they pump steam through the pipe to harden the resin, and presto—the pipe is, though slightly narrower, all but new. The crew runs an auxiliary pipe while they fix the leaky one. Workers can find leaks by stopping up pipes with sandbags, pumping smoke down a manhole, and then seeing where the smoke starts creeping out of the ground. Clearly, people have thought about this stuff a lot.

"It gets in your blood," said a senior engineer and inspector named Dave, who managed a construction site near my house. I had stopped by a sewer truck to watch a couple of guys hose out a pipe, which they followed to a manhole at the backyard boundary of a few properties. "I don't like the looks of that," one had said when, spooning out grit from the hole, he unearthed pieces of clay pipe. Rather than dig on several people's private property, the city decided to abandon the line running between the houses and reroute the flow to the end of the street, where it could join a larger main and head downhill. But since the flow had to go downhill, the engineers had to get wastewater to flow away from the manhole in a different direction. That meant, simply, digging a deeper trench in the direction they wanted it to go. They had to do the same thing on the line that received the new flow, so they were digging on two streets for a few weeks, and I occasionally stopped by.

I watched them carefully lower new green PVC pipes and check the slope. They use a laser to measure, with a sort of bull's-eye target at the end. The red dot right in the center means the pipe has the right slope. "We used to run string lines, length by length," Dave told me. "This makes it easier. A *lot* easier." They lay pipe on a bed of gravel, supporting it with rocks and pieces of brick to maintain the slope, unlike water pipe, which, under pressure, can just be laid in a trench and buried. Any pipe below 12 feet has to be ductile iron, to support the weight of the earth on top; same with any pipe that crosses a creekbed, hangs under a bridge, or does anything but lie directly on the earth. Even though sewer pipes start out low and have to keep going lower, in a city with no subway system there's not much other infrastructure in the way; 12 feet is fairly deep for Raleigh.

The Neuse River Wastewater Treatment Plant, southeast of Raleigh, discharges most of the 40-plus million gallons of water it treats every day in a state bordering on potable. Spread over 300 acres (and surrounded by 1,200 acres of farm fields for application of biosolids), the plant is big enough that to see it you have to tool around in a van; you can't walk it like you can the water treatment plant miles upstream. Superintendent T. J. Lynch started my tour with a drive to the head-works, where screens and vortex filters remove the floating junk and grit from the outflow of the twin 72-inch trunks flowing in from the sewer system. The floating stuff is more obvious, but Lynch emphasizes the basins that settle out grit: In a process heavy on pumps and pipes, grit is anathema. "Think about sand," he says. "It's abrasive. It will literally wear out your equipment." They fill three Dumpsters a day with grit and the debris caught by screening, all of which goes to the landfill.

Remarkably, though the air has a certain tang, it doesn't stink. "Ninety-nine-point-nine percent of it is just water," Lynch says. "We've just got to get that 0.1 percent out."

Outside the headworks Lynch points to a concrete basin almost the exact size and shape of a baseball field, sloping downward from the outfield to a low point at home plate: a 32-million-gallon equalization tank. The sewer system does not have water towers or storage tanks to accommodate regular fluctuations in wastewater volume (flow peaks at breakfast time and again just after midnight), so it stores water in the equalization tank during periods of high flow and, especially, storms: Lynch says, "It's not uncommon for us during a heavy rain to see our flow double." The equalization tank gives Lynch a place to put that excess flow. When the flow slows down again, he uses four enormous screw pumps to push the water to the top of the slope on which the plant is built—the rest of the way through the plant, gravity does the work. He shows off the pumps proudly. They're called "vertical turbine solids-handling pumps," but he notes that they use technology roughly unchanged since the time of Archimedes: turning screws to lift water.

From the headworks the water flows to primary clarifiers—tanks through which the wastewater flows extremely slowly, not unlike the settlement basins at the water plant, and with the same goal: allowing solids to settle to the bottom, creating a "primary sludge blanket," though here grease and oil also float to the top. Scrapers make a circuit along the surface, scooping grease into a small flume, then cycling to the bottom where they shepherd the sludge to its own pumps. Water cleanliness is measured by biochemical oxygen demand (BOD)—the amount of oxygen the bacteria in the water use to remove its organic impurities. The lower the BOD, the smaller the next basins can be and the lower the plant's operating costs. This is a crucial point, given how much energy the next step takes. That step is what Lynch calls "the absolute heart and soul" of his plant: the activated sludge process.

So after a few hours in the clarification tank, the water flows into aeration basins, six concrete pools of several million gallons apiece, the bottoms of which are crisscrossed by air nozzles. These enormous tanks of what looks like boiling brown sewage are just what you imagine when you think "sewage treatment." But it's not boiling: What's happening is aeration, which provides oxygen, in the presence of which bacteria love to eat poop. "We are bug farmers," Lynch says. Bacteria in the basins multiply rapidly, like the starter for sourdough bread. The wastewater provides the food, the nozzles provide the oxygen, and the bacteria feel like they're on a cruise: nothing but breathing, eating, and reproducing, with free food all day long.

This process removes all the harmful chemicals from the water—except nitrates, which feed algae in rivers. These algae propagate wildly and then die. "And the decomposition sucks up all the oxygen in the river, killing the fish. So now we're going into the same tanks and we put walls in there and we have different zones where we stimulate the bacteria to do different things" that remove nitrogen. After about a day of that, the water spends 2 days flowing very slowly through secondary clarification basins: a dozen large circular tanks, each the size of an aboveground swimming pool. "It's very quiet," Lynch says. "The bacteria settle down and create what we call the sludge blanket," which sinks to the bottom and is pumped out. The water trickles out through V-notch weirs around the top of the tank, by which point it has a barely yellowish tinge and no odor whatsoever.

We'll get to the next stage of water filtration, but what's more interesting at this point is what happens to the sludge. Most of it becomes RAS—return activated sludge—and rejoins new wastewater in the aeration basins, providing the starter for a whole new treatment reaction. Bacteria can go around the cycle half a dozen times, Lynch says, but eventually they become WAS—*waste* activated sludge. In the WAS stream, the bacteria go to four big covered tanks called aerobic sludge digesters, in which instead of wastewater nutrients they eat each other. We climbed up to the top of one of the basins and looked through a porthole inside: You could almost hear the screaming. Okay, not really; it's just a tank of sludge. "If it's good sludge, it's got that nice brown color—it's oxygenated, and it don't smell bad up here," Lynch says. If it's black, something's out of whack—it probably needs more oxygen.

Aerobic digestion, Lynch says, is actually inefficient—it costs money, since the plant has to pump in oxygen; anaerobic digestion, to which the plant hopes to switch, is the opposite: It generates methane, which the plant can use to generate electricity to operate its pumps and blowers; the waste heat from the generators can even help provide the heat the anaerobic digesters need to keep the bugs at optimum eating-each-other temperature. "There are plants now that generate their entire power needs from that methane," he says. "They pull no energy from the grid."

From the digesters we drive to the dewatering building—just as at the water treatment plant, the wastewater plant uses belt presses to squeeze the water out of the last, bug-eat-bug stage of the sludge. Enormous screw conveyors grind big pieces of the dewatered stuff along like the mixers in an industrial bakery. Lynch hands me a piece of what they call cake. It has no odor at all and feels a lot like inch-thick rubber, the kind used under playground equipment. Polymers are introduced to help coagulation and add to the rubbery feel. "Don't forget to wash your hands," Lynch says.

We leave the sludge and return to the water. Primary treatment is mechanical—settling; secondary treatment is biochemical—activated sludge digestion. Tertiary treatment combines mechanical and photo-chemical: The water flows to a dozen deep sand filters, which remove the remaining fine particles. The final hurdle the water clears is ultraviolet treatment. We walk over to a small, low concrete building, in front of which Lynch pulls up a flat piece of aluminum to reveal a 4- or 5-foot-wide channel of water flowing smoothly past banks of green-glowing UV lamps. They look much like fluorescent lights, though they have a self-wiping mechanism to keep them clean. "It doesn't kill [pathogens]," he says of the light. "It just scrambles their RNA. Sterilizes 'em." He mentions in passing an open concrete channel between the filters and the UV treatment, in which tilapia swim. "It keeps the duckweed down," he says. Once fish are swimming in your treated sewage, you've got to feel like you're getting the job done.

Out behind the UV building we finally reach the finished product: the effluent, flowing out in strong wide arcs into a canal from a dozen UV channels. The water seems to have a greenish tinge, but when Lynch fills a little water bottle and holds it up it looks utterly clear. Then we drive down toward the end of the line, where the effluent enters the Neuse River. There, in a tiny green glade at the bottom of the hill, the river bends into a cove, near the bank of which a few surface bubbles give away the presence of the underground pipe. Lynch says if you didn't know where the pipe was you could follow shad upstream to find it: "The water's warm and highly oxygenated," so the fish love it.

Lynch says the river is the natural place for the water anyhow. Every drop of Raleigh water comes from the Neuse watershed and ought to return there. "All we're doing," he says, "is what a river would do." That is, rivers are naturally self-cleaning, and the Neuse would absorb waste, given time and distance. Waste on the ground would be dispersed by rain and the water would be filtered through the earth, entering the groundwater system clean; matter that made it to the stream would become waterlogged and sink. "On the rocky bottom, bacteria live," he says, that feed off the nutrients in waste. "What happens in our plant is the exact same thing that happens in a stream. That's exactly where the process came from. We've just concentrated it," Lynch says. "It might take the river a couple hundred miles to accomplish what we do in a couple days." We've been talking about sewage treatment for 2 hours—about dewatered cake and grit screens and activated sludge and UV filters—and suddenly I understand.

WHAT THE RIVER DOES is exactly what a sewage plant does, and until around World War I most people didn't really think plants were needed at all. It was understood that watercourses were to some degree self-cleaning, that "the solution to pollution is dilution." But as populations increased, especially downstream, dilution stopped offering much of a solution. Chicagoans felt great about their famous flow-reversal of the Chicago River, sending their sewage into the Mississippi instead of into their own water supply of Lake Michigan. Predictably, the people of St. Louis were not as delighted. Their expression of dissatisfaction eventually landed them in front of the Supreme Court. Raleigh itself was sued in the late 1940s by downstream neighbor Smithfield. Smithfield won, and in 1956 Raleigh's first sewage treatment plant opened, treating 12 million gallons per day. The current plant replaced it in 1977; it's expanded since, and now it's expanding again.

Raleigh's sewage treatment will be limited not by space, but by nitrogen. In 1995 the state of North Carolina set limits on nitrogen based on totals for that year. Raleigh's plant released 1.3 million pounds of nitrogen into the Neuse in 1995, and its current limit is 49 percent of that total, or 676,496 pounds. In 2007 it released 233,061 pounds, its lowest total ever. Still, the state-mandated limit will keep dropping, and Raleigh's capacity to treat its sewage will probably finally reach its limit in pounds of nitrogen rather than in millions of gallons per day.

MODERN SEWAGE TREATMENT IS A BOON, of course, but it creates a new problem. If you treat sewage so effectively that by the time water leaves the plant it's almost drinkable, then what do you do with all the sludge you cleaned out of it? People have been fertilizing with their sewage since the ancient Athenians, but modern Americans seem to mistrust the process. As recently as 2006, when water-starved San Diego considered a water-saving measure to reintroduce effluent from its sewage plant into its reservoir—from which, of course, the city's water would still be treated before use—the *Union-Tribune* opined, "your golden retriever may drink water out of the toilet with no ill effects. But that doesn't mean humans should do the same." The practice would have made the reservoir no different than the Mississippi or the Neuse or any other source of water into which the effluent of cities upstream has been poured (water managers like to spout the true-enough-for-discussion statistic that by the time Londoners drink water from the Thames, it's been through seven sets of kidneys upstream; others repeat the same chestnut about New Orleans and the Mississippi). Two years later San Diego's mayor claimed the reuse measure was a waste of money and vetoed it. The city council overturned his veto, but it's clear: Even in the parched Southwest, people are frightened of wastewater reuse.

(In 2008, when Raleigh introduced a plan to save water by reusing effluent from the Neuse plant—by piping it only to large-scale users, such as universities, business campuses, and country clubs, and only for irrigation—some politicians resisted. They claimed to object to "subsidizing" large-scale users through lower rates for the reuse water. Fortunately, enough people remembered the drought; the system was built, using pipes foresightedly laid almost a decade earlier.)

Given that people feel that resistant to highly treated water, what on earth to do with all this sludge? New York used to dump its sludge far out in the ocean, a practice that didn't represent a huge improvement over dumping raw sewage, until that was outlawed in 1992, after which the city started shipping sludge by train to a Texas landfill. Plenty of cities still landfill their sludge. Raleigh chooses to follow the example of Milwaukee: More than 90 percent of its sludge is beneficially reused as biosolids (nationwide about 50 percent of sludge is reused). Some of Raleigh's muck is thickened on gravity belt presses and applied directly to fields as Class B biosolids (according to the EPA, this use requires a buffer between fields and the public, and they can't be used on crops for human consumption). Some of this was overapplied to the Raleigh farmland surrounding the plant in recent years; a series of poor practices resulted in groundwater contamination near the plant, so the practice was stopped, though the plant currently has the highest certification level of the National Biosolids Partnership (the NBP is a nonprofit comprising three national groups: Two represent the sewage treatment industry, which may not be the most objective source for biosolids practice assessment, and the third is the Environmental Protection Agency, which probably is).

Some primary sludge is dewatered and sold to a composting company, which treats it and sells it to agricultural products companies as safer, more highly treated Class A biosolids. The rest is mixed with lime, which raises the temperature high enough to pasteurize it, and sold to farms, institutions, and the public as Raleigh Plus, Raleigh's own version of Milorganite. Maybe I'll use some on my lawn. Nobody has any statistics on how it affects gophers.

CHAPTER 5

THE ASPHALT BALLET

Streets, Sidewalks, and the Highway Overpass

THE RUMBLE AND BEEP OF LARGE VEHICLES GOING IN REVERSE caught my ear one morning at breakfast, so I scrambled and within a few minutes my 4-year-old son and I were standing a block away from our house, watching a street become a street.

First, we watched the street briefly stop being a street. To resurface a street (Raleigh tries to get to every one of its streets every 10 or 15 years), you need a milling machine—in this case a Bomag BM 1300/30, which looks something like the walking transports in *The Empire Strikes Back*. It has four hydraulic legs, each with a little triangular tread for a foot, that extend so that the machine appears to stand on tiptoe; the conveyor belt for clearing away the milled asphalt stretches upward like a neck. Louie and I marveled at it.

Crawling forward smoothly, the milling machine lowered its mill— basically a spinning drum covered with thick, replaceable steel spikes— from its belly and the instantly pulverized remnants of what had been road began shooting up the conveyer, arcing as gracefully as the jet of a fountain into the back of a dump truck rolling slowly ahead of it. Like dancers executing a pas de deux, the two trucks moved gracefully together, taking a few inches off the top of—no kidding—New Road. That went on for about a day, after which the contractors did it again piecemeal, this time digging deeper, but only where the lower layer of asphalt was collapsing—over replaced water lines, for example, where the hole had been poorly backfilled and deep cracks showed the road had settled. Once the milling was done, the workers spent another day making sure the manholes and valve tops and other infrastructure poke-ups were at the right height for the new street.

Then came paving day: In front, a big red dump truck crept along, occasionally tilting to dump hot asphalt mix into the paver, a smaller green truck with a hopper whose lid spread open wide like the beak of a baby bird to receive the hot mix. The paver released the mix and automatically smoothed it (a worker had already spread "tack," a sort of glue that helps the asphalt bond to the pavement below it). Behind the paver, workers scraped the sides of the patch with shovels, putting the extra atop the steaming asphalt, which radiated heat at close to 300°F. Others used metal rakes to evenly spread it. Finally came the steamroller, packing down the fresh asphalt mix, its drum wheels cooled by water to help it smooth and compact.

As spectacle, it outperformed many theater and dance troupes I've seen, and Louie was deeply satisfied: Everybody made their entrances and exits, the gentle, driving rhythm rarely varied, and nobody ever lost track of what they were doing. The process moved astonishingly quickly. If you lived on New Road and you went out of town for a few days, you could come home to a brand-new street having missed the whole thing.

Street paving is a pretty mature science. Don't pave when it's below 40 degrees or so, because the asphalt cools too quickly and doesn't set up right or bond to the subpavement. One worker explained to me that a street usually has two or three levels of asphalt: The base course (and the intermediate layer if there is one, for high-traffic roads) is structural, designed to hold up the road but also to drain water if any gets in. The high-density top layer, or "surface mix," is waterproof. Most damage to asphalt roads comes from the freeze-thaw cycle, when water seeps beneath the edges of the road or into cracks and then freezes, expanding and separating the layers. That's how potholes start, the worker told me, and that's why a place like North Carolina, which freezes and thaws all winter long, has a rougher time with its roads than even some places up north, where the freezes last longer. Water doesn't need much of a hole to enter: A crew filling potholes told me they scan the street for any hole big enough to hold a marble.

The surface layer is also designed to resist skidding, wear, and the stress of vehicles driving over it. For details about the road surface—a mix of asphalt, sand, and gravel—a crew supervisor sent me to the *North Carolina Department of Transportation Standard Specifications for Roads and Structures,* a little red Bible-size handbook he carried in his pickup. Asphalt, it turns out, is the lowest grade of crude oil, which bubbles up from the ground in lakes: The La Brea Tar Pits in Los Angeles are asphalt, and there are other major asphalt lakes in Trinidad and Venezuela. Asphalt historians like to conjecture that the pitch Noah is described as using for the ark—and the "slime" used for mortar in the tower of Babel—were asphalt, though they refer only to the goo itself, not the gravel mixture we use in paving. But for information about modern road paving in Raleigh, I didn't need to go any further than to the City of Raleigh Web site.

There I found specific standards for residential streets. A 31-foot-wide street, like mine, requires a 50-foot right-of-way; the 5-foot-wide sidewalk that is required (on one side only) will tilt a quarter-inch per foot toward the street for drainage and be 3½ feet away from the curb. The road itself will slope away from the center, or crown, at a quarter-inch per foot; the compacted subgrade beneath the road will start 12¼ inches beneath the crown; the base layer of compacted crush-and-run (gravel mixed with sand) will constitute 8 inches; and the 2-plus inches of the top layers will include one layer of intermediate topped by a layer of finish grade. The Raleigh Web site shows simple cross-sections of street showing various layers and slopes, as well as string-line diagrams showing dimensions from curb to curb. Thousands of years' worth of distilled understanding of how a street works appears on-screen in seconds.

THE ROMANS PIONEERED ROAD ENGINEERING. To keep their roads dry, they built up the earth beneath the roadway a good meter above the ground; for drainage, they crowned the road in the middle and ran ditches alongside. A longer, paved road was called a Via, or Way—the famous Appian Way, for example. On these major roads, above the meter of earth came a layer of flat stones a foot or more thick; on top of that came one or more layers of mixed gravel and lime, and finally, a layer of flat paving stones. That's a lot of roadway; put it on top of that meter of initial height and you have a *way* that's *high* above the surrounding territory: We still call a long road a highway. Of course, all roads weren't given such major treatment. A North Carolina highway engineer told me to look at a kind of steamroller with low cleats used to compact earth beneath a gravel layer in modern paving. It's called a sheepsfoot roller. The Roman army, he said, traveled with flocks of sheep, who besides providing food, wool, and hid, had an additional job: The sheep would travel ahead of the soldiers, their hooves compacting the roadway soil, which the army (charged with maintaining the roads anyway) would cover with gravel.

Raleigh has been paving its streets since 1886, when the main street was "macadamized." John McAdam, a Scottish roadbuilder, had figured out in the early 1800s that instead of layer upon layer of different materials, the standard design for roads since Roman times, builders could simply lay down fresh crushed stone, compact it, and commence driving. He learned that two layers of stone freshly broken up into small pieces—the bottom layer about 3 inches deep, the top layer less than an inch—could rest directly on a prepared subgrade, with no base of large stones. Once compacted, the sharp edges of the fresh broken stone gripped each other, with dust and sand as a binder. This made a road as strong as the much more complex roads built on block foundations; the stone matrix drained well, too. The roads got better still when the tar leftover from the production of coal gas for street lighting turned out to be perfect for pouring atop macadamized roads to keep down the dust: "Tarmacadam," or "tarmac," entered the vernacular, though now we mostly use the word to mean airfields. Actual asphalt came into use in Europe in the 1850s and had paved Union Square in New York by the 1870s.

The strongest advocate for the new smooth roads was the League of American Wheelmen—a bicycle lobby, which during the 1890s became one of the nation's largest special-interest groups. Nowadays asphalt covers 93 percent of American roads; it's cheaper and less noisy than concrete, so we pave with concrete only where structural integrity is vital—on bridge decks, for example, or on high-volume roads pounded by truck traffic, like interstates. Amazingly, modern asphalt paving is more than 95 percent gravel—the smooth surface comes from the other 5 percent.

Apart from introducing smooth, dry roads to the world, McAdam's technique also provided a lasting cliché image. Because providing a steady stream of 1-inch rocks was rough work, departments of transportation nationwide made deals with their prison systems. Those chain gangs in stripes breaking rocks by the side of the road aren't just an image from cartoons and old movies: Those guys were real. The road boss carried a steel ring through which the smallest stones had to pass; failing that, a stone small enough to fit into a laborer's mouth was good enough. Convict labor started in North Carolina in 1887 and continued well into the 1950s, when it stopped nationwide (though it made a brief reappearance in the 1990s).

PHYSICALLY, A STREET IS SIMPLE: It holds the cars up and keeps them out of the mud. Conceptually, though, what a street ought to be, and how one ought to manage it, remains a work in progress. One of my favorites is Gavin Street, not a quarter-mile from my house. It's a little angled thing, running past a couple of new warehouses and a train yard, then taking a right by a boiler repair shop and an empty auto mechanic's, but what I love about it is that it's paved only with gravel. The city of Raleigh maintains 1,031.57 miles of streets, street superintendent Chris McGee told me, of which 5.97 miles (about 0.5 percent) are still gravel. There's something satisfying about a gravel road—maybe it's the plume of dust your shoes or tires kick up, maybe it's that satisfying crunching noise, or maybe it's just the reminder that once upon a time the whole world wasn't asphalt and concrete. When you're standing on a gravel road maintained by the same people responsible for six-lane streets with medians and turning lanes and $100,000 traffic signal systems connected by fiber optic cable to a central management headquarters downtown, streets that carry tens of thousands of vehicles per day, streets covered by stripes and lane markers, populated by signposts and reflectors, you look at roads in a different way.

Streets are organized according to some principles. They have a surface; they have a specific width; they have a certain number of lanes; access to them is controlled or it is not; they are one-way or two-way. The roads, like everything else, have their own taxonomy: Controlled-access divided highways like interstates are principle arterials; other enormous divided roads are secondary arterials. Next come thoroughfares (major and minor), which have few intersections with smaller roads; think of one of those wide streets leading out of town past endless strip malls: five or six lanes total, with turning lanes and sometimes a concrete median. Then come collector streets, two- to four-lane roads that feed traffic to the thoroughfares. Smallest are the local streets, two-lane roads whose only job is to provide access to your house and a place for your neighborhood kids to ride skateboards on when they should be in bed.

Gavin Street and Center Road, which is my street, are local streets. But when I consulted a planning map labeling the streets—arterials red and brown, thoroughfares blue and green, collectors in gentle purple—it shocked me to learn that the definitions slide around some: The neighborhood street I walk along to Gavin Street for my occasional gravel reveries is actually a collector street, not a local. I couldn't tell the difference—it's just another ordinary street, built in the late 1910s when my area was subdivided, and annexed to the city in the 1930s as homes were built.

But that got me thinking. I decided to pace the width of my street: It's 10 paces, or 30-ish feet, from curb to curb, or "face to face," as transportation engineers have it. Then I paced the collector road: 12 paces. That's an extra 6 feet. On the other hand, that street has no sidewalks at all—it's designed for cars, not for me.

Trying to understand my roads woke me up, just as looking at maps of the Pigeon House drainage system had gotten me to notice the tiny feeder creeks I had long unconsciously walked past. It also explained things. For example, like most people, I have favorite local routes to avoid this intersection or that crowded street, enabling me to pick my way among tiny streets so that I emerge on some thoroughfare or arterial well past the problematic intersection. I traced my little shortcuts on the map, and it turned out that every one followed collector roads. Collector roads have the job of ferrying people from local streets to thoroughfares. All this time when I thought I was so clever, I was just doing what the roads had in mind for me in the first place. The road has ideas, and it gently—or brusquely—encourages you to do what it wants. And a whole phalanx of engineers pay attention to the roads in their every particular. I asked one of those engineers to explain my streets to me, and he suggested that we meet at a busy intersection a mile from my house, where six roads come together in a little jumble of stores, restaurants, traffic lights, and utility poles.

So I walked up my local street (whose traffic count is too small to bother with—surely only a hundred or so cars a day), turned onto the minor thoroughfare (about 7,500 cars a day), and walked toward its intersection with a major thoroughfare (24,000 cars per day), where I waited for Eric Lamb, Raleigh's manager of transportation services, to explain what the roads were doing, and how, and why.

IN THE SUN, SITTING ON A BENCH IN A LITTLE PLAZA overlooking the multistreet intersection called Five Points, Lamb said, "Look at these guys. Let's see what they're going to do." Two bicyclists came through the intersection from one of the side streets, cutting across a combined seven lanes of traffic and pedaling off on another side street. They clearly kept their heads up and watched for traffic—no screeching brakes, no angry motorists—but they behaved in ways that make transportation engineers like Lamb shake their heads. "Did they have a green light?" Lamb smiled. "No. See? That's what we have to work with." Lamb wants to help everybody on the streets work together, but that requires a lot of compromise.

Lamb is a proponent of complete streets, a movement that works to plan streets for the benefit of pedestrians, bicyclists, and public transit as well as cars. "We're never going to get rid of cars," Lamb said. "Nor should we." Increasing fuel prices and population density, worsening traffic congestion, and improvements in transit convenience will eventually get more people out of cars, he says (he is echoed by most of the current generation of transportation engineers and planners), but even now a good street should provide space for sidewalk cafés for people to socialize, for walkers, for buses, and of course for cars. "We need to design the transportation system as a whole so that it serves all users equally: cars, pedestrians, bicyclists, and transit."

Which makes for quite a project, given that almost every street in

Raleigh was built during the mid- to late 20th century, during which engineers designed streets for cars and almost nothing else. You can see the history, if you look. "Sidewalk infrastructure is a passion of mine," Lamb said. "You can go around the city and tell when a street was built by the sidewalk measurements." Five Points, for example, the intersection where we sat, had the narrow, 4-foot sidewalks bespeaking post–World War I development, but at least each of the six streets coming together *had* sidewalks. "Five Points was one of the first developments outside the center city," he said. "Beyond that, you're going into some of the first auto-based, post–World War II development," and a lot of that has no sidewalks at all. My own house, I pointed out, less than a mile away, sits on a street with a sidewalk on only one side, but many of the neighborhood streets have none, since for decades Raleigh regulations didn't require them. Even now cul-de-sacs of fewer than 10 homes require none. Lamb understands: "Sidewalks cost money," he said, "but there's that subtext of telling the pedestrians they're second-class." No kidding: I love a little diner not half a mile from my house, but the streets on the way there don't have sidewalks, including one stretch along a busy street with no space at all beside the road as it climbs to a bridge. The bridge does have sidewalks, so if you make it that far you're in good shape, but it's just too dangerous to walk to the bridge. I love the diner but I've pretty much given up walking there.

"And remember," Lamb went on, "the city didn't build your street. A *developer* built your street." That is, since Raleigh was first hacked out of virgin forest in its planned, 1-square-mile grid in 1792, every expansion has come about simply because the population was growing: Developers bought property, subdivided, and hooked streets into the nearest roads leading into town—so initial roads grew in traffic and scope, sometimes widening, sometimes not. Raleigh's very first planning maps were made in 1922. Before that, the physical infrastructure of the roads just sort of happened.

A big part of the jobs people like Lamb do is try to recover from centuries of such helter-skelter development. Maintaining your streets involves more than just replacing the surface every decade or so. You also have to make sure the street is doing what the city needs it to do—and every generation defines those needs differently. A recent city project, for example, liberated Raleigh's main downtown street from decades as a failed pedestrian mall. Reintroducing traffic to the street satisfied a public clamor—but how much traffic? How many lanes? The city put in a single lane in each direction, plus on-street parking, allowing wide sidewalks for the rich street life it was trying to encourage, as well as allowing traffic, but preventing the street from becoming too crowded.

But even including pedestrians in the plans is new. "Transportation engineers like to define transport as the safe and efficient movement of goods and services," Lamb said. "That raises two problems. One is that safety and efficiency are sometimes mutually exclusive. The other is that nowhere in that definition does it talk about people. To make things more pedestrian-oriented, you have to make sacrifices in vehicular capacity. And there are a lot of people in my profession who are not prepared to do that yet. That exact debate is what's going on in transportation engineering."

Lamb described one large project currently under construction on a major downtown thoroughfare near North Carolina State University. The street has been the site of 24 car-pedestrian accidents over 5 years. The project aims to reduce traffic by removing one car lane, adding on-street parking, widening the shoulder to accommodate bicyclists, widening the sidewalk, and installing a median strip. Planners hope the car traffic will find its way to a parallel street added many years ago about a quarter-mile south—a secondary arterial that, though busy, has for some reason never absorbed the excess traffic from the thoroughfare. On the same thoroughfare the city is also replacing a complex intersection with a roundabout, which engineers hope will keep traffic moving but also slow it down. The simplest intersection right now, with two streets crossing, has 32 conflict points, where cars and people are not only moving at cross-purposes but can collide head-on; a roundabout will reduce the conflict points to eight—plus, since all the cars will be going the same way at slower speeds, any collisions will tend to be far less serious. The point isn't whether the roundabout will improve traffic, as planners hope, or become a catastrophic choke point, as opponents fear. The point is that transportation engineers count traffic, consider needs, address changes in transportation trends (say, an increase in bicycle use, or the city's hope to improve the business climate on a key street), and constantly tinker with the streets and how they work, trying things and seeing what happens.

We took a drive so that along the way Lamb could point out other street elements we don't think about unless transportation engineers tell us about them. Trees, for example—we drove by some lovely ones downtown, which grew along the curb or on median strips, but rare is the new major road that has any. This is because, Lamb said, about 250 miles of the city's major streets are actually on the state road system. Until recently the city maintained them and was reimbursed by the state; now the state, pinched for funds, has taken them back. State roads are considered highways and managed according to standards maintained by the American Association of State Highway and Transportation Officials (AASHTO). "Based on those standards," Lamb said, "these trees are going to kill you." That is, drivers hitting those trees at highway speeds would be killed. The North Carolina Department of Transportation might apply smaller lane width requirements—say, 10 or 11 feet instead of the 12 used on interstates—but DOT's current rules focus on moving traffic, not creating the kind of streets Lamb thinks Raleigh needs, which requires creative solutions. The downtown thoroughfare project just described went so strongly against DOT procedures that the only way Raleigh could proceed with it was for the state to yield control of a segment of the street to Raleigh.

In fact, DOT rules don't even necessarily encourage the kind of *highways* Raleigh needs, Lamb noted. When the state resurfaced part of I-440, the beltline around Raleigh, the city undertook to place landscaping in raised median planters. The DOT balked and significant negotiation ensued, resulting in a compromise in which the state reluctantly allowed Raleigh to plant the trees if Raleigh agreed to maintain them. Since then, Lamb said, engineers have noticed that an accident on one side of the highway results in a much smaller rubbernecking delay than before the trees came in. People don't see the wreck—they see the trees. No matter how organized the engineering principles, the roads are always ferrying people around, they'll always be changing, and they'll always be unpredictable. "The roads," Lamb concluded, "are the craziest infrastructure."

ALLOWING FOR THE POSSIBILITY that my neighborhood streets might just be crazy helped me to understand them. City historians and city engineers gave the same answer: The streets were built by developers whose motives for their design decisions are easily forgotten. This is true not only in Raleigh. Even the famous wide boulevards of Paris were not designed purely as an expression of grandness. "[Baron Georges-Eugène] Haussmann, who designed Paris, made wider streets in order to prevent the peasants from barricading the streets," Joe Hummer, a traffic engineer and professor at North Carolina State University, told me. Streets have ever evolved to suit their surroundings: "They just start out," one engineer told me, "and then they end up where they are."

We've had streets since we've had places to go, though the way we've managed them has periodically undergone sudden improvement. The first streets were nothing more than pathways beaten down by travel—Europeans exploring Africa described crossing the continent entirely on footpaths, and when Europeans came to North America they found the same thing: Native American footpaths a couple of feet wide. Naturally, worn paths grew muddy in rain, so many paths took advantage of the better drainage atop hills, becoming ridgeways—long paths along high areas.

When the first cities developed in Mesopotamia around 4000 BC, stone-paved streets soon followed; at about the same time, corduroy roads—logs laid across the direction of a road—showed up in swampy areas in England. Like almost all other types of infrastructure, roads took a step forward around 1000 BC with the Minoans of Crete, who built a flagstone road from Knossos to the coast. The ancient Chinese, Indians, and Assyrians also had extensive road systems.

But, as with much historical discussion of infrastructure, we have to go back to the Romans again. In *Ways of the World,* a history of the world's roads, M. G. Lay notes that Roman road builders combined skills from all over their empire: masonry from the Greeks, cement from the Etruscans, surveying techniques from the Egyptians, and pavement styles from the Carthaginians. In any case, all roads led to Rome, back in the day, because the Romans came up with lasting road-building solutions. (One of the titles Julius Caesar assumed was "director of the great roads.") The laws of the Twelve Tables, in the 5th century BC, had set rules for road width (8 feet where straight and 16 feet on a curve, improving sightlines and allowing space for carts that didn't steer especially well), though roads grew much wider as construction methods improved and traffic increased. By the time the Romans were done the world even had a basic standard of width: Limitations in axle length and the weight that unpaved roads could bear, along with the width of a standard team of draft animals, created a de facto standard of something under 7 feet that exists even today. Transportation engineers tell me that's what they use for a standard cars width in modern calculations: 7 feet per car, to be generous. Some stone roads in Greece and Malta show wheel ruts of approximately that width; those ruts in turn sustained the standard. Most roads had only one set of ruts, making passing and even turning something of a chore (even today we talk about the danger of being in a rut). Eventually, the standard width of roads was increased to about 18 feet so that two carts had room to pass. According to Lay, this standard also enabled a legion of soldiers to march six abreast. Moving armies has ever been a powerful motivation for building roads.

By the time the Roman Empire collapsed, it had built some 50,000 miles of good roads. Some historians partially blame the complexity and cost of the Roman infrastructure (including roads) for the empire's collapse, but whatever the reason, the Romans stopped maintaining the roads. The fact that so many of these original Roman roads remain today gives an indication of what a fine job the Romans did in building them, but over the centuries most of them sank back to their original swampy state. Rural roads were little more than rutted pathways that were swampy in the rain, dusty in the heat, and slowly eroding into deep ruts. After the end of the empire, most people in a poor and fragmenting Europe didn't have much need for long-distance travel. Long paths like the Silk Road provided opportunities for trade, but those were routes rather than roads; as for paving itself, many towns dug up the stones from Roman roads and built walls with them—so the Middle Ages, essentially, was an era of unpaving rather than paving.

ONE OF THE VERY FIRST THINGS the newly founded City of Raleigh did, in 1793, was to appoint an "overseer of the main Streets, leading from the Public square," to be in charge of managing the labor he was empowered to require of citizens (you could send slaves if you had them; if not, you could always buy your way out). The citizens of Raleigh still bear the responsibility for maintaining the roads in Raleigh, as do the citizens in every city and state—only instead of doing it themselves or sending slaves, they now do what only the rich used to do: They pay their way out of it. We call it taxes. The point is that if you want public streets, you'd better plan to take care of them, and unless you like the idea of your local streets overseer knocking on your door and telling you to grab your shovel because it's your turn for asphalt day, you'd better plan on paying for it.

The job of traffic engineers is to take the two goals that forever wrestle for supremacy on their desks—safety and efficiency—and turn the wrestling match into a ballroom dance. Traffic needs to move, but drivers, cyclists, and pedestrians alike need to be safe. In order to increase pedestrian safety, cars have to go more slowly, and the streets get clogged; if you focus on keeping the cars moving quickly, the safety of pedestrians and cyclists suffers. If you widen the streets to create a bicycle lane, pedestrians crossing the street have a longer walk, to say nothing of the squawks of property owners when you ask for 4 more feet of their real estate for the public right-of-way.

There are no simple answers. The current debate on bicycles, for example, includes proponents of separate lanes, proponents of completely separate paths—and those who believe that the best solution is simple pictograms of bicycles in the road: "Sharrows," Lamb calls them, short for "shared lane markings." They have what he calls a "marketing effect," reminding people that everyone needs to share the road rather than giving bicyclists a 4-foot ghetto with a boundary over which they and the drivers can immediately begin tussling.

If citizens don't fight about bicycles, they'll fight about something else. Raleigh performs traffic counts every year, and engineers tinker with streets that show excess speed or volume. To slow cars on local or collector streets (and encourage drivers to use thoroughfares instead), they put in medians that widen out periodically on one side or another, forcing drivers to slow down around the manufactured curves; they widen the curbs; they place extra signs. They try hard to avoid speed bumps, which Lamb calls "the nuclear option." People lobby fiercely for better traffic flow, but the minute a project is done, they complain. At one point I asked Lamb to name the most essential elements of his work. Asphalt and concrete? Design and planning? Speed and safety? "Money and political will," Lamb said. "Those two components dictate everything. I'm using physical engineering methods to solve social engineering problems."

SOLUTIONS ARRIVE WHEN TRAFFIC REQUIRES THEM. The first changing traffic signal predated cars, popping up in London in 1868—it had red semaphore arms and a red gaslight for "stop"; green meant "caution," during which you were supposed to go carefully. Red and green were already conventions used in marine and railroad traffic systems. Salt Lake City installed lights in 1912 that required an operator; the first electric signal was introduced in Cleveland, in 1914. In 1920 the Detroit police introduced four-way, three-light traffic towers (they really were towers, in the middle of the street), which they began automating in 1921. (The Detroit police department had already invented the stop sign, in 1915.) By 1922 Houston had several electric signals controlled from a central tower. In 1928 progressive systems came along, replete with pressure-sensitive actuators buried in the road, not unlike the electric induction loops that detect vehicles today. Denver installed a computer-controlled system in 1952, and we've been complaining about poorly timed lights ever since. Today, the National Traffic Operations Coalition estimates that up to 10 percent of all traffic delays nationwide are caused by poorly timed signals.

In the Traffic Control Center on the second floor of the Raleigh police headquarters, you can see real-time traffic control. The enormous projection TV in the center of the main wall of the darkened room runs the Weather Channel, and each of the 11 TVs running in rows along the top and sides of the big one shows the view from a traffic camera along one of Raleigh's main streets. "We have access to 60 NCDOT cameras," says traffic signal system manager A. P. Humphries. "And five are ours, that the city owns." At the moment the screens show no lines of stopped cars at any of the intersections. The real action is on the computer.

Almost every single one of Raleigh's 510 traffic signals is connected by copper wire or optical fiber to Humphries's traffic control computer. Humphries taps a couple of keys and up pops a map of Raleigh, with hundreds of little squares of red, yellow, and green indicating where signals are and what phase they're in. Humphries answers the first question without being asked: "We look for a green band," he says—a long stretch of green lights, where cars can keep moving through a corridor. Creating those green bands on computer screens, and thus on the streets, is the goal of the traffic signal system. The Raleigh Traffic Control Center tries to time lights on about 15 major roads, Humphries says. He makes clear that putting in more traffic signals is not his department's goal. In the first place, signals don't necessarily reduce accidents ("you sometimes increase rear-end collisions"), and they don't improve capacity—engineers estimate that just putting a four-phase signal (red, yellow, green, left turn) at a simple crossing decreases road capacity by 30 percent.

But once the signals are in, Humphries's office follows fairly simple, commonsense rules in controlling traffic. Lights are timed according to actual traffic speeds, not speed limits. Main streets have priority over cross streets ("though you still have to get those cars off the side streets and into traffic"). Pairs of one-way streets are by far the easiest to time; timing the lights is much more complex when you have two main, signal-coordinated streets crossing, say, or three main, coordinated arteries wreaking havoc with the cross streets. On the other hand, every signal can change cycles as many times a day as necessary—you can have a morning rush pattern, followed by a midmorning break, then a lunch rush, then a lull, then early afternoon, late afternoon, evening, and late-night patterns, all scheduled on the signal itself—in the brushed aluminum box hanging from a utility pole or standing on a street corner—and managed by the central computer and, of course, Humphries and his staff. Accident on Wake Forest Road inbound during the morning rush? They can give the cross streets nice long greens to encourage drivers to find another route. Construction midday cutting a two-lane street down to one lane? They can lengthen a green to allow the usual number of cars, only in a longer line, time to make it through. All day long, they keep an eye on the screen, an eye on data, and an eye on the cameras, and they adjust when necessary. "Any time a road is revised," Humphries says—widened, narrowed, clogged with traffic from a new school, closed because of a water main break—"we recalibrate." If a signal goes offline, it doesn't just start flashing; instead it reverts to its standard pattern for that time of day.

The other engineers chime in about why every driver in the world is convinced the lights are mistimed, not timed, or aggressively anti-timed. For one thing, the induction loops in the street that electromagnetically perceive your car and tell the system you're there (in those cuts in the asphalt you see at most intersections) usually don't work on a main street during coordinated runs. The cycle doesn't change if a lot of people want to turn left at a busy intersection during rush hour—each signal is on a cycle that keeps it right where it needs to be in relation to the ones behind it and before it on that green band. But if nobody wants to turn left, the system may release the main street early, to keep the traffic moving. So, since people in that early-release packet then have to wait at the next light, they think the lights are out of sync. Conversely, if there's a long line of cars at a left-turn signal and the guy in front of you is talking on his cell phone and eating a Krispy Kreme and it takes him a while to get going, the signal might "gap out"—pick up the gap in traffic, figure there's nobody else waiting, and change—and leave you stranded for another cycle. Drivers are unpredictable, and any approach the control engineers take to timing lights holds surprises. They run models and do calculations, but in the end they always end up in the same place: on the street. "You have to go out and ride it," Humphries says. One engineer drives and the other holds a laptop computer running a program. "You start the program, and hit a key when you hit each intersection." The central traffic control computer can do a lot, but it can't act like a driver.

So: DESIGN, PLANNING, PAVEMENT, SIGNALS, SIGNS—traffic professionals think about every element of the ride to work that you mostly make
unconsciously. When the subject is roadways, the first thing many Americans think of is not their local commute, but the Interstate Highway
System. William Randolph Hearst suggested a system of interstate roads
as early as 1906, and most sources link the system to the Federal-Aid
Highway Act of 1938, when, after years of public debate, the Bureau of
Public Roads (predecessor of the Federal Highway Administration)
undertook a study of the feasibility of building superhighways along
three east-west and three north-south routes. But the idea of interstate
roads really got its start long before that.

The Cumberland Road, the very first federally funded interstate highway, was authorized by Thomas Jefferson in 1806 and built between
1811 and 1818. It ran from Cumberland, Maryland, to Wheeling, West
Virginia. People called it "the road that built the nation," given that it
cut the travel time from the East Coast to Wheeling to 2 weeks, down
from 6 or 8 weeks up- or downriver. Unfortunately, maintaining the
road cost money; the federal government could not constitutionally collect tolls, so by the 1830s it had handed responsibility for maintaining
the road back to individual states, which naturally turned to tolls to raise
revenues. (The term "turnpike" refers to the long staff that blocked the
way until the traveler paid.) As traffic increased in the mid–19th century,
the ill-maintained Cumberland Road became rutted and worn. With the
railroads available for long-distance travel, rural roads functioned mostly
as farm-to-market roads, maintained, if at all, by those who used them.

But the same "good roads" movement supported by bicyclists that
helped improve city streets included rural roads; by 1912 Congress had
passed a post roads act meant to improve the roads by which the mail
traveled, and in 1916 it provided the first federal aid to states for road
construction. The Bureau of Public Roads described 90 percent of traffic
as local and encouraged the states and counties to improve the roads
used by interstate traffic rather than building a special interstate system.
The Lincoln Highway from New York to San Francisco, the country's
first actual cross-country route, established in 1913, followed mostly
unimproved roads and took about 30 days to travel by car: "If trouble is
experienced," the 1916 guide published by the Lincoln Highway Associ-

ation counseled about a particularly hairy spot in Utah, "build a sage-brush fire. Mr. Thomas will come with a team. He can see you 20 miles off." The Lincoln was largely a publicity stunt, unfunded and barely even identified by signs (the name was sometimes painted on barns, rocks, and such). Similar trails popped up throughout the country—routes mostly in name, with occasional signage, little paving, and few amenities. Just the same, at least conceptually, these routes existed: the first true incarnations, perhaps, of Thomas Jefferson's National Road.

IN 1917, SOMEONE IN WISCONSIN GOT THE IDEA to number the roads. Suddenly, instead of telling someone to turn left at the first road past the bridge that used to be painted silver, you could say, "Stay on Route 70 until you get to Route 64, then turn." Other states quickly got the idea, and they also began emulating Wisconsin's determination to hang regular signs marking the way. Before long, the US government got into the act. In 1921 Congress passed a federal highway act offering to fund 50 percent of the cost for states to improve the 7 percent of their roads that carried interstate travel. The US routes were numbered simply, with odd numbers going north-south and even ones east-west; the low numbers started in the east and in the north.

That worked great, and asphalt roads stretched across the country. But of course as cars became more prevalent (there were fewer than half a million on the roads in 1910, nearly 10 million by 1920, and 26 million by 1930; in 2007 there were 136 million, plus another 95 million light trucks like SUVs, pickups, and vans), and as newer and larger trucks trundled over—and virtually demolished—the two-lane asphalt highways, Americans recognized they needed a highway system that could support the enormous new volume and weight of traffic. The Federal-Aid Highway Act of 1938 spawned the Federal-Aid Highway Act of 1944, authorizing 40,000 miles of highway meant to connect "the principle metropolitan areas, cities, and industrial centers, to serve the National Defense, and to connect at suitable border points, routes of continental importance." Congress got around to actually funding all that work with the Federal-Aid Highway Act of 1956, which directed a portion of gas and other user taxes to a highway trust fund, from which the federal government would pay 90 percent of the costs of road building. The act also legislated virtually all the elements we associate with interstate travel today: at least two 12-foot lanes in each direction; a wide paved right shoulder; controlled access; and a traffic speed of between 50 and 70 miles per hour. The numbering system followed but inverted the US route system—that is, the interstate east-west routes used even numbers and started in the south, with I-10, finishing with I-90 along the Great Lakes, and the odd numbers started with I-5 in California and ended with I-95 on the East Coast, along the route of old US 1. Numbering conventions took into account most other issues, too: A spur gets an odd first digit (395 goes into Washington but not back to 95), and a loop or parallel road gets an even one (440s encircle both Raleigh and Nashville; the reused numbers are okay because they're in different states). With funding established, construction got started and it hasn't stopped. Today the system includes 46,726 miles and connects just about every-where to everywhere. Though it almost didn't reach Raleigh.

Focused on internal road improvements—the North Carolina state road system is the country's second largest, behind Texas—and perhaps a tad overproud of its Southern dislike of federal interference, North Carolina simply didn't hustle after routes during the planning of the interstate system. Thus Raleigh was one of only six state capitals originally not linked to the interstates. Not until the success of Research Triangle Park in the 1960s did North Carolina petition for interstate extensions; in 1968 the state received permission to start building, but I-40 didn't finally connect Raleigh to the rest of the system until 1988, and I-40 didn't complete its journey from Barstow, California (at I-5) to Wilmington, North Carolina (on the coast, 120 miles east of Raleigh) until 1990.

THE INTERSTATE SYSTEM BROUGHT RALEIGH more than just something else to fight about with the federal government; it also brought bridges. Running through rolling hills and over small creeks, Raleigh roads mostly avoid the few deep places in the landscape; a lovely 1872 bird's-eye-view map of Raleigh shows not a single bridge. Most of our bridges are at highway overpasses, and almost every one of them is a steel continuous stringer/multibeam or girder bridge: your garden-variety flat bridge made of a concrete deck mounted on horizontal steel girders and supported by vertical concrete pilings. It's about as basic as bridges get, using no arch, no trusses, no suspension. It's a log across a stream.

Bridges make the big news in roads. After the 1967 collapse of a bridge over the Ohio River at Point Pleasant, Ohio, that killed 46 people, the Federal Highway Administration (FHWA) in 1971 created national bridge-inspection standards. The 1983 collapse of 100 feet of the I-95 bridge over the Mianus River in Connecticut helped intensify the early 1980s spasm of interest in our crumbling infrastructure much as the 2007 collapse of the I-35W bridge in Minneapolis did in recent years. Yet as it happens, none of those collapsing bridges was a standard highway bridge, and investigations into each failure identified specific design flaws. So even though bridge failures make us reflexively look at our local highway bridges and worry about maintenance, lack of mainte-nance didn't cause the catastrophic bridge failures that have seized our attention. Just the same, rightly or wrongly, bridge failures have become popular evidence that infrastructure *isn't* working.

So now we pay more attention. According to FHWA guidelines, each state now must inspect every one of its public road bridges that is longer than 20 feet at least every 2 years. The FHWA maintains the National Bridge Inventory (NBI), listing the almost 600,000 bridges on federal, state, and county roads. The NBI database lists 468 bridges in Raleigh. And though the government pays attention to all those bridges, we're still running a little longer on "check" than on "fix." The 2009 American Society of Civil Engineers Report Card for America's Infrastructure gave bridges a grade of C—26 percent of bridges nationwide were judged structurally deficient or functionally obsolete; in North Carolina the number is 31 percent. Now, a bridge might be judged as a failure because its traffic has grown to exceed its design capacity, slowing traffic but not endangering drivers. On the other hand, a bridge might still be sound, but only just. Most steel stringer highway bridges are designed to last 50 years, and a good many of Raleigh's were built in the 1950s and '60s, so Raleigh—like all of North Carolina, and like the rest of the country—has plenty of work to do on its bridges. The one between me and that diner looks like it's in pretty good shape. I still can't walk to it, though.

You can look at the roads from so many angles that you lose track. In downtown Raleigh the streets have wide sidewalks, but commonly not wide enough for the sidewalk cafés and rich street life that the current boosters want. Eric Lamb, sitting at the pleasant Five Points intersection so close to my house, pointed out both that nodal, walkable developments such as this one aren't the kind of streets Raleigh is building now and that every time the city has considered improving Five Points traffic flow, it runs into such a maelstrom of conflicting neighborhood demands that it backs off.

The answer to congestion used to be more car lanes and more roads; now people think that just draws more traffic: So is the answer *fewer* roads? Chances are, we'll never arrive at a final answer. People complain about traffic flow until the engineers manage it on major arteries with signals; then people trying to use the cross streets complain. "Everybody wants two traffic signals," NCDOT engineer Dewayne Sykes told me. "One at their street, and one at their work. And they're always green." Give me a bike lane when I'm riding—but if I'm driving, I want that bike lane back. Everybody wants more public transportation to improve traffic, Sykes said—as long as someone else is taking it. Same with parking: The current thinking is that to improve traffic flow and street use, parking should cost more on the street than it does in a garage: Drivers will use the garage unless they're in a terrible hurry, in which case they will gladly pay the premium for street parking. In practice, though, people often get irritated if they have to park in a garage. Some current thinking, especially that of the late Dutch traffic engineer Hans Monderman, also suggests the counterintuitive approach that driving improves and safety increases if you put up fewer, not more, signs and signals—unfamiliarity slows everybody down. A thought-provoking idea, but other tactics work too: Julius Caesar instituted what you could call the first congestion pricing in 45 BC, when he banned unauthorized vehicles from Roman streets between 6:00 a.m. and 4:00 p.m. In London today, drivers are glad to pay a fee to drive into the city during congested hours; their program has worked fine. New Yorkers, on the other hand, refuse even to try it.

Joe Hummer, of NCSU, left me with a final thought about roads. "The speed of traffic through the middle of our big cities has not changed in 5,000 years," he said. "It's basically walking speed. We had chariots for a while, then streetcars, then buses and cars, but we manage to slow everything down to about 4 miles per hour. Whatever the technology, we find a way to gum up the works, and walking speed is about the best we can manage." It's true—walk along one of Raleigh's downtown cross streets for a few blocks and you can often hold a conversation with a driver going the same way.

Unlike with water pipes or electrical wires, no matter how we adjust capacity and demand, there's a natural speed to traffic. "The reason for that," Hummer says, "and maybe the big difference between streets and other infrastructure, is that the streets we give away. They're free for the taking and first-come, first-serve. Everything else has a meter, and we charge for use." We've got a gas tax, of course, though at 18 cents a gallon it scarcely presents a hardship. "Ways to charge people to use this particular street at this particular time would give us a chance to get out from under that."

We seem to have found the way to build a street or a highway. We've figured out the necessary basic markings and signs, signals and movements. Trail, pathway, dirt lane, gravel road, asphalt street, superhighway: If there's one thing we can do, it's make a street.

We just can't agree on what to do with it.

CHAPTER 6

THE BLUE GLOW

Heating Water and Turning Cranks

MY CHILDREN ARE FUELED ALMOST ENTIRELY BY MACARONI, not electric power, so it's probably not fair to say electricity wakes me in the morning—usually my clock radio goes off long after they do. Once I'm up, though, electricity rules my day. It powers the pumps that send the water to my faucet and the heat that warms it, to say nothing of the processes that cleaned it back at the plant. Electricity runs the lamps that enable me to see what clothes I'm putting on. It powers the kitchen radio I listen to while pouring cereal (and the transmitter that pumps the signal to me from the station), the microwave that warms the oatmeal, the refrigerator that cools the milk. It runs the pumps that gas up the car that takes the children to preschool, and all day long it runs the air conditioner or space heater that keeps my office comfortable enough to work in, the lights that enable me to see my notes, the telephones that enable me to talk to others, the computer that I work on, and the millions of servers that connect me to people and information by keeping the Internet running.

And all because a couple of clever people sat around and figured out how to whack uranium molecules into pieces, harvest the energy from that transition, heat water with it, use the resulting steam to turn a crank, use the crank to spin a magnet within coiled copper wires, and then harness the electric current that results. Other plants use coal to heat that water, still others use oil or gas or water falling from a dam, but everybody is turning cranks, creating current, and running that electricity through wires to houses so that people like me can run their toasters.

Naturally I wanted to follow the electricity from the nuclear plant to my house, so I called Progress Energy, which provides power to Raleigh as well as much of the rest of North Carolina and other southeastern states. A Progress representative said they'd be glad to show me around the Harris Nuclear Plant, the one closest to me, which churns out 900 megawatts of power, enough to fuel 550,000 nearby homes. But I would have to wait a few weeks, because the plant was getting new fuel assemblies.

My power plant was turned off.

Hold on. The telephone on which I spoke to them still had power, and the computer on which I worked still had power, as did my air conditioner and refrigerator and television and toaster. What do you mean, the power plant is off? "Despite your proximity to the Harris plant," the friendly media relations director told me, "not all of your electricity comes from that plant." I shouldn't have been surprised. After all, even the water people couldn't say exactly how my water reaches me, and, unlike the electrical grid, every water plant in the country isn't connected by a vast grid of pipes to every other water plant. I had barely gotten started, and already there was so much to understand.

Some things I could easily wrap my mind around. Getting power to my toaster takes three systems: generation, transmission, and distribution. Generation happens at the plant, which I could go visit once they turned it back on again. Distribution starts at the substation a block and a half from my house, a half-acre of gray equipment with porcelain insulators that buzzes all day and night like a hive of bees, out of which come the power lines that run up and down neighborhood streets on utility poles that also carry telephone wires and other cables. My own electric power comes from a wire that runs from a utility pole straight to my meter. The transmission lines travel on higher poles, high enough that the current can't arc to the ground or trees: The Eiffel Tower kind that look like mechanical space aliens holding wires in their six or so arms are carrying transmission lines. Progress has 60,000 miles or so of distribution lines, but only about 6,000 miles of transmission lines. The transmission lines connect utilities and regions together, and every company or entity manages its share of them in centralized energy control centers that share information nationwide.

AFTER CONSIDERING THE WATER, SEWAGE, AND STORMWATER systems that flow around us and beneath our feet—what you might call the primary infrastructure—you barely have to change terms to discuss the electrical system.

The electrical grid is not unlike the water grid. The power plant is the equivalent of the treatment plant; transmission lines are the huge pipes bringing water into the city; the substations that transform the 115 or 230 kilovolt (kV) electricity from the transmission lines to the 12 or 23 kV electricity in the distribution lines are the equivalent of pumping stations and water towers, managing and distributing supply. The water companies have to make sure the pressure is right in each zone so it doesn't pop the hoses off people's washing machines or do other damage to pipes and valves, and pipe size affects water pressure and the rate of water flow; the electrical grid works exactly the same way.

For example, electricity traveling through wires is measured just like water traveling through pipes: While the water moves in cubic meters per second, the flow of electricity is measured in amps, which can be thought of as electrons per second. Pipes are measured by diameter, with smaller diameters slowing flow and causing higher pressure, whereas greater diameters allow freer flow; wires have resistance, measured in ohms, and wires provide less resistance the bigger they are. And as the force of the water is measured in pressure—pounds per square inch—the "pressure" of electricity is measured in volts. Much like the grist mill that gets its power by tapping the energy of water as it falls from greater to less potential energy, voltage measures the difference between two states of electric excitement—between two wires, say, or a wire and the ground. A big difference equals a lot of electric potential—just as water high up has a lot of potential energy. And like water, electrical energy follows the path of least resistance to either get back to its source or get to the ground, which is why you never want to provide a route, like, say, your body, between a charged line and the ground. A vital equation describes the relation of those forces: The current equals the voltage divided by the resistance. That is, raise the voltage and you get more current; lower the voltage, or raise the resistance (by using less-conductive or smaller wire) and you get less current. To increase the current, you must either raise voltage or reduce resistance.

Once the water comes out of the faucet you're happy. But with electricity, once it flows out of your plug or socket, you're just getting started. Because you don't want a bucket of electricity; you want that electricity to do work, which means you want it to provide power. In a way, resistance, in that original equation, is power. If it just flows through a wire, the only work it has to do is to overcome the resistance of the wire. An electric toaster, though, or a lightbulb, uses wire of high-enough resistance that the current generates heat to make toast or light to illuminate your desk. Electricians measure power in watts: 1 volt flowing at 1 amp will give you 1 watt of power, and 75 of those watts makes one lightbulb glow in my office reading lamp. The power company measures those watts as I use them—leave the light on for an hour and I've used 75 watt-hours. My downstairs air conditioner is rated at 3,500 watts, so when I let its compressor run for an hour, I've used 3,500 watt-hours, or 3.5 kilowatt-hours, which is how Progress Energy bills me. The refrigerator requires about 100 watts most of the time, though five times that much when the compressor is running. An average home in the United States uses approximately 1,000 kilowatt-hours a month, and our home, with two kids keeping the dishwasher, clothes washer, and vacuum cleaner running pretty much full-time, is about average.

The last thing you need to know about electricity and the way it differs from all other utilities is that the electricity runs only in a loop. It can't dead-end at my toaster: It has to find its way back to the power plant through a return wire, forming a circuit. And again it will complete its circuit by following the path of least resistance, which is why you don't ever want its path of least resistance to be through you. We're all very glad the smart people look after it for the rest of us.

SINCE I COULDN'T GO TO THE PLANT AND FOLLOW MY ELECTRICITY HOME, I started at my house and worked backward. My electricity meter is a gray box with a face-size glass bubble attached to the outside back wall. It looks like a node from some science-fiction organism. Ours is one of the old meters—it has toothed metal gears grinding away, as low tech as a stem-winding pocket watch. Soon someone will replace it with an electronic meter that, through the Smart Grid everybody talks about, will be able to communicate with both me and Progress via the Internet. Through the electronic meter, Progress and I will be able to control individual appliances we agree to share, allowing me to run them when electricity is cheapest and allowing Progress to turn them off if peak load gets too high on some hot August afternoon.

But that's far off—we don't have a Smart Grid yet. As lineman Randy Clifton was quick to point out, the current grid is as dumb as the utility posts it hangs from. Clifton and John Peel, the manager of the regional operations center for northern North Carolina distribution, walked me through my little corner of the grid to illustrate. Peel showed me the headquarters where people work during a storm or other emergency. Customers imagine NASA Mission Control, but for keeping track of where lines are down and power is out, the cutting-edge technology is big maps and pushpins. "People think they don't need to call when their power goes out," Clifton said. "But we want them to call—that's how we know what's gone out."

They do have tools to know what's going on. Peel pulled up the GIS map of my neighborhood and traced my power from my substation to my house, noting something I never had: that the transmission line going from substation to substation marches right up my street, on 80-foot poles that I had never even noticed; the distribution line hangs beneath it on the same poles. It's "underbuilt," Peel said. The 115 kV transmission line required nothing more than a higher pole to keep it out of the way, but that height had allowed it to escape my notice. The grid wasn't the only thing that needed to get smarter in my neighborhood.

As I read on a Smart Grid informational flyer, "Alexander Graham Bell would not recognize today's phone system with our cell phones, wireless transmission towers and the texting craze, but Thomas Edison would be completely familiar with our electricity grid." Before contemplating the potential wonders of the Smart Grid, I wanted to learn about how electricity gets from the power plant to my house today. Edison wasn't around to explain it, so I turned to Clifton and Peel.

They started with some basics. First, the power plant generates power in an alternating current at around 23,000 volts, or 23 kV; then a big transformer yard at the plant steps it up to 230 kV to go to the grid. A transformer, by the way, works pretty much exactly like the generator at the power plant. A change in magnetic field causes electric current. So the power plant generator spins a magnet within wire coils, causing current. A transformer simply uses the current in the lines to power an electromagnet within another loop of coils. That current causes the change in field to generate current in the new loop, and differing coil ratios change its voltage: More coils equals more voltage. The transformers lose only about 1 percent of the power as they make the change up or down. The power makes its way along the transmission lines to substations, where generators step it down, usually to 23 or 12 kV, and then separate it into a bunch of streams heading out into neighborhoods: These are the primary distribution lines, the wires that go from pole to pole down the street. From those, more transformers—those ubiquitous canisters hanging on the poles—step the voltage down to 120 volts and send single lines to individual homes. That's secondary distribution—the wires to specific homes and businesses. A neutral wire does double duty, not only completing the circuit and providing the electricity with a route back to its source utility, but also providing support for the wires from the transformer to the home. It's grounded both at the utility pole and at your house, so it's safe; the other lines running to your house are not safe, which is why they're insulated—about the only insulated lines you'll find between the power plant and your house.

Another weird secret is that electricity travels in phases. Think of the pulses of alternating current—say, in your 120-volt (V) home line—as a sine wave, going up and down from +120 V to –120 V 60 times a second, which means the voltage curve constantly crosses the line at which it has zero voltage, or no current at all. That's not a big deal at home—your lights, for example, flicker fast enough that you can't see it. But large-scale industrial machinery hates that constant starting and stopping, so electrical plants generate electricity in three phases—think of three sine waves starting slightly out of sequence, so no two ever hit the zero mark at the same time, much less all three. That makes large electric motors, such as the ones that run elevators, work better. So the wires along the transmission and distribution grids travel in threes. If you've stopped at a utility pole and wondered why the metal letters A B C were nailed to the pole, in one order or another, that's why: When linemen string the wires, they mark the poles to show in what order the wires are strung. Also, because appliances like stoves and dryers run on 240 volts, the transformers on the poles transform the current into two phases, giving each house the capacity to run 120 V appliances on one phase or the other and 240 V appliances across both phases together.

Now, about wires, which linemen call "conductors": First, they're made of aluminum, which is a good conductor, lighter than steel, and cheaper than copper. Second, they tend to be braids of wires rather than single wires: Because of a phenomenon called the skin effect, the electricity tends to run on the outside of the line rather than all the way through it, so instead of one big line, the conductor is made of groups of smaller ones. Two 1-inch-radius wires have the same surface area as one 2-inch-radius wire, so they transmit the same power, but the 2-inch wire is double the area in cross-section, so it weighs and costs more without transmitting more power. The wires aren't insulated, either: Aluminum doesn't rust.

BEFORE HEADING OUT TO THE STREETS, Clifton and I walk around his warehouse. Progress Energy installs and maintains the streetlights for the city of Raleigh, so here I see streetlight bulbs and parts as well as a selection of switches, insulators, spools of line, and a huge variety of insulating gear—blankets, gloves, and so forth. My favorite piece of equipment is what he calls a shotgun stick: a telescoping fiberglass pole that linemen use to open or close switches on utility poles in order to isolate a section for work or repair or to reroute power to suit changing needs.

"With Smart Grid [technology]," Clifton says, "we'll be able to do with the distribution grid what they can do at the Energy Control Center with the transmission grid"—change routes, open and close switches, and control current flow at distant substations, directly from their computers. But for now, if a distribution line starts overheating on a hot day and Progress wants to reroute some of its power, trucks have to roll and linemen have to get out of them and reach up with long sticks to open and shut switches on utility poles. It seems amazingly low-tech, and it will be one of the first things to change as the grid smartens up. Clifton notes that along many streets, a Progress-owned fiber-optic cable runs below the power lines—evidence that the future, including controllable switches, isn't far off.

We finally load up into his truck for a tour. Clifton shows me the truck that augers holes in the ground and plonks utility poles in them like a sowing machine on a farm. We see a crew solving a problem in a buried line using a machine called a thumper, which sends pulses of power into the line; the line should jerk and make a noise where the fault is, which the workers aboveground will hear so they know where to dig. There's general agreement from the guys standing with the thumper in the hot asphalt parking lot that underground wires are four times more expensive to install and 10 times harder to maintain than overhead. "With this, you're blind," says one worker. As Clifton says, "Overhead is ugly, but it's accessible: If line's on the ground, guess what? Call two bucket trucks, four guys, splice it up, reattach it, and you're gone." Still, most new developments prefer underground wiring, and that's the future. Computers do a better and better job of estimating where faults are—both above- and belowground—but the linemen still prefer a line they can see.

As we drive, Clifton points out transformers and switches hanging on utility poles and fuses made of tubes of animal horn fiber: If a silver wire inside the tube overheats and arcs, it melts some of the horn fiber, which releases a gas that pops out the bottom of the tube, kicking open a spring-loaded catch to disconnect the line. Those, not transformer explosions, are the pops people hear during lightning storms when wires go down and circuits overheat. Actual transformer explosions would spray oil over the surrounding yards; the fuses are designed to prevent exactly that. He shows me thick parts of the line where splices have been made, basically aluminum wraps crimped together, and points out how many utility poles are within inches of the curb: a good thing, because it gives utilities a fighting chance not to be trimming trees every year, but a bad thing because cars hit them all the time, "and we have to fix what they tear up. Dump trucks, garbage trucks tear our stuff down. People put Dumpsters under our lines," which then get torn down by inattentive trash truck drivers. Clifton drives hunched over the steering wheel, looking up at the wires. "I'm always patrolling," he says. Even on vacation, he watches the lines: "I'll say, 'I'll be damned.' I'll stop and call the local utility." He laughs. "How sick is that?" But he doesn't know a lineman who doesn't do it.

Finally, we drive to my own substation. The power comes in on tall steel towers, which seem to gently lower their lines over the surrounding fence to the machinery, like Rapunzel. In the middle of the station, between 20-foot scaffolds, Clifton points to two big gray boxes, each about half the size of a semitrailer: The wires reach the scaffolds, then descend to the boxes, which are covered with fans and grilles to distribute heat. The boxes are transformers that supply nine different switches, each leading to a feeder line heading into a particular neighborhood. Steel girders hold up what looks like a grape arbor of square aluminum poles, which are buses: conductors that connect the transformed power to the switches (and capacitors, arranged on two smaller arbors). All the switch boxes and circuit breakers have smooth, rounded stacks of porcelain insulators, so with the switches, the superstructure of girders, and the atmospheric buzz of the transformers, the whole substation has a satisfactory, Frankenstein's laboratory feel. Peel had identified for me on his GIS the circuit that runs to my house and now we identify it by switch and pole, following it a block and a half to my house.

Of all the things Clifton explains to me, I find nothing as satisfying as his reading of a utility pole. On the corner of my lot, not 5 feet from the iron pipe that my surveyor had tied with snappy pink ribbon, stands a tall wooden pole with a bewildering array of lines, braces, and knuckle-size yellow numbers stuck on a metal shield: utility pole D239 BL. Farther up are two hand-size aluminum digits nailed into the pole: 13. "That's for the transmission department," Clifton says; this pole has two numbers because it is underbuilt: The three transmission lines, each hanging off nine shiny brown insulators that look like Fiestaware soup bowls, are fastened to the top of the pole, a good 80 feet up. Below the transmission lines are the three smaller distribution lines, two on one side of the pole and one on the other, each on a single white insulator barely jutting out from the pole. Below them is the neutral wire. Clifton identifies another wire as Progress-owned fiber-optic communication cable.

Beneath that is a streetlamp—number 10, by the label—and below that what is plainly a cable line, with loops of wire hanging from the pole. Next, a forearm-width telephone cable snakes its way up the pole from underground: It's identified by a case hanging from the cable just off the pole that's labeled with the numbers 1714—the number of the house that would stand next to mine, if one were there. More cables farther down are simple support braces—mechanical engineering, not electrical, Clifton says. And below that is the part of the pole where you put up the sign about your missing dog. Clifton shows me the drill holes at the base where a subcontractor tests the pole for density every few years (the company fills the hole with a treated dowel afterward) and tells me that the average pole is sunk a good 6 feet into the ground, though a transmission pole like this one goes 12 or 14 feet deep. Finally he points out the copper wire running down the pole from the neutral wires, providing a ground should the pole or wires be struck by lightning. There are no transformers or switches on this pole—my own power actually sweeps up to a pole on my neighbor's lawn, from which it hops to a transformer on a pole across the street.

CLIFTON HAD NOTED THAT AT THE Energy Control Center (ECC), managers could remotely control activity on the transmission lines, so that was the next place I needed to go, though it was also a place Progress was much less comfortable showing me. So I can't tell you where it is, though I can tell you it's hiding in plain sight and you'd drive by it a thousand times before it crossed your mind that anything important was going on there.

In a small conference room at the ECC I speak with Randy Wilkerson, director of energy control, who gives me a brief but dizzying seminar on the mechanics, economics, and politics of power generation, transmission, and distribution. Then he steps to the wall and presses a round, red, thumb-size button. A motor hums at the back of the room and, slowly, a curved wall of teak slats slides away, revealing floor-to-ceiling windows overlooking a cavernous room. It feels like the moment in a James Bond movie when the captured Bond realizes just how vast is the empire of the villain, just how maniacal are his plans.

Workers move between three desk stations, each surrounded by arcs of computer screens, six or seven per station; on a riser at the back sits a man at a master station, with more screens. At the front of the room on a wall 30 feet tall and 60 feet wide is a diagram with glowing red and green lights, long straight lines of green, yellow, and blue, and labels here and there: cities, plants, connections, lines.

It's the grid.

We talk about it, we read about it, we opine for long hours at cocktail parties about its nature and needs, and finally I got a chance to have a look at it. Not the whole grid, of course—this is just the part managed by Progress. The electrical grid as we think of it actually covers the entire North American continent, from the US-Mexico border all the way to the polar ice cap (Mexico has power, it's just not connected to the US grid). It's broken into two huge units, each a complex hodgepodge of many states, companies, and regulatory and supervisory bodies, and a few smaller ones. The two main groupings are the Eastern Interconnection, which extends from the East Coast to a line roughly paralleling the Nebraska-Wyoming border, and the Western Interconnection, which goes from there to the West Coast. There are also three smaller ones: the Texas, Alaska, and Quebec Interconnections.

Wilkerson had been telling me for quite some time about the enormous complexity of the interconnected power grid, and I even followed much of what he told me, but it all slipped away when that teak panel whirred into a pocket in the wall. He explained what I was seeing. The blue lines—there were only a few—were 500 kV transmission lines carrying power on long interstate journeys; the much more common green lines were 230 kV lines connecting power plants to substations and each other, and the spaghetti tangle of reds was the 115 kV lines that go everywhere—the low-voltage high-voltage lines, if you like. Pointing to a blue line heading north out of the Progress grid, Wilkerson said, "That's part of a major 500 kV loop that runs all the way through Ohio. Dominion takes that." Dominion is a Virginia power company that hooks up to the Progress grid near the Virginia-North Carolina border. (I eventually drove out to look at that line: behemoth steel lattice towers a thousand feet apart, conductors hanging down from long strands of insulators. I'd driven beneath them for 17 years without seeing them.)

And mind you, this map shows only the transmission grid.

A system that's been developing along its own path for more than 100 years is going to be complex. Wilkerson explains the desks in the giant room of the ECC: The guy on the right is keeping track of generation, looking at all the different power plants Progress has running at its 32 generation sites. The guy in the middle manages transmission services: He keeps an eye out for whether Progress will need to move large amounts of power into or out of its service area; if it does, Progress's own transmission lines won't suffice to move it. "A Progress marketer has to get on the Internet to get access to its own transmission line," Wilkerson says, a result of a 1996 deregulation act that it was hoped would turn the national electrical grid into a freewheeling free market of electricity on which you could buy your power from New York today and California tomorrow if the price was right. The complexities of the grid have prevented that—yes, electricity travels at the speed of light, but the choke points between various areas of the grid and the complexity of keeping the load balanced have rendered that utopian free market impossible so far. Just the same, federal regulation of transmission lines requires a first-come, first-served access, so the companies play by the rules.

The guy on the left, Wilkerson says, sits at the reliability desk. "He goes through each element, 873 different contingencies, every 10 minutes." Wilkerson does not pull the number 873 out of the air: That's the actual number of issues—"breakers, generators, lines, buses, lines to other utilities"—that that guy has to consider every 10 minutes.

"All we want to know is, if a voltage drops by 5 percent or a line nears 90 percent capability," Wilkerson says, "what would I do?" If a line neared capacity, what switches could be opened or shut to reroute power to users on other lines? What users could be convinced to lower their consumption? If a power plant had to shut down how could power be rerouted to its customers? Progress is obligated by the North American Electricity Reliability Council (NERC), which manages the entire North American grid, to have a contingency plan based on existing conditions. That way if a line goes down or a plant trips, the center is implementing a plan, not thinking about what to do. "Now, if that contingency were to occur, I've got 30 minutes to execute that plan and get out of that contingency, or I'm in violation of reliability standards," Wilkerson says. That is, if a line goes down and another one overloads, the plan organizes the response that will get the line out of overload, and they have 30 minutes to redistribute the load. At minute 31 they start paying fines.

NERC was authorized by the Federal Energy Regulatory Commission (FERC) after the blackout of 1965 left 30 million people in the Northeast without power and the industry decided that reliability standards would be a good idea. Subsequent blackouts—the 1977 New York blackout, the 1996 blackouts in the West—encouraged the strengthening of regulations, and the 2003 blackout, North America's largest ever, leaving 50 million people in the dark from Ohio to Ontario, finally turned NERC into a federally certified organization that can create standards and assess penalties. (SERC, the other ERC, by the way, is a sort of sub-ERC covering the Southeast; there are subsidiaries even to that—North Carolina is part of VACAR, the Virginia-Carolinas Reliability Agreement). Power flows easily within local areas, and only slightly less easily within an interconnection; metered tie lines connect different utilities or multi-utility groups, so they know constantly whether current is flowing into or out of their section of the grid and adjust their generation accordingly.

If that all sounds somewhat cobbled together, that's exactly right:

Electric power is nearly 130 years old, but the grid, the continental inter-connection of utilities, is barely 50. "In the 1940s," Wilkerson says, a Progress operations manager "figured out how to tie the first line to AEP [American Electric Power, another power company] at Danville—then to Duke Power at Durham, and the loop kept growing." Before then, your local power company provided your power, and if it had problems, you had problems. "Across from the 42nd Street Oyster Bar used to be the old Raleigh Electric Company," he says, referring to a lovely industrial build-ing downtown that has in recent years held a series of failed restaurants. "That was the old steam plant. If that went dark, so did Raleigh."

Engineers elsewhere figured out similar connections from region to region, recognizing that they could provide greater reliability by hooking their systems together. More than 211,000 miles of high-voltage transmis-sion lines—lines of 230 kV or more—march across the continent along various trails, keeping the 830 gigawatts of power flowing to nearly every-body on the continent. The entire system generates alternating current at 60 hertz, which means that the current alternates 60 times per second. A sudden shift in load, whether from generators going offline or lines disconnecting, causes minute fluctuations in that rate, and the people at those desks in the giant room at the Progress ECC and others like it across the continent jump out of their chairs and say, "What just happened?"

The 2003 blackout was caused by someone not having a contingency plan up to speed. Hot days cause high power use, and transmission lines stretch when they heat up from the extra current running through them. A transmission line run by an Ohio utility stretched enough that it brushed tree branches, arced to the ground, and failed. Because the util-ity didn't detect the outage quickly—an alarm didn't go off at its ECC—and didn't report it to regulators and other utilities, additional lines overheated, stretched, and failed, surprising operators who hadn't been warned; generators with nowhere to put their capacity automatically shut down, further overheating other lines as electricity tried to make its way to increasingly underserved markets. Utility companies with their eye on the ball caught the problem and protected themselves, which is why the blackout didn't spread south; others got caught. Progress, buff-ered by an intervening agency, was fine, though Wilkerson got a call:

"The Harris plant manager called me and said, 'The frequency just shot up to 60.1.' I said, 'Uh-oh, check Florida.' They called back and it wasn't Florida, so I said, 'Uh-oh, it's up north.'" Wilkerson dismissed terrorism, he says, since multiple facilities had clearly been affected at the same moment. "More than likely, it's a system operator problem. Because every blackout in the country I've studied was caused by a system operator operating beyond their first contingency."

SO THERE'S THIS ENORMOUS TANGLE of electrical lines connecting everything to everything, and we can all use our computers and make toast, but if somebody at a utility company makes a mistake, 50 million people's homes and workplaces go dark. To understand how we got to this point, we need to start at the beginning.

Raleigh got its first electrical service in 1885, when the Thomson-Houston Electric Company ran a generator out of a railroad car factory, erected poles, and in December hung lights on Fayetteville Street, making Raleigh North Carolina's first electrified city (the newspaper described a cheer, and "hundreds of spectators . . . looking with interest at the powerful radiance"); best of all, electric lights could hang directly over intersections, rather than standing at the side like gaslights. But because the electric lights were dimmer than people had hoped, the city kept the old gaslights as part of its street lighting strategy for decades, using them for streets away from the city center. Street lighting, by the way, has been going on since the Romans practiced it, and it spread to other Mediterranean cities in following centuries. London instituted rules requiring certain citizens to light their homes for street safety starting in 1416; as early as 1697, New York required during the dark of the moon that "every 7th house doe hang out a lanthorn and a candle in it." Englishman William Murdoch found in 1792 that burning coal gas could be harnessed to provide light, and gas lighting spread to North America when Baltimore began using coal gas in 1816. Prior to this, oil or candles had fueled streetlamps. When Raleigh got its first gas lamps in 1858, Raleighans preferred "the brightness of gaslight to the dripping dimness of the old style," according to one newspaper editorial. Although it took gas lighting a half-century to make it to Raleigh, electricity reached Raleigh barely 3 years after Thomas Edison opened the world's first commercial electrical utility in Manhattan in 1882, serving 59 customers within a mile of his generating plant.

Edison, searching for a profitable alternative to gas lighting, had advocated direct-current (DC) electricity, whereas George Westinghouse and Nikola Tesla preferred alternating current (AC). In the 1880s and '90s they contested a bitter and sometimes bizarre "war of the currents." Edison's DC plants were the first to send electricity to market, and their remarkable success at powering homes in New York City, New Jersey, and elsewhere led to many imitators. Westinghouse was soon installing AC systems in Massachusetts and western New York. When Tesla invented a motor for alternating current that was not the equal of the DC motors that Edison's more-established plants supplied but their superior, Edison responded by working with one Harold Brown, another DC supporter, who sought to demonstrate the dangers of AC by electrocuting a series of dogs with AC power. When alternating current continued to gain adherents, Edison responded in 1903 by using it to electrocute an elephant named Topsy at Coney Island.

Topsy died in vain. Alternating current outperformed direct current in several ways. Most important, it solved the problem of long-distance transmission. Because any conductor has some degree of impedance, electric current heats wire as it travels through it, wasting energy during transmission, and higher current (not higher voltage) heats the conductor more. The formula for power simply multiplies current by voltage, so the way to keep the power high without heating the wires too much is to increase the voltage, keeping the current low. Transformers can easily step up the voltage of alternating current for transmission and step it down again for local distribution and use; you just can't do that with direct current. Thus Edison could serve customers only within a mile or so of his plants, after which power loss along the wires was too great. When Westinghouse built an AC hydroelectric plant at Niagara Falls and in 1896 ran wires from it 15 miles to Buffalo, the war of the currents effectively ended; though Edison continued to advocate for direct current for years, his company, General Electric, finally switched to alternating current (though not soon enough for Topsy), and the world had a standard.

In most cities several companies competed for customers. In Chicago, for example, 28 new electric companies were founded between 1887 and 1892. But as electricity raced from being a luxury to a necessity, companies gobbled one another up and local and regional power companies emerged that were large enough to undertake the financial investment of building plants, planting poles, and stringing wire (or burying it—an 1888 blizzard in New York caused so much damage that the city required all subsequent lines to be buried). Those companies then stimulated demand by selling electrical appliances (irons and vacuum cleaners were the most popular early on) and starting streetcar lines, which would not only use power but also provide ticket revenue. Because water power was used to generate much early electricity, Woodrow Wilson in 1920 signed the Federal Water Power Act, which created the Federal Power Commission (which eventually became FERC), and power, at least in the cities, was on its way to becoming a fact of life. In 1907, only one of every twelve American dwellings had electricity; by 1932, two of every three homes had it, eight of ten in cities.

The countryside was electrified much more slowly. Companies that could economically run wires down city or suburban streets lined with customers ignored isolated farms. Only in 1936 did the Rural Electrification Act of the New Deal address the fact that 90 percent of all farms in the country lacked access to electricity. Low-interest loans enabled farmers and other rural residents to create cooperatives, building small plants or running wires to existing systems. As a result, by 1941 more than 35 percent of farmhouses had electricity. By the 1940s individual power company grids were connecting with each other; in 1957 nuclear power plants joined the coal, hydroelectric, and gas and oil plants that were already up and running, and we had the completely ubiquitous electrical system we now take for granted.

PEOPLE USED TO WORRY A LOT MORE about nuclear power irradiating us all than about mountaintop removal coal mining or carbon footprints. Given that, I found it hard to explain my reaction to the deep, quiet concrete pool inside an enormous concrete room within the concrete containment building at the Harris Nuclear Plant, about 15 miles southwest of Raleigh, where they keep spent fuel assemblies. Twenty-three feet of still water covered the used fuel that engineers had removed from the reactor about a month before. They hadn't had a chance to move it to longer-term storage pools, which are off the route of tours for interested parties, so my getting to see the spent fuel was something of a coup.

"If you tried to swim down there," said plant operations manager John Dills, his voice echoing in the vast, gray room, "just to touch it, by the time you reached the fuel you'd be dead." And yet my response was exactly the opposite of the fear I might have expected.

That response: "Oooh." The spent fuel emits beta particles (electron-size bits emanating from the nuclei of still-radiating atoms), which travel faster than the speed of light in water. Those particles cause water molecules to briefly enter a polarized reorientation toward the beta particles and then to snap back to their regular chaotic disorganization. That snapping back emits energy that our eyes pick up in the blue spectrum, so the water glows blue, somewhere between the dim luminescence of a grow light and the staticky glimmer of a black-and-white TV screen in another room.

You can't take your eyes off it. Partly because it's pretty, partly because it represents a staggering amount of energy, and partly because it's dangerous. The dangerous part the plant has under control—before you drive into a nuclear plant, they not only stop you at a security wall out front, they put a mirror beneath your car and swab you, possibly for explosive residue, though they won't tell you exactly for what. "Put it this way," said the cheerful guard. "If you had bought a bag of fertilizer and put it in your trunk last week, we'd know." The next set of guards I went through had machine guns. Which didn't bother me. I had already been to several plants and establishments that are very important to the city and the most severe security I had encountered was a rolling gate. While this seems reasonable to me—you can protect only so much, and at the water plant you're better off thinking about treating the water than keeping out bad guys—a nuclear plant is a different story.

Dills fairly radiated just the kind of competence you want in the people creating nuclear power. "Everything is identical to a fossil fuel plant," Dills said. "The only difference is the heat source." That is, the reaction boils water and the resulting steam turns a turbine. "You remember a pinwheel?" he asks. "This is a $30 million pinwheel." That's the cost of the turbine itself. The Harris plant cost $4 billion by the time it opened in 1987, 16 years after Progress Energy announced it. Progress broke ground in 1978, and the next year came the Three Mile Island partial core meltdown in Pennsylvania; all the resulting changes in the plant's design, construction, and management of nuclear energy came as change orders. "We were going to build four reactors for a billion dollars," Dills says, smiling. "We got one reactor for $4 billion." But the plant is built, it runs, and he believes the Three Mile Island accident made it safer.

Dills talks a mile a minute as we go into increasingly secure buildings, through full-height security turnstiles and enough metal detectors and pat-downs to get me into a dozen airports. "The reactor produces heat," he tells me as we stride through concrete hallways and tornado-proof doors while neutrons bang into the uranium-235 atoms in the fuel assemblies. With every step we pass pipes. The entire plant has the feeling of the water treatment plant, only giant and loud: The noise is from pumps and the turbine. Whereas the largest pipes in the water plant were about 60 inches in diameter, conduits in the nuclear plant run about 60 feet high. The similarity to the water plant isn't totally surprising, because water systems make this plant run.

The plant contains three water loops. The first loop, heated by the reactor, never leaves the reactor building. Under pressure, the water remains liquid instead of boiling into steam, which is why this plant type is called a pressurized water reactor. The second loop—the "feed water"—is boiled by the heat from the pressurized loop, then fed through the turbines. After it leaves the turbines, a condenser cools it so it can reenter the steam generator as water, which improves the heat transfer and the efficiency of the plant.

The third water loop is the one people most associate with nuclear plants: 6 million gallons of water that cycle through the condenser, which is cooled by the iconic concrete cooling tower to about 98° F. Dills takes care to get two points across: The water in the cooling tower never enters the radioactive portion of the plant, and the cooling tower isn't part of the nuclear reactor. In fact, it's built far enough away from the plant that even if it keeled over like something in a Monty Python animation it wouldn't touch the reactor building. Although plenty of fossil fuel plants use those same arcing concrete towers, Three Mile Island made them the symbol of the nuclear industry. Dills can tell as many people as he likes, but people still see cooling towers and think "nuclear plant."

Inside, it feels like a huge water plant inside thick concrete walls, only with everything on a massive scale. The Raleigh water plant produces about 60 million gallons per day when it's going close to full-bore. The pumps circulating water into the Harris condenser run about 30 million gallons *per hour*. The condenser itself is about 150 feet long, and the three pumps feeding it look like the boilers for a steamship. The conduits leaving the condenser are about 60 feet tall. "It takes 58 megawatts just to make the energy," Dills says. That is, nearly 8 percent of the energy the plant generates goes right back into keeping the plant generating energy. The turbines (there are three of them) look almost exactly like locomotive engines a child would draw: vast metal cylinders, only about four times the size of a steam engine, covered in thick, shiny blue industrial paint.

MY HEAD IS SPINNING at that point, so naturally that's when we enter the control room and I get the speech: The control room is pressurized, so if there's a catastrophe clean air will flow out rather than irradiated air flowing in. It contains food and water enough to last for 30 days. The 3-foot concrete walls surrounding the building and the tornado-proof doors aren't enough; the control room door is bulletproof. "Did it click?" someone asks as the door closes behind us. It did, and we look around.

The control panel that angles across the front of the room looks like something on a *Star Trek* set—that is, everything about it says '60s and '70s electromechanical, not LCD digital. It's like one of those old washing machines that had buttons for "rinse" or "suds" that used to light up during the cycle. Of course the controlling mechanisms are computerized and utterly up-to-date, but the displays and signs are still very much analog: curving meters with fluctuating red needles, panels with printed words that light up, glowing red lights. "It's robust and it works," Dills says amiably. "And it's all safety grade."

To step off the tile floor and onto the carpet right in front of the control panel you need the express permission of the shift manager. Permission having been granted, I clasp my hands behind my back and gingerly inspect temperature gauges and coolant pump indicators as Dills gives a basic lesson in reactor physics. Neutron population multiplied by fuel equals power, so they control the reaction by controlling the neutron population. Control rods above the fuel assemblies absorb neutrons, and if power is lost gravity will drop them down, stopping the reaction in a second or two. A second way to control the reaction is with boron, which eats neutrons; the engineers dissolve boric acid into the reactor coolant to control the reaction. Too high and they add boron; too low and they add pure water. If the unthinkable happens the reactor will SCRAM— automatically drop the control rods and shut down, with sirens and lights and everything. A red phone on the desk provides a direct link to the Nuclear Regulatory Commission, and there's a duplicate control room, exactly like this one in every particular and connected in real time, 3 miles away, in case something goes unimaginably wrong inside the plant. When I ask about the word "SCRAM," Dills says that though the very first nuclear reactor at the University of Chicago in 1942 included several safety systems for inserting control rods into the uranium pile, the final safety system was a rod hanging over the pile on a rope, and a man was given an ax to cut the rope if all else failed: Super-Critical Reaction Ax Man, or SCRAM. Ha ha, but when you look it up, that ax guy actually existed. Whether the acronym formed in that way or was a back-formation from the more usual, and under the circumstances completely understandable, usage of the word "scram" is almost irrelevant. Anyhow, I didn't touch anything.

The rest of the plant tour showed me things I had come almost to expect: the enormous mazes of water pipes and electrical and communications lines for meters, supervisory control and data acquisition programs, and the like. "We have a tremendous infrastructure just for the plant," Dills told me. The plant cleans its own drinking water from the reservoir on which it sits and runs its own sewage plant. And of course the complex includes two monstrous buildings with 6.5 megawatt diesel-powered generators to keep the plant going if it somehow becomes separated from the grid.

Leaving a nuclear plant is almost as difficult as getting in. You are checked for radiation in so many ways and at such fine levels that you are warned to wear only cotton clothing because the massive walls are made of concrete, which slowly exudes radon gas; the static electricity in noncotton clothing gathers that radon to it and the dosimeters pick it up, which had happened to a television reporter not long before my visit. Having been forewarned, I kept to nice, comfortable cotton and got out fine.

THE HARRIS NUCLEAR PLANT, like almost any modern power plant, creates 900 megawatts of energy, generating enough electricity to power at least 500,000 houses. Thousands of people manage that power 24 hours a day. The engineers in the energy control center take the pulse of the transmission grid, Wilkerson told me, *every 4 seconds,* making sure that the demand and the supply remain equal, because electricity cannot be stored. "This is the only business in which your customer can demand and consume your product before you can manufacture it," Wilkerson told me at the ECC. The minute the power plant generates electricity, it joins the grid and is consumed; in fact, the pressure of people consuming energy helps drive the generators to increase production. Those constant snapshots let managers know how their power supply and demand stack up, which lets them know when to turn generators up and down, like the managers at the water plant adjusting supply to demand by turning pumps on and off. And just as the water, sewer, and traffic guys have their peak and valley usage times, power use follows particular patterns, both daily and seasonally, which engineers spend a vast amount of time managing. "It's almost entirely driven by weather," Wilkerson told me.

He drew a graph. In winter, domestic power use goes up overnight, as the temperature goes down and heaters click on in the night; the daily peak is in the morning, when hot water, shavers, blow dryers, micro-waves, electric ranges, radios, televisions, and computers join the heaters that have been running all night. Use diminishes during the day as the temperature rises, then begins climbing again starting at dinnertime: Lights go on, somebody's in the kitchen cooking dinner, everybody else is engaged with one screen or another, and maybe somebody's running a load of clothes through the washer and dryer. Evening reaches a second, smaller peak around 9:00 p.m., with streetlights on and hot water for baths and showers; then it diminishes again until around midnight, when overnight heating causes it to start rising again.

Summer has a less complex curve, with morning use climbing slowly through the day and reaching a lower but longer peak from about 6:00 to 9:00 p.m. with dinner and appliance use, then diminishing through the night as the air conditioner doesn't have to work as hard. Until the 1940s, all electrical utilities had their peak demand loads in the winter; with the growth of air-conditioning since then, almost all regions now peak in the summer (in the South and Southwest, air-conditioning can account for some 40 percent of power use in summer). And, Wilkerson explained, regulated utilities are obligated to provide all their customers with all the electricity they need at the moment of peak demand—but if they build too much capacity, regulators may not allow them to charge their users for the investment. Thus, Progress has to be able to provide all the electricity its customers need at 6:00 p.m. on the hottest day of August, one way or another—which, most of the rest of the time, leaves it with generating capacity to spare.

It's a constant management problem. Progress runs its cheapest-to-operate plants—nuclear plants—full-time. Coal plants run a little less cheaply, but Progress also runs them virtually all the time. Various types of gas and oil plants are more expensive; the most expensive and dirtiest, called "peaker plants," run only when Progress desperately needs them, during periods of highest demand. Of course, some of them need to run for several hours before their boilers are ready to produce power, which keeps Progress managers and demand forecasters glued to weather reports. Finally, for the highest demand peaks, Progress can buy energy from other utilities more cheaply than it can generate it, so in its downtown headquarters Progress has teams buying and selling energy contracts 24 hours a day. (In fact, they do this regardless of peak loads—weather differences and the type and price of fuel used for generation by different neighboring utilities make energy prices fluctuate all day long, and traders make contracts for as little as 15 minutes' worth of power at a time.) Utilities manage peaks in other ways, too—they have agreements with major users, such as factories and office buildings, and they contact those users in times of need: They'll make a phone call to a factory and ask it to shut or slow down on a hot August afternoon, or ask an office building to allow its air-conditioning to creep up to 78° from 74°F.

WHICH BRINGS US BACK TO THE SMART GRID. "Smart Grid" is a catch-all term for the many ways in which improved communication, transmission, and distribution technology will give both producers and consumers greater control over power generation and use, ideally encouraging conservation as well as efficiency: Utilities like to refer to the Smart Grid as a virtual power plant, improving use patterns instead of building capacity. When the grid smartens up, for example, Progress can make agreements with its large customers to render those peak-time phone calls unnecessary—Progress managers and computers will simply be able to control, say, skyscraper air conditioners or manufacturing plant processes, cutting them down or off in order to reduce load. Same for consumers: The Smart Grid will add meters and switches, controllable through the Internet, that will enable the grid to respond much more effectively in real time to changing demand loads. Progress has already started putting devices on the air conditioners of individual users. If the load on the Progress grid gets too high, Progress can turn these air conditioners off for short intervals, then restart them. Customers say they never notice the brief caesuras. At one demonstration I attended, the representative of a company that creates Smart Grid software said that if even 20 percent of homes participated, the savings would equal all the renewable energy currently generated.

POWER COMPANIES HAVE MANY GOALS FOR THE SMART GRID. To start with, it will encourage distributed generation—home solar panels and windmills, for example—and allow people who generate power effectively to sell energy back to the grid. It could use the combined power of the batteries of electric cars as an extra hedge against those load peaks: That is, you charge your car overnight, when load is low; during the day, if it's plugged in, when load is high you can use the battery to run your computer or lights. (Utilities do this themselves with hydroelectric plants, running the generators during high-load times and spending that cheap energy overnight to pump water back up into the dam and store it for the next day's high-load use.) The Smart Grid will be self-correcting—when a tree brings down a power line, it will automatically reroute the power, something that right now requires workers to drive to utility poles and pull switches. It will also, through a Web site, keep you apprised of the cost of your power. So, on that hot August afternoon when Progress is itself buying power because even its highest-fuel-cost plants can't keep up with demand, your power will cost you a lot, at night, when everybody is asleep, power is cheaper. With this information, users can choose to run dishwashers and washing machines when power is cheap, not when it's expensive. Pilot projects of systems allowing customers to set monthly use targets are already in place, and they're saving customers money.

That nobody's quite sure how all this stuff will work on the large scale doesn't faze anybody. I went to a demonstration where a professor of electrical engineering told me that all that stood between us and implementing all Smart Grid technologies was breakthroughs in electricity storage (batteries that can stay powered for long periods and store large amounts of energy), solid-state transformer technology, and semiconductor technology (silicon can't handle the high voltages the power grid requires). When I wondered whether that might not be like saying that all we need to solve our traffic problems is the coming breakthrough in human-shoulder-wing technology, he just smiled. Like most of the other people in the power industry I spoke with, he is sure it will happen, and that it won't take long, either.

BUT POWER IS NOT JUST ELECTRICITY—there's always one more grid. Across the street from my house one day I noticed a hole in the pavement, maybe 3 feet by 4 feet. Parked next to it was a van from the gas company, and going inside the hole was what looked like a slim yellow snake, writhing rhythmically into the dirt. What I was seeing, the guy running the compressor that drove the machine told me, was modern utility connection. The service connection running to the house from the gas line beneath the street had sprung a leak and needed to be replaced. Backhoe? Trencher? Not anymore. His HammerHead machine used pneumatic power to drive a piston head into the earth at the end of a high-density plastic pipe. That head whanged itself forward at the rate of about half an inch per whack, moling its way beneath the driveway all the way to the gas meter at the side of the house. At my stunned reaction, the guy just laughed: This is small potatoes. Trenchless pipe installation is a major element of all infrastructure work now. I encountered some of it when I watched the installation of a cast-in-place pipe along a troubled sewer line; my surveyor, Sherrill Styers, had told me that various trenchless technologies are now responsible for a significant portion of emergency calls, when some automatic mole pounds its way through a pipe wall or snaps a cable somebody didn't know was there. Just the same, the idea that you could dig a little hole in the street and reach your gas meter that way still struck me as delightfully Jules Verne.

That was all the natural gas technology I saw up close. When I reached out to the local natural gas utility for a chance to see what they did, I was politely but firmly told that in a post-9/11 world, they "no longer share specific details about our pipeline infrastructure," though they offered several useful Web sites I was welcome to consult. So I reached out to the public utilities commission.

Bill Gilmore, deputy director for natural gas for the Operations Division of the North Carolina Utilities Commission, laughs when I tell him that the gas company refused to divulge the location of their local pipelines. "We have pipeline safety laws that require us to put up pipeline markers where they cross major roads," he says. In fact, there's one half a block from my house, a big, floppy plastic strip telling me not to dig there without calling the gas company. A weird 7-foot brown pipe also sticks straight up from the ground there—a pressure relief valve. If the system pressure gets too high, gas vents out the top of the pipe, which is covered by a lid that snaps back to cover the vent; a little metal flag flips over, though, to leave evidence that the release occurred. What's more, the distribution center—what's called the city gate, where the pipe leading into Raleigh separates into many smaller pipes bringing gas under just about every street—isn't actually very hard to find. It's out west of town past the fairgrounds, and it has an enormous white tank, festooned with a huge logo for the gas company, that is connected to a small processing building before branching out to a pipe structure that vanishes underground. (The processing building is where they add the stink—it's called mercaptan, and it's added so that a gas leak has that unmistakable odor. Gas is naturally odorless, so the stink prevents potentially deadly leaks from going unnoticed.)

The Chinese had discovered the properties of natural gas by 200 BC, when they were already piping it through bamboo chutes for cooking, heating, and light. The Delphic oracle and the biblical burning bush may have been flaming natural gas seepages, but Westerners were almost 2,000 years late to the table, with William Murdoch's late-18th-century revelation about the potential of coal gas. In 1821 a well in western New York was providing gas for street lighting, though because gas required pipelines to be transported, almost 4 decades passed before anyone thought to start a company to produce it. When electricity took over from gas street lighting at the end of the 19th century, gas companies repurposed their networks of buried pipes and began promoting gas's domestic uses, such as running stoves and water heaters. The first long-distance pipeline went into service in 1910. During World War II, hastily constructed pipelines brought oil from Texas to New York to replace oil that couldn't be safely transported by ship; after the war the government retired the pipes, and natural gas companies began using them.

The natural gas system functions similarly to the way the water system would if the country had only a few monstrous water plants that served the entire nation instead of one for each town or city; it also resembles the electrical grid in that it breaks down into three separate parts: gathering systems, which are like power generators, and then transmission and distribution systems. The whole thing is fairly simple, if the transmission of an explosive substance under pressure for thousands of miles can be called simple. Wells gather the gas and pipe it to processing plants that clean it of impurities such as water and sulfur dioxide. The plants—most of them in Texas, Oklahoma, Alaska, and western New York—then pump it under a pressure of 600 to 1,200 pounds per square inch (psi) in 30- to 43-inch buried steel pipes; compressors along the way, run by gas in the pipeline, keep up the pressure. Mine gets to me from the Gulf of Mexico on the Transco pipeline, the only pipeline that serves North Carolina, which Gilmore says has surely the poorest natural gas delivery system in the Southeast and possibly in the nation: In the late 1980s a third of the state's counties had no natural gas service at all. The state saw that it was losing opportunities to draw industry and so has invested in extending intrastate pipelines that run from Transco to North Carolina's major cities. When it gets to that city gate, the gas company steps down the pressure to a couple hundred psi and moves it to my house in tiny pipes starting out in the 12-inch range and coming down to as small as 4 inches under my street. Then it comes up my driveway to that little gas meter that keeps track of how many cubic feet I use per month. (Gilmore tells me that at the city gate the gas company measures not just volume but also the heat content of the gas, which varies by day, and does some arithmetic to bill me for the heat content of the gas I'm using.)

Beyond my meter, with its bent Rube Goldberg pipes going in and out, and the relief valves I occasionally see, the only gas infrastructure to keep an eye out for on the public streets is valve covers—exactly like the water valve covers, little circles lending access to valves that service workers can control. Gilmore tells me one more amazing thing. Just like every other infrastructure stream, gas use has peaks and valleys. "Before electric generation the curve used to look like a saw," he says, peaking in the winter and cratering in the summer, year after year, when gas was used mainly for heating and cooking. Now electric generation peaks in summer, so the curve has evened out some, but gas still runs much faster in winter. To respond to that, my gas company has two types of storage: seasonal storage and peak storage. Just as the roads are designed to be safe in the rain, at night, for someone driving a little too fast and the water system is designed to be able, at

the busiest moment of the busiest day, to still have the pressure to supply water to fight a major fire, the gas system is designed, Gilmore
says, "to serve heat-sensitive customers on the worst possible winter
day." Seasonal storage is a portion of each day's gas purchase that's
pumped farther up the pipeline into a depleted gas reservoir in Pennsylvania; come the cooler temperatures of autumn and winter, the
company pumps that gas back into the pipeline and uses it to heat my
house. Peak storage is liquefied natural gas stored in the tank at the city
gate that can come to the rescue on what they call the design day—the
coldest day of winter, which for Raleigh will be a day when the average
temperature is 10° or 12°F.

But pipes travel underground; perhaps grid-crazy, I keep my eyes
skyward, gazing at my street's poles and wires. Maybe it's because the
one in my yard, a transmission pole with no cross arms, gets lost
among the pines in front of the house, but I had simply never paid any
mind to the wires that festoon my street. Now, standing in my driveway, I can trace the two rows of standard cross-arm poles up my street,
then see them crisply head in opposite directions when they reach the
corner; I can see the transmission wires, rather elegantly in comparison,
swoop up the street, crossing whenever it made for a shorter span—wires
cost money, so shorter is always better. At the intersection with the big
street they cross again and then, span by span, disappear down a hill. It
looks somehow majestic, like seeing an elk leave a clearing and bound
into the woods. I counted no fewer than 15 electrical wires running up
and down my street, not counting telephone and cable-TV wires or the
guy wires holding up the poles themselves. Being that close to a substation, I should have noticed it before, but like my street's lack of storm
drains, this is the type of thing that comes to you only when you decide
to take a patient look around. I liked it.

I felt connected.

CHAPTER 7

THE BIG RAVIOLI

Why Future Archaeologists Will Find Our Trash
Somewhat Perplexing; or, Thank God for the
Union of Concerned Scientists

THE 1930S WERE A TOUGH TIME in a lot of ways, but the decade was a
golden age for new and better ways to collect, haul, and dispose of
garbage. In 1937, in an effort to keep the rats down and the capacity up,
the director of the Fresno, California, landfill came up with the idea of
compacting each day's waste and covering it with dirt. This was the birth
of the sanitary landfill—and the same process, updated, is still the basis
for trash heaps worldwide. Every day starts with bulldozers quickly
clearing as much dirt as they can off yesterday's trash, and every day ends
with that dirt—and some new, of course—being thrown back on.

Also in 1937, the city of Knoxville, Tennessee, improved its trash
pickup system by purchasing a new kind of truck. Patented in 1935 by a
local resident for use in the construction business he ran with his broth-
ers, the truck automatically picked up and emptied out containers into a
hopper on its back. In a world of increasing packaging and refuse, a bin
that required little manpower to empty was a godsend. So George Dempster's "Dumpster" didn't remain a Knoxville secret for long.

Meanwhile, in Michigan, Gar Wood Industries took the compaction
idea mobile in 1938, improving the standard design of closed trash
trucks (which kept litter, pests, and odors down) by adding hydraulic

compactors. Gar Wood's Load-Packer truck was the first version of what you or I would instantly recognize as a modern garbage truck.

These three innovations constituted basically the first changes to trash management since the first caveperson said, "Let's put that pile of shells and junk out behind the cave—it stinks!" And we haven't changed much since. As for whether that constitutes progress or not, the jury is still out.

I SO WANTED THE MORNING MUSTER OF THE RALEIGH TRASH TRUCKS to remind me of the helicopter scene from *Apocalypse Now.* I imagined a general turning of keys and grinding of engines in the parking lot full of trucks, a slow, balletic staggered arc toward the exits, the swelling strains of "The Ride of the Valkyries" as dozens of trucks rumbled out in formation to attack the recycling, trash, and yard waste from a quarter of the city (the Raleigh Solid Waste Services Department handles a quarter of the city each day, leaving 1 day a week for problem solving).

No dice. I arrived on a Thursday morning, as arranged, to meet the two-man crew of my 769-home recycling route and the driver of my 850-home trash route. But Thursday is meeting morning at Solid Waste Services, and guys kind of filter out, in their green mesh vests and make their way to trucks in dribs and drabs. You never really notice it, but a low engine growl murmurs the whole time, and suddenly you notice that the parking lot is mostly empty of its 100 or so white trucks—including truck 1339, which will get my recycling. In the chaos nobody seems able to point me toward the one that will get my trash, so I jump in my car and start trolling. The people in the front office have given me 2-foot-square GIS maps of the SW1 quadrant of the city, with my routes highlighted, so I know where the trucks must be.

First I go home. I know from my son's delighted cries every trash day that the recycling truck usually comes by before 10:00 a.m. and sure enough, at 9:25 I hear the grumble, the squawk of brakes, and the sounds of a bin being emptied. Soon, around the corner rolls truck 1339, a white LaBrie Top Select recycler. The driver, Kendall, jumps out at every house to pick up the green recycling bin from the driver's-side curb, dumping it with a splash of breaking glass into a long bin along the side of the truck;

the other guy, John, trots along next to the truck and empties the bins on the other side of the street. Raleigh only recently switched from curbside sorting to single-stream recycling; the workers used to have to separate paper from everything else. Now that they don't, Kendall and John move so swiftly that by the end of a block they've left me behind, even though the truck has stopped once so that the bins on each side can slide up, flipping the unsorted contents into the truck's hopper with the help of spidery arms, then return to the sides. I'm just watching and I can't keep up.

But I know where they're headed, because I've already visited what the solid waste guys call the murph—the materials recovery facility, or MRF—and seen one of the most amazing machines this world has to offer.

A BACKHOE PATROLS THE CONCRETE TIPPING FLOOR of the 45,000-square-foot shed of the Sonoco MRF in southeast Raleigh. As soon as a truck pulls in and tips its contents into the pile that spreads over the floor, the backhoe pounces, scooping the recyclables into a Dumpster-like container called a metering bin that shakes the contents up, performing the counterintuitive job of mixing the different recyclables together.

Jim Foster, plant manager, smiles at my disbelief. "In the truck the stuff naturally stratifies," he says—heavy glass settling to the bottom, nearly weightless plastic bottles bubbling to the top—but the computer-automated reclamation processing system, the surgical-scrubs-green machine that dominates the shed, works most efficiently if the materials enter in a steady stream, not waves of one material or another. The metering bin, he says, increased the system's efficiency by 20 percent.

Foster walks me literally through the machine, up and down metal stairs in what feels like a cross between the superstructure of a small battleship and a well-scaffolded three-story Rube Goldberg machine. From the metering bin a conveyor carries the stream past two workers wearing ear protection and hard hats who pick out cardboard and throw it into a hopper; they also pick out and discard recycling unacceptables like wires, plastic flowerpots, pizza boxes (grease queers the deal), and crockery or glassware shards, which melt at different temperatures than food-container glass. (Raleigh plans to shift within the next couple of years from 18-gallon basket-style household recycling containers to 95-gallon wheeled bins that, like trash bins, can be emptied automatically. This change is expected to increase diversion by up to 30 percent—currently the city recycles about 28 percent of its waste—and save money by cutting recycling collection to every 2 weeks and preventing the inevitable injuries workers sustain in lifting and dumping. Sonoco just expects to see more garbage in the recycling stream, because those large containers will be too hard to resist.)

The conveyor then feeds into an escalator-looking thing called an agitator or an elliptical machine, on which rotating elliptical rubber disks bounce the recycling stream up an incline. Light items like paper effortlessly climb the ramp and flip over the top: The plant's workers call paper recyclables "overs." Heavier materials—glass, plastic, metal—bounce around and fall into hoppers, so they're called "unders."

Overs—papers—are then baled and used by Sonoco's own paper plants or sold to other sources here or abroad; paper can be recycled seven times before the fibers have been broken too many times to be useful, and Asian countries love American recycled paper because it's usually had only one or two uses. Unders—mostly cans and bottles—go by conveyor to a crusher, which breaks glass and separates it from the metals and plastics; a magnet picks out ferrous metals like tin cans. Then the stream flows past a new optical sorter, which recognizes different types of plastics and blows them with puffs of air into different metal mesh hoppers. (Polyethylene terephthalate, or PET, is group 1—clear containers like drink bottles; high-density polyethylene, HDPE, is group 2—milk, juice, and shampoo containers; Sonoco stops there, accepting only products with a neck, though many other types of plastic can be recycled by different types of facilities.) The installed optical sorter hasn't worked well yet, so instead three workers scramble to manually separate the plastics.

Finally a remarkable device called a rare-earth magnet beneath the conveyor kicks out aluminum cans with audible pops. What's left—paper that filtered in with the unders—then flitters down off the end of the conveyor like a gentle, constant snowfall into a pile near the entry to the machine, from where a backhoe occasionally shovels it over to the rest of the paper. Workers crate metal for smelters; machines crush and bale plastics, paper, and aluminum for shipping. Aluminum brings about $1,000 per ton, Foster says, "but we ship a [20-ton] truckload of cans every 10 days." Newspaper brings only $45 per ton, but the plant bales five truckloads a day. There's money there.

But they work hard for the money. Raleigh drops off about 1,500 tons per month at Sonoco, but that's only 4 days per week. Sonoco gets materials every day, both residential and commercial, from all over the region. Moreover, Sonoco isn't first a recycler, but a packager; its recycling business got started to supply it with cheap raw material. "We really want the fibers," Foster says. "The City of Raleigh is fortunate, because we *need* this. This is all we used to do. We were solely here to feed our paper mills." As the recycling industry has changed, Sonoco has responded: "First we went after textiles, then mainframe computer cards, then green-bar printouts." And though Sonoco has just invested deeply in the automated single-stream system, Foster raises fundamental questions about recycling practices.

"Recycling is not at the curb—that's not recycling," he says. Recycling is processing (what his plant does) and, especially, reuse. "The first thing [manufacturers and people] need is to *buy* recycled," he says, to create a need for products made with recycled materials. "We do it the other way, so far—we go get it and try to find something to do with it." That is, he's in a raw-material business, in essence mining our garbage, but instead of going after what he thinks will be useful, he takes whatever Raleigh wants to exclude from its waste stream, then tries to find someone to sell it to. Consider glass. "Glass is 27 percent of our weight" in incoming recyclables, he points out, "and it's of zero value to us." That is, there's no shortage of sand, the main ingredient in glass, so recycled glass, which has to be sorted for color, saves a bit of energy but otherwise isn't of much value to glass manufacturers. But Raleigh wants to keep glass bottles out of its landfills, so glass goes in the recycling bins, ends up on Sonoco's tipping floor, and goes through the machine, where it's filtered out. Sonoco hauls it to a local glass reprocessor, and if the pittance the reprocessor pays covers the fuel required to drive it over there, Foster counts himself lucky.

Sonoco has been bidding for—and winning—Raleigh's recycling contracts since 1992, and the numbers change from contract to contract. Foster recalls the 1986 and 1987 garbage ships—the barge *Mobro*, from New York, which for 7 months failed to find a place to dump its trash and finally burned the load in Brooklyn; and the *Khian Sea*, which left Philadelphia with a shipment of ash from a trash incinerator in 1986 and wandered the seas until 1988, with most of the ash ending up in the ocean. These highlighted what some perceived as a growing solid waste crisis, which sparked recycling programs everywhere. "But paper mills were set up to use trees," not recycled paper, he says, so the market instantly flooded. "We couldn't take paper for, like, 6 months," and paper collected for recycling ended up in landfills.

But paper mills have adapted, and it's the same situation for every material that comes in: Each material brings a specific price, which changes according to market forces. Sonoco's current contract with Raleigh has Sonoco paying the city $16 per ton of materials dropped off. They negotiated that contract in 2008, when Sonoco was selling $1 million of material per month; now, "these commodities have dumped so much that our sales are like $300,000 a month," Foster says. "We just bid the city of Durham," right down the road, he continues. "Charging *them* $25 per ton." It's like fuel hedging by airlines—you sign long contracts, and everybody takes a chance. New factors constantly affect the process, either intended (Wal-Mart decides to change its packaging) or unintended: A 2007 expansion of the 2005 federal highway bill, for example, extends tax breaks for use of blended fuels beyond transportation uses. A vile substance called "black liquor," a by-product of paper pulping that's mixed with diesel to form fuel that paper mills reuse to run their plants, turns out to qualify. As a result paper mills suddenly qualify for billions of dollars of tax breaks if they use trees, not recycled paper, and the value of recycled paper plummets. City councils, state legislatures, and Congress may also change recycling regulations. Raleigh's doing well in its current contract and it swore it would never pay a per-ton processing fee, but Foster expects that the next contract will include one, with Sonoco and the city splitting any resulting revenues when sales are greater than the processing fee.

Some cycles are more predictable. Newspaper has diminished from 63 percent of Sonoco's stream in 1995 to 50 percent now—Foster blames the decline of subscriptions rather than a rise in other recyclables. Tonier subdivisions send in more corrugated cardboard: "They're shopping online," he figures. Foster takes me to a quiet room overlooking the automated processing system so I can watch as long as I want. "I mean, look at that stuff," he marvels. "It's just rolling in. And it's gonna keep rolling in whether this facility is running or not." Yes, it will—in 1960, recycling amounted to 6.2 percent of total municipal solid waste in the United States; in 2007, that was up to 24.9 percent. Add in the 8.5 percent that was diverted to composting facilities in 2007, and nationwide we now reuse more than one-third of our solid waste. (Besides recycling paper, plastic, and glass, Raleigh sends dozens of truckloads of yard waste daily to a recycling center where the waste is processed and sold back to citizens as mulch, compost, and wood chips.)

That still leaves about 169 million tons of solid waste for the United States to dispose of every year. What do we do with it? As late as 1941, a government survey found that more than a quarter of American food waste was being fed to hogs. After a disease outbreak resulted in more than 400,000 swine being slaughtered, this practice dwindled. By the 1970s, barely 4 percent of food waste went to swine; current EPA documents don't even mention it as a strategy.

BUT THAT'S SOMETHING OF A HISTORICAL ANOMALY. For most of their early history, American cities relied on herds of free-roaming pigs for their waste management. Not rural areas, mind you—cities. "They are the city scavengers, these pigs," wrote Charles Dickens in *American Notes for General Circulation* (1842), describing pigs on Broadway in New York City. "They are never attended upon, or fed, or driven, or caught, but are thrown upon their own resource in early life, and become preternaturally knowing in consequence." Pigs ate the copious food waste thrown into the streets; hogs could eat even the dead horses that collapsed in the street and were left to rot.

Wandering pigs may sound a little extreme, but until the Industrial Revolution, most solid waste was food scraps. Not much else was being discarded beyond some torn clothes, broken tools, and pieces of pottery. Depending on how you look at it, solid waste is either the newest or the oldest problem we've got. On the one hand, until the 20th century, when we started to use disposable razors and plastics and endless layers of packaging, nobody had much to throw out. On the other hand, we've been coping with trash since we first started hanging around in one place long enough to generate it: Stone Age trash heaps called middens, which contained oyster shells and bones and dated from as much as 140,000 years ago, have been found in southern Africa. The Minoans, 3,500 years ago, dug holes for their trash. By the 5th century BC, Athens had begun what is considered the first organized town dump, a mile away from the city walls. Most trash, of course, consisted either of completely biodegradable wastes like food, bones, and shells, or things like broken pottery; valuable metals were mostly reused, and few people had much more to throw out.

By the time of the Roman Empire, most trash was thrown into the streets and washed into the sewers, where rats ate and bred and caused pestilence; the Tiber occasionally became so full of refuse (including dead people and animals) that slaves had to dredge it. Things only got worse with the collapse of the empire. By the Middle Ages "rakers" in London made their livings by hauling off refuse and making use of what they could; by the 1800s they had been joined by "toshers," who went through the sewers looking for useful items, and "mudlarks," who did the same on the riverbanks. The poet Baudelaire romanticized the *chiffoniers*, or rag pickers, who scavenged the trash heaps of Paris for linen used in paper-making and other useful raw materials, but their lives were not very romantic. Most people were so poor that almost no usable cloth was thrown out: Hospital regulations in the Italian town of Perugia required that the clothes in which people died be passed on to their families. The average chiffonier in 1760 was estimated to find less than 5 pounds of rags per day.

People weren't much richer—or cleaner—in the early United States. Benjamin Franklin in 1792 created the nation's first garbage collection service, whereby servants (slaves, according to some sources) gathered the refuse of Philadelphia's 60,000 residents and dumped it in the Delaware River, undoubtedly to the chagrin of the city's downstream neighbors. A century or so later, disgusted residents of Alexandria, Virginia, attacked and sank barges carrying the trash of Washington, DC, to a downstream dump site. Around the turn of the 20th century, New York was still dumping its trash in the harbor, and Chicago dumping its in Lake Michigan. Cities that collected trash (it was by no means the norm) commonly dumped it in vacant lots. Sometimes ash and garbage were used to fill in swamps, as at New York's famous Fresh Kills landfill. Nobody worried in those days about leachate contaminating the groundwater; leachate *was* the groundwater. (Fresh Kills, by the way, took New York's garbage from 1948 to 2001, becoming not only the world's largest landfill but also, according to some, the largest pile of anything ever made by humans.)

Georgetown, in the District of Columbia, passed one of the nation's first laws regulating trash in 1795: You couldn't dump it in the street, and you couldn't just leave it cluttering up your yard. Since there was no municipal service, residents had to haul their trash away, usually to vacant lots or open dumps outside of town. But in general, 19th-century America remained a trash-in-the-street world. And "trash" included horses and their by-products; one Chicago engineer estimated that during an 8-hour day 1,000 horses left behind 500 gallons of urine and 20,000 pounds of manure. In 1880, in Boston, the ratio of people to horses was about 25 to 1, and if we take that as an average nationwide ratio then Raleigh, with about 10,000 people, would have had some 400 horses leaving 200 gallons of urine and 4 tons of manure in the streets every single day. This happened in every city: In 1900, there were 3.5 million horses pulling streetcars, carts, and wagons in American cities. The horses that dropped dead at work were commonly left where they lay or hauled off by scavengers for rendering. Some cities passed laws protecting carrion animals like vultures.

It sounds disgusting—and by all accounts it was—but at least most of the refuse cluttering up the streets was biodegradable. Anything useful was reused, and the food, manure, and dead animals rotted into the ground or were washed away by rain. As cities started devoting more resources to providing clean water and sewers, public health boards got more power and turned their attention to solid waste. George Waring, the man who had designed the Memphis sewer system that channeled sewage separately from stormwater and led the way toward separate systems throughout the country, moved to New York and became the commissioner of street cleaning. He urged the city to take over the management of solid waste, which it did, even instituting early waste stream management. New Yorkers were expected to use three containers: one for garbage (including food waste), one for rubbish, and one for ashes from coal or wood fires. Other cities followed suit, mostly dumping the rubbish and ashes and feeding the food waste to hogs. Just the same, solid waste remained what the *American Journal of Public Health* in 1925 called the "orphan child of sanitary engineering." But continued interest in city planning and beautification, along with better understanding of health and sanitation issues, led to improvements in municipal trash collection and to sanitary landfilling, the compacting truck, and the automatic lifter, and now it seems as though we've known what we were doing forever.

WHEN I MOVED TO RALEIGH in 1992, one of the celebrated elements of its high "quality of life" was twice-weekly backyard-trash pickup, plus a third pickup for yard waste; when I bought my house, the previous owner showed me which part of the front garden the trash workers would expect me to keep clear for their path, and I always did. In 2004, when Raleigh changed to once-weekly fully automated pickup using 95-gallon wheeled bins at the curb, some of my neighbors were furious. But the Raleigh Solid Waste Services director told me it was the best decision he'd ever made: He saves $3 million per year in calls for missed collections by three-man crews and another $2.6 million in workers' compensation claims; he can't wait to make the same change in recycling.

The Raleigh fleet of garbage trucks includes several kinds of trucks—standard rear loaders, used mostly downtown, where there's no room for the sci-fi arms of the automatic trucks; the side-loading recycling trucks; and a couple of different kinds of special pickup trucks, for everything from appliances to sofa beds: The small ones are called pup trucks and the larger ones are called knucklebone trucks, or knucklebooms, for the articulated pickup booms they use to drop even the heaviest refuse into the hopper.

But the main truck Raleigh uses is the fully automated kind that workers call a one-armed bandit, in which a lone driver goes from house to house deploying a skeletal mechanical arm to pick up the big trash bins and upend them in the hopper. When the truck came to collect my garbage one day, I introduced myself to driver Michael Walden and told him I planned to follow him for a while.

By my watch, the truck emptied a bin about every 18 seconds, which made perfect sense: Walden said he would hit about 850 houses in less than 5 hours. Add in lunch and a trip to the transfer station to drop a load, and that's a day's work. Walden would drive up one side of a street and down the other, signaling to me when he was pulling into an inter-section just to turn around, and occasionally backing up a street to avoid such a turn. Both maneuvers are dangerous, and the department plans to install route-design software that will enable the office to plan routes so that, like delivery truck drivers, garbage truck drivers might make only right turns, avoiding busy roads when possible.

The truck bumped cheerily along, the automatic arm's three hinges enabling it to stretch farther for a bin depending on where the customer had left it and whether parked cars impeded access; the fingers—two on one side, one on the other—closed gently around a bin, just tight enough to cause a little bend in the bin wall. If you think of the bottom of the truck as the arm's shoulder, the arm folds closed with its elbow at the top; by flexing only the elbow and the wrist, the arm not only can grasp almost any bin, but also can dump it without worrying about entangle-ment in overhead electrical or telephone wires. At each stop, as the arm plucked the bin up and dumped it into the hole at the top of the hopper, the truck rocked agreeably from side to side, like a happy 1-year-old.

When the arm put down a bin, the fingers would gently stabilize it. Now and then Walden would get out of the truck to pick up a piece dropped from an overfull bin or to right a toppled bin, but otherwise he just kept moving. I watched for about half an hour before he signaled to me that he was heading for the transfer station.

The transfer station is just what it sounds like: not the landfill, but the spot where garbage trucks drop their loads. The city dumps its waste in landfills owned by the county and run by private services. When the North Wake Landfill closed in 2008, after about 25 years in use, the location of the new South Wake Landfill would have vastly increased the driving time for trucks to dump, so the city built the transfer station, basically a long, low shed with a hole in the floor. Walden pulled onto the scale at the entrance and I quickly parked my car and jumped into the cab with him. While we drove the semicircle around the transfer building, he told me it took about 2 weeks to learn to use the arm and that the truck holds several tons of compacted garbage. Then we backed onto a concrete tipping floor and hydraulic pistons slowly tipped the hopper while Walden crawled the truck forward, watching through the mirror as he deposited his load. Once it was done, he leaped out and took a quick peek to make sure the hopper was empty, then headed back to finish his route. At the transfer station, backhoes pushed the trash into an open spot on the floor, beneath which sat the bin of a semitrailer. When the trailer gets packed good and full, it is driven to the landfill.

ATOP THE MOUNTAIN OF MULTICOLORED TRASH at the active cell of the South Wake Landfill in Apex, just southwest of Raleigh, I watched semitrailers wriggle out from around enormous 20-ton rectangles of garbage from the Raleigh transfer station, like skins shedding snakes instead of the other way around. The carcasses of trash were immediately set upon by heavy-duty machines, the coolest of which, hands down, was the Caterpillar 836H Landfill Compactor, a 60-ton, 33-foot-long bright yellow object of desire with 55-inch-wide drum wheels 67 inches in diameter. And that drum wheel diameter doesn't include the 13-inch-long cruciform steel cleats, 35 of which stick out of each wheel. If the 836H wore black lipstick, you would call it a Goth steamroller. "The cleat tears the stuff up smaller, and the drum does the compacting," said Troy Mitchell, the landfill manager for Waste Industries, the private company that manages the landfill for Wake County. The 836H was slightly bigger than the 826H, which trundled around next to it on the heap; the 826H weighs a mere 40 tons. "The 836 is better because of the tons per hour it can handle," Mitchell continued. The South Wake Landfill gets about 1,500 tons of trash per day, but it doesn't come in at 187.5 tons an hour—there are rushes during the day, and the 836H helps keep up during rushes.

Unless there's a serious problem, the 836H never sets down its U-blade to push trash—a bulldozer takes care of that. ("See?" said Chrissie Koroivui, who led our tour, explaining the difference between the 836H and the bulldozer. "That one is a smusher, and that one is more of a pusher.") Said Mitchell, "If he's not smashing he's doing something else, and we want him smashing." Air space is everything for a landfill owner: It's a landfill's only resource, and every cubic foot of trash compacted is another cubic foot of space the landfill operator can sell, which is how the landfill makes its living. So someone has the job of driving that magnificent beast with those 13-inch cruciform steel cleats over and over load after load of trash.

THE TOUR OF THE LANDFILL started in a trailerlike building at the entrance, where Koroivui showed me and two bloggers in sundresses a scale model of the base of the landfill. The site is first prepared with bulldozers so that it tilts downward toward a sump, where the water that trickles through the garbage collects and can be pumped into a receiving sewage system. An enormous percentage of the effort involved in making a sanitary landfill goes toward collecting and managing this water, known as leachate ("garbage coffee," Koroivui called it). In the early days of landfills, water trickled through the bottom of the landfill into the ground below, eventually finding its way into the groundwater system. This is not a bad thing when the trash doesn't contain much that is noxious. But when trash includes plastics, diapers, pharmaceuticals, and other household nasties, the leachate becomes dangerous, and landfills must not only capture and manage it but also monitor the surrounding earth for evidence of its escape.

Waste Industries estimates that it costs $250,000 to $350,000 per acre to prepare a landfill site to receive its first garbage. In the first step, the South Wake model showed, a bottom layer of compacted earth is laid to form a solid base. Atop this is a layer of 2 feet of compacted clay, which must demonstrate a permeability rate of less than 1 by 10^{-7} centimeters per second, and according to North Carolina law, the clay has to be at least 10 feet above the nearest aquifer. But leachate isn't supposed to even reach the clay, much less soak into it, because above the compacted clay is a 60-millimeter-thick liner of high-density plastic. Koroivui showed us a piece; it feels like about five Pringles cans' lids fused together. Engineers lay the plastic liner in strips about 15 feet wide, welding the strips together with heat fusion machines and sealing each seam twice an inch or two apart. On top of the liner is a layer of what is called geocomposite: a kind of plastic latticework with woven fabric something like springy, resilient dryer lint. On top of all of those liners lie 2 feet of protective dirt, which keeps sharp pieces of trash (or the 836H) from poking through the liner. In the dirt layer lies a system of 6- and 8-inch perforated pipes surrounded by gravel, like French drains.

The leachate travels downhill through these pipes to the sump, from which a pump sends it to the sewage treatment plant. The decomposing garbage in the smushed, anaerobic environment of the landfill generates landfill gas, which is about 60 percent methane and 40 percent carbon dioxide. The landfill manager places wells to collect that gas, which can be either burned in flares to keep the methane (a powerful greenhouse gas) from polluting or, ideally, captured, cleaned, and sold as energy to some nearby customer.

The South Wake Landfill covers 180 acres, of which 26 acres constitute the current Phase I. An acre or so is used for dumping on any given day. A couple of decades from now, when the 1,500 tons per day the landfill collects has added up to a 15-million-ton mountain of trash, they'll "entomb" it by welding 40-millimeter-thick plastic liner to the bottom liner, creating a single giant ravioli of trash completely sealed from the environment. Then a couple more feet of earth go on top of the pile, which by that point looks something like a Mesoamerican pyramid. Grasses are planted to keep the soil in place, and then everybody looks at it, hikes to the top, and enjoys the view. No trees are planted, because roots are dangerous to the liner. Nothing is built, since the mountain, several hundred feet high, will settle by some 30 or 40 feet as time goes by. The gas wells continue to operate, and wells surrounding the landfill are monitored for both migrating leachate and creeping methane—this monitoring continues for 30 years after the landfill is closed.

LANDFILL ENTOMBMENT RAISES THE PROSPECT of perplexed future archaeologists, who will wonder why we took such enormous care to make sure our trash lasted for, basically, geologic time. Of course, maybe they'll love us for it. Modern archaeologists, after all, find the trash pits of ancient societies and try to extrapolate history from crockery shards and fragments of discarded buildings, clothing, and tools. Future archaeologists will have not just the remainders but, likely, the trash itself. Research like William Rathje's famous Garbage Project, in which he and his University of Arizona students treated landfills like archaeological digs, has uncovered decades-old newspapers still readable and hot dogs and banana peels undegraded after many years. A banana peel exposed to sun, water, and air will compost in a few days; even a plastic bag will photodegrade given enough time and exposure to the elements. A modern landfill, however, spares garbage from the elements.

In a laudable effort to protect people from the poisonous chemicals and metals that can leach from landfills, government "overreacted to the problem," says Mitchell, the landfill manager, by introducing environmental regulations that "slowed the degeneration process down so much that we'll have to deal with a little bit of gas and a little bit of leachate forever. So now we're rethinking that." Bioreactor landfills recycle leachate back through the landfill, keeping garbage wet and bacteria active, which both speeds degradation and encourages settling. Adding air to the mountain of trash further encourages degradation; adding water alone—keeping the environment anaerobic—also encourages the production of landfill gas, which not only increases landfill air space but creates more usable energy. The closed North Wake Landfill near Raleigh sells its landfill gas to a neighboring plant; the South Wake Landfill already has a nearby factory interested in purchasing the gas once it's available in great enough volume. Landfills in Florida, California, and North Carolina are already experimenting with different types of bioreactors, and reuse of landfill gas appears to be here for the long term.

Landfills, of course, aren't the only destinations for solid waste. In 1940, St. Louis was described as treating *negative* 20 percent of its sewage, because in addition to dumping all of its raw sewage into the Mississippi it also ground up and dumped its food waste. Dumping solid waste into waterways has virtually stopped since the 1972 Ocean Dumping Act (the source of the famous Syringe Tides in New Jersey in 1987 and 1988 ended up being not ocean dumping but the Fresh Kills landfill), but of the American municipal solid waste that isn't recycled or composted, some 18 percent is incinerated. Incineration is expensive. While Raleigh pays $33 per ton to dispose of its waste in the landfill, cities in the Northeast commonly pay two or three times that if they wish to incinerate theirs, which is why northeastern states ship their garbage to the South and the West. Incineration reduces the weight of garbage by 70 to 85 percent, but leaves behind toxic ash that still must be landfilled. And waste-to-energy plants, expensive to build and run, generate controversy not only regarding pollutants but also because the higher tipping fees they charge to offset their costs can send haulers scurrying for other options, creating political battles over whether trash may cross county or state boundaries. Which is why about 82 percent of Americans' garbage that doesn't get composted or recycled goes to landfills.

Many cities built incinerators at about the turn of the 20th century: When people didn't think much about air pollution, incinerators looked like a great solution. Those became less popular in the 1930s and beyond, as did plants that practiced what was called "reduction" of waste, which used chemicals to turn organic waste into grease. The expense of running those plants—and the unspeakable odors they emitted—limited them to large cities and eventually doomed them. The last competitor to landfills went by the wayside in the 1950s, when rampant hog diseases caused states to pass laws requiring people to cook any garbage they planned to feed to hogs. Compared to a stinking reduction plant, an expensive incinerator, or a swine cafeteria, a landfill starts to look like the answer to a prayer.

MY WIFE AND I GOT MANY WONDERFUL GIFTS when a second baby came our way, but none meant as much as *The Consumer's Guide to Effective Environmental Choices,* produced by the Union of Concerned Scientists. The organization pulls no punches: If your region is cramped for landfill space and has plenty of water, use cloth diapers; if it's pinched for water, use disposables. The EPA says disposable diapers, including those for adults, constitute about 2 percent of landfill volume. The Environment Agency, the United Kingdom's equivalent of the EPA, in 2008 estimated that over the 2½ years of an average baby's diaper use, cloth diapers actually have a larger carbon footprint than disposables, given the resources consumed by washing cloth diapers in hot water. So, in my drought-susceptible town that just opened up a brand-new 25-year land-fill, I'm not just getting away with using disposables. *I'm actually help-ing the planet by doing so.*

Disposable diapers represent only the highest-profile representative of the unsettled nature of trash disposal. Since the voyages of the *Mobro* and the *Khian Sea,* Americans have worked hard to solve a garbage crisis that may or may not exist. Environmentalists point out that modern landfills concentrate lead, mercury, and countless other poisons in leach-ate; landfill managers note that the leachate is not just contained and managed—and monitored for decades after the landfill is closed—but that new developments like bioreactors will recycle leachate, create energy, and help compact trash. Others note that sooner or later those landfill liners will leak, and that sooner or later—maybe much, much later—the leachate will find its way through the plastic, through the clay, through the ground, into the groundwater.

It's hard not to have conflicting thoughts about waste disposal. It's good that the United States recycles a third of its garbage—but to a recycler stuck with raw materials he can't sell, it's bad. The average American generated 2.68 pounds of solid waste per day in 1960; by 2007, that had increased to 4.62 pounds per day, which is bad. But factor in recycling, and over the same time period the amount the average person puts in a landfill per day has decreased slightly, from 2.51 pounds per day to 2.5 pounds per day, so that's good. The number of active landfills has dropped from 7,924 to 1,754, indicating that space for our trash is shrinking, which is bad. But the remaining landfills are much larger, and they are all lined and monitored in accordance with state guidelines based on EPA regulations, so that's good. Unless you're thinking about when they eventually leak.

At the Wake County landfill sites, Raleigh residents can recycle all electronic equipment, tires, appliances, and lead-acid batteries. According to Wake County managers, none of that stuff is shipped to Third World countries where unprotected workers wade into toxic piles of smashed computers to recover metals and other reusable ingredients, so that's probably still good. Unless it's not—after all, it was good when cities recovered land by filling swamps with garbage, until that turned out to be bad. The Fresh Kills landfill in New York closed in 2001, so that was good, at least if you lived in Staten Island; now New York pays $124 per ton to put trash on the train to Virginia and South Carolina, which is either good or bad, depending on how you feel about the price and whether you live in New York, Virginia, or South Carolina. After 9/11, Fresh Kills came out of its brief retirement to receive the remains of the World Trade Center. That's too awful to think about.

But think about it all we must, and people will think about it plenty as we continue to generate trash and need to find places to put it. I learned a lot about trash the summer I spent in college working for my local sanitation department, and I learned a lot more going to Wake County's open and closed landfills and watching my trash and recycling make its way from my house. But I learned the most about trash in 1986, when the municipal garbage collectors in Philadelphia, where I lived at the time, went on strike. For nearly 3 weeks the trash piled up, and the flies and rats and stench quickly multiplied until the city resembled a Hieronymus Bosch painting. People in vans and pickups sold their services as carters, hauling trash to places nobody cared to ask about, often just throwing it on piles of trash in other neighborhoods. People smuggled trash in car trunks to New Jersey or snuck it into commercial Dumpsters. Things never quite got medieval—the strike was settled after 20 days—but merchants started guarding their Dumpsters, temperaments went from anxious to toxic, and the smell went off whatever charts they use to measure smell.

Trash pickup, called the "orphan child of sanitary engineering" as long ago as 1925, seems like a small, mechanical matter—collection, transport, burial. And truly, had Philadelphians tried to tough it out for 3 weeks without sewer service or freshwater, things would have gone much, much worse; trash service isn't sewer or water.

But that's all it's not. Nobody knows exactly what we'll be doing with our trash 100 years from now, but it's a cinch that we'll be collecting it and getting it out of town. If nothing else, think of the service we're providing for future archaeologists.

CHAPTER 8

EVERYTHING, EVERYWHERE, ALL AT ONCE, ALL THE TIME

By the Time You Read It, Unless You Already Have a Wireless Chip Implanted in Your Head, This Chapter Will Be Laughably Out of Date

AFTER MONTHS OF AVOIDING THE CONSTANT SCARY WARNINGS that on June 12, 2009, our television would no longer be able to receive broadcast signals, my wife and I finally gave in, used our government-issued $40 coupon, and bought a digital converter for our big old analog television. We paid a few extra dollars for a special digital antenna. Then we hooked everything up, and for about 5 minutes we were highly impressed by the newfound clarity of our television shows.

But the reception immediately went downhill. Some stations used to occasionally fuzz in and out, becoming briefly blurry or staticky. Now they froze, broke into freaky patterns of shifting colored squares, or jerked along in an unwatchable stop-and-go like *Max Headroom,* the hiccupy mid-1980s sci-fi show. Fortunately, before we blew any more money on pre-digital upgrades, one evening our old television emitted a little snap and went silent, offering for video only a bright dot at the center of the screen. We took it to the recycling dropoff, bought a digital-ready flat-screen, and found no improvement in our reception. For the briefest moment we considered what the government

Web site suggested—mounting a rooftop antenna and turning it to maximize reception for each channel—but since that never worked even in the 1970s, we joined the modern age. We gave the converter box and the rabbit ears away and called the cable company.

Which meant we got a visit from a nice young man in a white van, its back filled with rolls of cable and boxes of tags and tools. He climbed up a ladder to the utility pole across the street, put in a simple filter to block the programming we weren't paying for, and hooked us up with the most basic package, including little more than local channels. The company called this bare-bones package "Broadcast Cable," which I laughed about, being old enough to remember the time when that would have been like saying "chocolate vanilla," or "positive negative"—cable and broadcast were the two opposite ways you could receive television. Of course then came satellite television, and the Internet, and by the time my wife and I hooked into cable television it was only the third service the cable company was providing to our house: We already got broadband Internet service and VOIP (Voice Over Internet Protocol) telephone from them. The guy showed me the little plastic tags he put on different taps from the cable, identifying which services a customer received: a blue one marked "HSD" for high-speed data, for the Internet; white, marked "VOIP," for telephone; and, for television, plain black, with the last two numbers of my street address as identifier. Our cable, up on that wallet-size tap hanging from the wire, looked like a little charm bracelet.

The smart grid press materials said that Alexander Graham Bell would not recognize today's phone system. Neither do I: When I was born in 1959, we had a big, black metal telephone, which you rented from the phone company. Now there are landlines and cable companies, wireless telephones and the Internet, and each one of those industries is turning into all the others at light speed while renting one another's time and wires. Mr. Bell would not be the only one having a hard time keeping everything straight. I'm connected to everything in this world by a constant torrent reaching me through wires and fibers and radio waves, and I despaired of ever being able to tease the different elements apart.

BUT TEASING APART THE DIFFERENT ELEMENTS turns out to be the exact wrong approach: a complex, changing admixture of content and communication coming to—and from—me by various means has been the norm, not the exception, since the dawn of long-distance communication. Alexander Bell's early telephone systems promised not just the capability to talk to people at a distance, but a delivery method for news and entertainment. In an 1876 piece entitled "The Telephone," the *New York Times,* thinking far ahead of its time regarding infrastructure, suggested the following: "Before many years we shall probably . . . read advertisements . . . of houses to let in which hot and cold water and Baptist preachers are laid on in every room; of others fitted throughout with gas and congressional orators; and still others in which the front parlor is telephonically connected with the Academy of Music, and the back parlor contains a series of instruments by means of which fifty eminent preachers, of different denominations, can be kept constantly on draught," about as uncanny a prediction of 500 channels of cable as you'll find. The *Electrical Review and Western Electrician* in 1909 suggested "pretty soon we'll be able to flop over in bed mornings, turn on a telephone-like arrangement and listen to a summary of news from all over the world without getting up out of bed." It didn't predict theme music by B. J. Leiderman, but it didn't miss much else. In 1911 the New Jersey Telephone Herald opened shop as, according to the *Times,* "an institution which calls itself a newspaper and yet has no printer's ink and no print paper." Yeah, like that could ever happen.

File that all under "nothing new under the sun." Although the Roman army was known to pass simple messages via smoke signals from tower to tower, until the late 1700s communication generally traveled no faster than a horse could run. That was the speed record until 1794, when Frenchman Claude Chappe figured out a method by which people standing on a series of towers about 10 miles apart, over the course of the 143 miles between Paris and Lille, could view through a telescope the positions of a pair of rods atop a neighboring tower, then copy the positions to relay them to the next tower, thus sending coded messages. The system, originally called a semaphore but changed to telegraph, soon went nationwide. Similar systems sprang up, and by 1796 the British could pass a message from London to Portsmouth and back in 15 minutes. Americans followed suit, of course—Telegraph Hill in San Francisco gets its name from a semaphore tower that signaled information about ships entering the Golden Gate.

The technology for communication at a distance took its next step forward with the invention of our more common conception of a telegraph. Samuel Morse made the first electromagnetic telegraph in 1838, and the first long-distance message was sent in 1844. Morse's invention used a simple direct-current circuit: The sender closed a circuit that sent power to an electromagnet miles away, which made at first a mark on paper but eventually just a loud beep. The telegraph was an instant hit. Long-distance lines soon linked eastern North America from New Orleans to Halifax. Telegraph companies strung more than 12,000 miles of line within a decade. In 1861 the telegraph reached the West Coast, following the Central Pacific Railroad line. The Central Pacific line itself followed the North Fork of the Platte River, in an example of infrastructure following geology; next along the Platte came US 30, then Interstate 80, all following the same natural route. The American Society of Civil Engineers, in the book *Me, Myself, and Infrastructure*, notes this common occurrence. "The physical and spatial pattern established by infrastructure is strengthened by vast economic, social, and emotional investments," the book notes. "This means that paths endure."

A scientist demonstrated telegraphy in Raleigh in 1844, even before Morse sent his first message, and the wire from New York to New Orleans reached Raleigh in 1848. Local newspapers immediately began printing occasional dispatches received by telegraph—and papers throughout the East doing likewise created, that same year, the Associated Press, the forerunner to every information network since then. Inventors soon created the duplex telegraph, which allowed a single line to manage two signals at the same time, one from each direction. Thomas Edison followed that in 1874 with the quadruplex telegraph, which handled four signals. This was the dawn of multiplexing—the practice of using one wire (or wave) to carry multiple messages, now fundamental to all telecommunication.

By 1857, Cyrus Field was working on laying a transatlantic cable, which took several tries—he had problems making the cable strong enough to support its own weight as it descended thousands of feet to the ocean floor. Field finally succeeded in 1866, and in that year Queen Victoria and President Andrew Johnson sent each other telegrams. Congress gave Field a gold medal, and the mural on the inside of the US Capitol rotunda shows Venus holding up the transatlantic cable (the Nautilus even encounters it in *Twenty Thousand Leagues Under the Sea*). Soon it was only *a*, rather than *the*, transatlantic telegraph cable; by the 1940s there were 20.

IN 1876 ALEXANDER GRAHAM BELL hooked up a diaphragm to an electromagnet. The movements of the diaphragm caused changes in the electromagnetic field, and thus changes in current that would move along a wire. When the signal got to a listener on the other end of the wire, the changing current would move the diaphragm on the receiving end and recreate the sound. Instead of transmitting only electrical pulses, wires could now communicate actual sound, earning that prescient hyperventilation from the *Times*. Telephone companies, franchising Bell's patents, sprang up everywhere: Raleigh's first telephone conversation took place in 1878. Barely 2 years after Bell told Watson, "Come here, I want to see you," word had spread sufficiently for Western Union managers in Raleigh and Wilmington to agree to hook telephones to their telegraph cables. During church one April Sunday, a congregation in each city sang hymns to the one in the other; after lunch the managers set up four telephones and allowed people to chat as they wished. That fall, telephones were the hit of the North Carolina State Fair.

In 1879 the same Raleigh Western Union manager set up a local phone exchange, connecting some 50 subscribers who learned to "tap the button firmly several times" to get the attention of the "switchman," then wait for a bell to ring indicating the switchman was on the line. He'd then ring the bell of the subscriber you wished to reach and patch you through, and you'd tap the button again to let him know you were done. Maybe Raleighans didn't have much to say—anyhow, the town scarcely covered a square mile, so there wasn't much distance to cover if you didn't have a phone. The business failed within a year, and Raleigh went quiet until 1882, when Southern Bell showed up in town. By 1887 Raleigh still had only 111 telephones.

The early Bell loops were simple: You picked up the handset and talked to the operator, and the operator patched you through to whomever you wanted to talk to. Lines ran to Durham in 1899 and to Fayetteville in 1901; by 1900, with Bell's patents having expired, Raleigh had three different phone networks—thus the image from old movies of a harried businessman picking up and slamming down several phones on his desk. By 1913, though, AT&T had established itself as fundamentally a monopoly—it was obligated to connect with competing local systems, but the growing backbone connecting cities belonged to it alone. Adding amplifiers to lines enabled signals to travel long distances, and the first cross-country telephone call took place in 1915; the first radio "networks" sent their programs to member stations over the AT&T lines.

In 1922 the final Raleigh competitor sold out to Southern Bell, and Raleigh, like everywhere else, became a one-phone-company town. In the 1920s the rotary dial telephone allowed electromechanical switches to begin replacing operators in central offices: Each click along the dial was like a tap on a telegraph. I remember when I was a kid being able to dial a 3 by pressing the cradle button three times quickly instead of rotating the dial. If I called my mom on Mother's Day in 1979, there was still a good chance that at the central office, rows of clacking switches would sort the call: If you dialed 9-3-2, the machine would recognize the 9, then direct the call along to the next level of switches, which would recognize the 3, and so forth. Dial 0 and the machine sent you directly to the operator. Dial a 1 and you went to the special long-distance switches, which immediately set about decoding a three-digit area code to figure out which far-off central office to point the call to, where the whole process started again. At the end of all that, the bell on my mom's phone would ring and I'd be off the hook for another year. That system was in play by the early 1920s. By 1927 telephone calls crossed the

Atlantic, between New York and London, via radio waves (a transatlantic telephone cable wasn't laid until 1956).

SMOKE SIGNALS ARE WIRELESS, but electronic wireless transmission got its start in 1888, when Heinrich Hertz of Germany proved the existence of radio waves. By 1894 Guglielmo Marconi was sending Morse code signals on those airwaves; he was sending signals across the ocean by 1901. The wired progression from the telegraph to the telephone took almost 40 years, but over the airwaves we moved from sending beeps to sending the human voice in only 6: The first vocal radio transmission was sent in 1900, when, from an experimental station in Maryland, Reginald Aubrey Fessenden asked an associate a mile or so away whether it was snowing. (The associate telegraphed back that it was.) Fessenden is also credited with the first-ever radio program broadcast, when on Christmas Eve 1906 he played the violin and read from the Bible; the broadcast reached ships hundreds of miles out to sea. Weekly radio broadcasts reached the very few listeners able to pick them up in San Jose as early as 1909.

What was happening was simple. The AC electrical grid at 60 Hz (oscillations per second) creates a magnetic field and pulses out waves of energy (that's part of what causes energy loss along electrical lines), and a radio tower does the same thing. An AC generator electrifies the antenna and alternates the current, and the antenna emits a wave at a desired frequency. The 60 Hz of the electric grid lies in the very-low-frequency range. Initial radio broadcast stations worked in the medium range, which we now call AM radio—from 500 to about 1700 kilohertz, or about a million oscillations per second. Just as Bell's microphone modified the signal on the telegraph wire, the input of the radio studio modifies the wave radiated by the antenna—"AM" stands for amplitude (height) modulation, so the signal from the studio causes the carrier wave to grow higher when the sound is loud, and lower when it's soft: It modifies the amplitude. The radio receiver detects the signal and plays the content.

During World War I the US government shut down all nonmilitary radio transmitters, but after the war radio grew rapidly, with the first recognizable commercial radio stations appearing in 1920. Radio broadcasting in Raleigh began in earnest in 1924, and the station that began broadcasting then still broadcasts today—it's a 50,000-watt talk-radio giant called WPTF, with three enormous red-and-white antennas just west of town: One, a beefy 600 feet tall, broadcasts during the day; the other two, smaller and spindly, broadcast at night, when, to forestall interference with radio stations in Boston and San Francisco, the station manipulates the phase and power of the two transmitters to directionalize its broadcast. AM radio waves bounce off the ionosphere at night, which is why you can hear stations from so far away (and why a station in Raleigh needs to worry about interfering with broadcasts from Boston and San Francisco). The directionalizing works, sending the signal only south: "We've been told people can hear us in South America at night," the WPTF director of group operations told me, "but they can't hear us in Wake Forest," 30 miles north. FM radio got its start after World War II, when technology had improved and could manage higher-frequency waves, which could carry more information with greater fidelity. Those higher frequencies, however, create smaller wavelengths that do not bounce off the ionosphere—to generate its long waves, an AM radio antenna tends to be a huge, self-supporting tower, insulated from the ground, but an FM antenna is usually a much smaller animal: a rod a few feet long, mounted way up on a tall tower, usually supported by guy wires.

Lower-frequency, longer AM waves can travel along the ground and bend around the curvature of the earth, but a higher-frequency FM signal, with its shorter waves, needs to reach you directly—FM is what engineers call "line of sight" technology. A large building or the curvature of the earth can prevent you from receiving the signal, so FM can reach only what the transmitter can "see." In Raleigh, that often means putting antennas up on hills southeast of town, where three fierce, battleship-gray "big sticks," as they are known in the lingo, stand as high as 2,000 feet, their metal structures and dozens of guy wires making them look more like missile gantries than broadcasting equipment. Transmitters for different radio stations share these antennas. Patrolling police officers sometimes gauge the strength of storms by riding by to hear the sound the wind makes in the antenna guy wires.

Television and radio broadcast at very similar frequencies—they're in the very high frequency, or VHF, range of the electromagnetic spectrum, which is why if you're poking around at the bottom of your FM dial you can often find the audio of a television station. The spectrum describes all the electromagnetic radiation we experience, from the highest-frequency (10^{20} hertz), inconceivably tiny gamma rays about the size of an atomic nucleus, on one end, to the very-low-frequency (10,000 hertz or so), very long (a kilometer or more) waves of AM radio, to even larger, lower-frequency waves emitted by maritime navigational signals on the bottom end. Visible light is right in the middle of the spectrum; radio waves, television waves, and microwaves are lower-frequency, longer-wavelength radiation than light; x-rays are higher-frequency, shorter wavelengths.

By the mid-1950s people had figured out how to piggyback not just sound but visual information on emitted waves, so Raleigh had a couple of television stations, and eventually those signals were beamed from the tall towers southeast of town; people either had an antenna on the roof or rabbit ears on top of the set, pulling the signal out of the air and turning it into programs. That's the exact level of technology I had when I bought my house, and it worked just fine until June 2009, when the world went digital. The electromagnetic spectrum has only so much space—each television channel takes up a 6 megahertz block of the spectrum, and the federal government has managed the spectrum, which is a public resource, since it began issuing commercial radio licenses in 1912. The 1996 Telecommunications Act addressed the need for higher quality and more spectrum for burgeoning wireless communications by planning to change television broadcasts from analog to digital. A digital broadcast stream takes up much less space than an analog stream— that's why broadcast stations suddenly have three or four mini-channels now: The switch to digital gave them a lot more space to fill and still freed up spectrum space for other technologies. Further advances in digital technology will only increase what programmers can offer and continue to decrease the bandwidth they need to offer it.

Unlike analog broadcasts, which degrade as distance increases and reception diminishes, getting increasingly fuzzy and staticky, digital broadcasts get briefly hiccupy and jumpy and then simply vanish, as though the signal had disappeared. Broadcasters call this the cliff effect, since reception goes from fine to worthless as though falling off a cliff. And though I live close to downtown Raleigh, even the major stations had trouble, caused by what I have heard described as "packet sway": On windy days, trees between me and that 2,000-foot tower sway enough that packets sent by the digital transmitter reflect off the trees at different times, arriving at my house sufficiently off-kilter that the decoder in my television can't keep up and gives me its best guess in those big, jaggy squares called "macroblocking." All ancillary stations either macroblocked, froze, or vanished—classic cliff effect. And that cliff effect is why I needed to get my television signal on a cable. I signed up for cable television for exactly the same reason its very first customers did: Because the signal on the airwaves wasn't reaching my TV.

Telecommunications isn't water, sewage, or roads, but it's almost as essential. Take away phones, video, broadcast, and the Internet and our culture would cease functioning. Try to travel without making reservations on the Internet or by telephone. Try to do business by face-to-face conversation or postal mail for a month and see how well that works. Your bank won't even know how to reach you to tell you you're broke. Somewhere between "What hath God wrought" and online video chats with your grandkids, communications became utterly essential.

I GOT A TELECOMMUNICATIONS HISTORY LESSON from a yogi named Pat Hourigan, vice president of network operations for the Carolina region of Time Warner Cable. Hourigan is an immensely cheerful man with an Ernie Kovacs mustache who loves to describe his colleagues in the cable industry as a gang of cowboys who wouldn't take no for an answer and in 50 years have turned what was originally a giant version of the old rooftop TV antenna into the content-providing, service-intense, indispensable utility cable has become. In the late 1940s, when television first came out, he explained to me, furniture store owners wanted to sell televisions. But in places like the hills of Pennsylvania, the line-of-sight television signals weren't reaching homes.

"So they built what were then known as community antennas," he said. They put great big antennas on poles on hilltops and connected them to multiple houses using the kind of flat, two-conductor antenna wire that people 50 and over remember from their childhoods. "They had a greed motive," he laughed. "Why would you buy this whiz-bang TV if you could only watch one show?" Similar things happened in many hilly parts of the country; in Ithaca, New York, Hourigan told me, utility companies were so nonplussed by the wires an early cable supplier wanted to hang that they refused access to telephone or light poles: "So he literally went tree to tree." Of course, as broadcasting spread, even smaller towns began to have their own stations, so it might have seemed that the nascent industry was doomed: "Who would *pay* to get TV reception?" Hourigan laughed. But by the late 1950s the providers had learned that their hilltop antennas could pick up multiple signals even from far off—their customers received many more channels than their local-broadcast-only neighbors. Suddenly cable had something to sell, especially since it had switched from using that flat antenna wire to using actual cable.

Coaxial cable, perfected in the 1930s at Bell Labs, improves the transmission of radio frequency waves over wire by containing the wave within the cable. That is, just as the conductors carrying electrical power, alternating at 60 Hz, function to a degree as a broadcast antenna, so too do wires carrying the much much-higher-frequency waves (measured in the millions of hertz) of radio or television transmission, losing their signals rapidly. But coaxial cable runs two conductors down the cable, one surrounding the other, separated by an insulator making it almost impossible for the signal to escape. Not only can the cable carry many signals, but the signals last must longer.

In 1972 a Pennsylvania cable provider began broadcasting a new premium service called Home Box Office (HBO). Cable systems could now offer not just improved reception and extra broadcast stations, but, also unique programming—something broadcast viewers couldn't get. Cable became more than just community antennas. Most historians use HBO's first-ever satellite broadcast, the 1975 Muhammad Ali–Joe Frazier fight billed as The Thrilla in Manila, as the defining event showing that people would pay for content delivered instantaneously via satellite. The first satellite broadcasts had taken place in the 1960s, but only in the 1970s, when satellites with multiple transponders were launched, did they become cheap enough that almost all broadcasters could use them.

Nowadays, though cable companies pick up local broadcast signals from ordinary broadcast antennas, cable headends—that's what the industry calls the main source of signal in a region—get most of their signals from satellites. And communications satellites relate to broadcast transmitters just as GPS satellites relate to surveying monuments: They do the exact same job, just from way higher up. A satellite in geostationary orbit, moving in perfect harmony with the rotation of the earth, seemingly motionless 22,236 miles above the equator, basically sends a signal that everybody on a continent can pick up. It's like a 22,000-mile-high broadcast antenna. You point a satellite dish at it and never have to move it. My neighbor's dish system points at one geostationary satellite or another. So do the 11 huge white antennas at the Time Warner Cable headend in Durham, where Hourigan has his office. Each can look at up to six satellites, and each satellite has up to 24 channels—and further advances will only increase the number. "Could you even watch that much television?" Hourigan said.

HOURIGAN POINTED THOSE DISHES OUT from the back door as he showed me around his facility. Thumb-size coaxial cables ran from the various dishes into the building along a track that looked like a ladder full of garden hoses. Next to the field of white dishes was a tall silver tower, atop which hung a white microwave antenna. I had told Hourigan that from my bedroom window I can see an antenna tower—it blinks all night long, warning away airplanes, but it isn't a radio or television tower, and though it has mobile telephone antennas on it, that clearly was down not its original purpose. Hourigan explained: It was the old microwave relay receiver for the Raleigh-Durham Time Warner link. Microwave relay antennas are those scoop-shaped or round dishes you see atop AT&T buildings, television stations, and broadcast towers. Using extremely high frequencies and tiny wavelengths, microwave systems transmit enormous amounts of data in a straight line. Lines of microwave relay towers crossed the country in the 1950s in the first long-distance telephone alternative to wires, and many television and radio stations still use them to transmit their signals from studio to transmitter. But they're a line-of-sight technology, which means that pairs of antennas face each other across 20 miles or more and shoot signals back and forth—electronic versions of Claude Chappe's telegraph towers. Time Warner runs the signals over fiber-optic cable now, but it rents out tower space for cell phones and corporate communications—truck dispatch antennas and the like.

Hourigan was keen to point out the facility's support systems: the dual generators that fuel the headend in a power outage; 700 tons of air-conditioning to keep the racks of computers that run the network cool; the complex air management system that in the event of fire lowers the oxygen level—"so you can live but the fire cannot"—rather than sprinklers that would destroy computer equipment. The system also scrubs air of impurities. "I scrub the air, I scrub the power, I scrub everything," Hourigan said. "It's like veal or Kobe beef—this is our lifeblood: This is what we *do*."

By "this" Hourigan meant the rooms full of servers into which he finally led me, through a biometric security door that recognized his fingerprint. The television side had rows of metal shelves holding columns of computers that looked like old component stereo systems: machine after machine after machine, each about the size of an unabridged dictionary, popping with little red and green LEDs indicating various statuses, all connected by cables of yellow, blue, gray, green, on little aluminum tracks. One box bore a tiny white label that said ESPN, another DURHAM CITY SCHOOLS. These are called digital content managers, which take the signals from the dishes, separate the streams into particular channels, then route them to different packages and customers. Each machine in the rows of servers had a sticker with a bar code, and each wire did too—"so you can scan that with a handheld bar-code reader and understand what that wire's going to do," Hourigan said.

"And we do all sorts of downstream processing," Hourigan continued, sweeping his arm toward more machines. "Compression, commercial insertion, processing to clean up," he said. Descramblers of the satellite signal; scramblers to secure the outbound signal; routing switches and combiners that mix signals into the packages in which they're pumped to customers. "Rows and rows of all that crap." Fiber-optic line carries the compressed, cleaned-up, processed signal from the headend out through the system, hanging from poles or running through conduits reachable by manholes. On coaxial cable, Hourigan said, the signal can travel 10 or 15 miles before requiring amplification, and after a few amplifications the signal degrades sufficiently that it is unacceptable. "Our general solution was just to build another one of these headends 50 miles away." Which was expensive. "And all that equipment cost me the same whether I had a million subscribers or two people." What changed all that was fiber-optic cable.

A GENIAL ENGINEER NAMED MITCH COLTON takes over, at the Time Warner construction headquarters. He tells me that the cable from the headend emerges from underground in Raleigh less than a mile from my house. At this hub, the digital signal is amplified with virtually no loss of quality, enabling that single, expensive headend to serve an entire region. Signal travels on fiber-optic cable as light, not as electrical impulses. Each fiber in a cable is a tube of glass, through which light pulses bounce back and forth millions of times per second, carrying digital signals over tremendous distances with extremely low loss of signal strength. This technology actually predates the telephone: European physicists found that beams of light shining through a flow of water bounced back and forth within the flow, though they didn't know why—they used it to illuminate fountains. (Bell even invented a "photophone" in 1880, which used a diaphragm to modulate light shining on a photosensitive cell, which in response sent a signal to a speaker. This was actually the first wireless telephone call.) Not until the 1950s did scientists successfully clad the fiber with a surface that was perfectly reflective on the interior, which meant that the signal could travel almost indefinitely. The invention of the laser in 1960 gave the technology its perfect transmitter; by the mid-1970s fiber had begun appearing in telephone networks. When the AT&T telephone system monopoly was legally dismantled in 1982 and the new long-distance competitors—Sprint, MCI, and so forth—raced around the nation laying cable, the cable they laid (and strung) was fiber-optic. The lines were often laid along rights-of-way owned by railroads—both Sprint and Qwest, in fact, were originally subsidiaries, at different times, of the Southern Pacific Railroad. "If you want to see the basic routes of the trunk lines" for long-distance telecommunications, one source told me, "you just look at the original government land grants to the railroads." Natural gas supplier the Williams Companies, on the other hand, ran fiber-optic cable through decommissioned pipelines.

Having so many advantages over wire, fiber-optic cable has ever since been making its way from long-distance paths closer and closer to homes. Because it's made of glass, it emits—and experiences—no bleed signal, like electrical conductors or coaxial cable; in fact, on utility poles, the first safe zone beneath the electrical wires is reserved for cable (telephone wires, commonly of copper, go below that).

From the Time Warner headend, fiber-optic cable runs all the way to the hub nearest my house: Hub Q, it's called on Colton's map, and it's one of 45 hubs Time Warner manages from the central Carolina headend. At a hub, either in a building or a bedroom-size controlled-environment vault underground, the trunk splits into several smaller cables, each with its own laser and transmitter and other pieces of processing equipment, that snake along utility poles into different neighborhoods radiating away from the hub. Hubs mostly do the same things headends do: Sort signals, scramble them, clean them up, and send them along.

Hub Q is buried. Big boxes of climate-control equipment sit on a concrete pad on the lawn of a building, and a manhole leads beneath. Fiber-optic cables climb utility poles nearby, and one cable follows a collector street about a mile until, across another main street, it reaches a node. A node, Colton tells me, translates the optical signal into radio frequency signal using photoreactive sensors. Each node can serve several hundred customers. The node serving my neighborhood, about the size of a large dictionary, hangs from the cable about 18 inches from a utility pole, looking like a big version of the transformer on the power cord to my printer. I followed the coaxial cable to the tap near my house, and finally to that single line looping between my pine trees and down to a little box on the front of my house, where the guy who hooked it up also stuffed a few extra loops of cable, so that if a connection goes bad or more work needs to be done he doesn't need to string an entire new line.

YOU SEE SIMILAR LOOPS OF EXTRA LINE all along the cable system, at nodes, at amplifiers, at poles—anywhere a splice might be needed. You can tell the fiber-optic cable because the loops are wound around frames that look a bit like snowshoes (the cable guys call these extra loops "shoes"). The fiber can be gently looped without problem, but the frame prevents it from kinking, which would destroy the connection. Colton loves fiber, and he agrees that the day when it reaches our houses is inevitable. Just the same, it comes with problems of its own. "For long-haul stuff, it's fantastic," he says. "But if you need to break into it for a new node"—he shakes his head—"it's a *mess*."

In a trailer near his headquarters, he demonstrates a fiber splice for me. First he rips a tie-line that opens the protective jacket, or "pipe," of a 36-strand loose-tube cable, revealing five tubes, three of which are active: one blue, one orange, and one green. Fiber organization uses 12 colors in a specified order. Each tube contains 12 fibers, clad in those same 12 colors. Splicing a 36-strand cable, he says, takes a couple of hours. To demonstrate, he slices open the blue tube and spreads out the 12 fibers within. He holds the blue strand up to a lamp: It's about the width of a thick hair. He takes out a little wire stripper with the finest hole imaginable, closes it, and strips the fiber; the cladding comes off like dust. The fiber itself is about the thickness of the thinnest, fairest hair you've ever seen.

He spreads open a splice box, clamps it to the shelf, and cuts the end of the fiber with a little chopping machine called a cleaver, that gets the end perfectly straight. He then slides the fiber into one side of an FSM-40S Arc Fusion Splicer. Another fiber goes into the other side, and a tiny LCD screen shows the magnified image of the two pieces of wire as the machine slowly moves them together and then, with a bright burst of light, fuses them; the fusion takes about 11 seconds, though the preparation took about 5 minutes. That's one fiber, and the cables Colton works on get big enough to carry 288 total fibers. Ribbon fiber makes life a little easier—it carries 12 fibers in a tiny ribbon half the width of your pinky nail. "On ribbon, you splice 12 fibers at once," after a single preparation of the whole ribbon. The fiber itself, Colton says, is surprisingly durable—if you kink it you'll break the connection, but if you unkink it, because it's inside all those layers of cladding, it'll work again, though never as smoothly as unbroken cable; fiber guys commonly say that if you need to attenuate your signal, just wind the fiber around your finger and then unwind it. Colton says cable is very fragile if you bump it from the side, but if you tug on it it's stronger than you are: "If you took a piece of bare fiber, wrapped it around each finger, and pulled?" He smiles. "It would cut down to the bone."

THAT FIBER IS WHERE CURRENT TELECOMMUNICATIONS LIVES—in many ways it makes modern communications possible, and everyone involved agrees it's a miracle. "In terms of capacity," Hourigan told me at the headend, "we've given up trying to do the math. The first optical links for cable were 1 G [1 gigabyte per second] standards; it's 10 G now," which is about how much data the hard drive on an average personal computer held in 2000. "And people are shipping 40 G fiber before it's approved. One hundred G will be approved soon enough. Think about that—100 gigabytes per second. You didn't use a 100 gigabytes on your data connection *this year*—and that's happening each second?" To get a handle on that amount of information, consider this commonly cited metric: 1,000 gigabytes is 1 terabyte, and 10 terabytes will hold the Library of Congress. The complete contents of the Library of Congress would take just under 2 minutes to transmit on a 100 G fiber. "And that's on *one fiber*," says Hourigan. "And there are millions and millions of fibers." There were about 85 million miles of fiber cables, in 2000, and that number has certainly multiplied.

Of course use catches up to capacity, but the technology leaps forward so rapidly that at least in fiber, capacity seems prepared to keep up with demand for a while. Because of that, the last pieces of my cable service Hourigan treated almost as afterthoughts. Once the programming is digital and the cables can handle tens of gigabytes of information per second, moving digital bits of information around just doesn't seem that hard.

I ask about my Internet service and he shrugs: Among the machines in his vast, air-conditioned stacks of bar-coded servers are cable modem termination systems—machines that capture the signal from my computer, via the cable modem at my house, and connect it to the fiber network stretching worldwide. My computer breaks all information I send to the Internet, whether it's an e-mail or a photograph of my kid on the swings or a video chat, into tiny packets of bytes; each packet has a header, carrying information about where it's going, where it's from, and how to reassemble it upon delivery. His machines sort it and send it on its way.

A network engineer at my Internet service provider (ISP) pretty much agreed with Hourigan: "We got more bandwidth than we know what to do with," he told me. "Every year we see more and more bandwidth." ISPs and other companies treat the lines of the fiber-optic network like nice, wide, well-paved highways. Of course we pay for them, basically with connection fees, some of which the ISPs pay to the companies (Sprint, Qwest, MCI, and the rest) who lay and maintain all those wires and fibers.

The story of the Internet is familiar: In 1969, the Advanced Research Projects Agency (ARPA) at the Department of Defense worked out a system to link computers at the Universities of California at Los Angeles and Santa Barbara, Stanford, and the University of Utah in Salt Lake City. The computers used lines leased from AT&T to make the connections, and engineers developed a technology called packet switching—that is, they sliced communications up into tiny packets of information; routers at points of connection sorted them and moved them toward their destinations—all virtually instantaneously. That technology eventually got the name IP—Internet protocol—which we still use. The ARPAnet grew rapidly, and router technology along with it. By about 1993 the World Wide Web had turned the Internet from a computer nerd thing to an everybody thing, and ISPs started offering connection to that service. From the start, customers connected, as the original ARPAnet did, over existing telephone lines; what service providers offered was a way in: The first routers were actually called gateways.

Each tiny packet goes the way the routers determine will be the fastest at that microsecond—an e-mail I send to my wife from my home office to hers will at the very least go to Atlanta and back since Atlanta is where my ISP has its processing machines, but pieces of it will likely travel different routes, only to be reassembled on my wife's machine 30 feet of physical distance but uncounted thousands of packet-wire miles away. My connection reaches the Internet over cable, but ordinary twisted-pair wire works just as well, and the cable company or the telephone company shoots information to the ISP's home processors, wherever they are, and they fling bytes hither and yon without regard for boundaries. The Internet isn't really infrastructure—it *runs* on infrastructure, but if the routers that do the work are infrastructure then you might equally well say that your refrigerator is part of the electrical infrastructure. Just the same, to get a sense of how information gets around, I went to a Web site and performed a "traceroute," by which a distant Web site sends a signal to my computer—it "pings" me, in the patois—and then lists all the different computers the signal visited on its way to me and how many milliseconds it spent at each. From Tustin, California, my ping stopped at 16 computers and took 1.5 seconds.

As for my VOIP telephone calls, a special modem at my house slices my calls into standard IP fragments, then flings them at the address of the person I'm calling. Somewhere between here and there my VOIP provider has to have access to a gateway to what telecommunications people call the POTS—the plain old telephone system—but that's the only slight complexity. Anyhow, DSL—and digital subscriber line—service now has telephone companies supplying Internet service at speeds comparable to cable, and AT&T's U-verse pumps programming over its lines. You can now get broadcast, telephone, and Internet over cable, over fiber, and over plain old copper telephone wires. Before the end of my life—and probably within the next 10 years—both cable and telephone providers will run optical fiber directly to my house, at which point, given the rapidity with which new laser and computing advances come along, my access to content will be all but unlimited.

WHICH BRINGS UP ANOTHER THING I needed to understand about the tangle of communications systems bathing my house in radio frequencies and electric signals and bits of data: multiplexing. When inventors turned those very first telegraph wires into duplex wires so operators could send two signals at the same time, and then turned them into quadruplex wires, that was the dawn of electronic multiplexing: getting more than one signal on a single line. People tell you that the Internet is a packet-switched technology and the POTS is a circuit-switched technology, by which they mean: that the Internet sends around data in tiny little pieces, whereas the old phone system makes a circuit between me and my mom on Mother's Day and we control that circuit as long as we're on the phone, whether we're talking or not. That's true, but only to a point.

From my house, those unused telephone lines—dead since I switched to VOIP—actually do run up to the thick wire running from pole to pole along my street. There they join other wires from other houses on my street, running in a thicker bundle until they go underground at a pole at the corner and then emerge across the street and partway down the block at what's called a cross-box—one of those green metal cabinets filled with tiny copper wires that you sometimes see the phone company technicians sitting in front of with a diagram. That spot is actually the last point on this earth where electronic communications is simple. Each house in the neighborhood has a connection on that tall board in there, and when someone makes a call on a landline, the call goes over wires and through that board to join an even thicker cable of more of those tiny copper wires going downtown, to the central office. Downtown, the wire encounters, instead of the old switchboard with its rows and rows of clacking switches, rows and rows of humming computers, not at all unlike the rows of computers I saw at the cable headend. And the uncountable wires seem to carry a comforting message: One set of wires connects one person to one other person. Cables as thick as your thigh—sheaves of up to 7,200 pairs of copper wires—snake along the walls on the same kind of metal trackways that in the cable headend carried only finger-size Ethernet cables of different colors.

But the phone system isn't simple. For one thing, from the cross-box to the central office, the system doesn't run one connection per house: It runs many fewer, figuring that the odds against everyone in the neighborhood being on the phone at the same time are astronomical. If 9/11 or something like it comes and everybody picks up the phone, I might actually get that fast busy signal telling me there's no room for my call—the most recent time that happened here, I'm told, is when a thin sheet of ice covered Raleigh's roads at lunchtime, causing the schools to let out early and every single school bus and parent in the county to begin driving at the same time—and then slide into one another at the first intersection. Everybody used their cell phones to call home, and then every home phone called every school, and there weren't enough lines, so the road system and the telecommunications system both failed—a doubleheader.

Beyond the central office, multiplexing grows far more complex. The telephone company has traditionally used both frequency-division multiplexing—piling calls of different frequencies onto the same wire and separating them at the other end just the way your television plucks out of the cable only the signal you tell it to—and time-division multiplexing, which works with the signal much like IP data: breaking a voice signal into tiny fragments and sending the fragments of many conversations over the same wire, where they're decoded on the other end. And for fiber-optic cable, engineers have reached dense wave division multiplexing, whereby they send data streams on one fiber at different wavelengths of light, each wavelength carrying as much data as the entire fiber could have carried with unmultiplexed light. It all seems unspeakably 21st century until you remember that they were doing it in the 19th century—and that the first multiplexing occurred in ancient aqueducts in Libya built by the Romans. Producers of olive oil in the mountains who wanted their product shipped to Leptis Magna on the coast poured it into the aqueducts: Oil and water easily separated out at the other end.

THERE'S ONE MORE PIECE TO THE TELECOMMUNICATIONS PUZZLE: wireless communications. At the base of the bell tower of a church near my house, two thick plastic conduits snake out of the ground, climb up the inside of the brick tower, and disappear in the cross at the top. No special connection to God: They're the power and data cables leading to a mobile phone transceiver, and that's only 1 of probably 50 transceivers within a few miles of my house. Throughout telecommunications history, the pendulum has swung back and forth from cables to airwaves. From signal beacons and Chappe's telegraph to copper wires, then to broadcast antennas, then to coaxial cable, then to microwave relays, and now we have fiber optics on the ground and satellites in the air. The two push each other along; microwave towers replaced strung telephone cable, but then fiber optics pretty much replaced microwave towers. Now cell phone technology provides less an alternative to landlines than an adjunct to them. Not long ago my long-distance phone call on a landline would have spent most of its time in the air; today, my mobile phone call spends almost all of its time on a wire or fiber somewhere— telecommunications types give this the delightful name of "backhaul." So with fiber optics seeming to signal the final victory for wires, naturally the airwaves made another assault.

The first telephone calls across the Atlantic and Pacific oceans went over radio waves, and by World War II the Allied and Axis armies both used two-way radios—walkie-talkies, which required a backpackful of equipment to run. Each used a specific pair of frequencies—one each way—to communicate with a base station (radios that use the same frequency for talk in both directions enable only one person to talk at a time; think CB radio or the toy walkie-talkies your kids have). If you wanted to talk to someone on another walkie-talkie, the dispatcher at the base station had to "patch you through," much like the original operators on the telephone system. Got that? Mobile device, specific frequencies, base station, patching through. That's your mobile telephone network right there.

Fundamentally, my mobile telephone is nothing more than a tiny little radio transmitter and receiver in my hand, though it broadcasts and receives on areas of the spectrum that broadcast stations don't use. That spectrum is everything to cell phone providers: Where fiber purveyors treat bandwidth like drunken kings rolling around in treasure stores full of gold coins, "the precious resource in the wireless network is the spectrum," Jerry Jones, a network engineer for AT&T's wireless services, told me. "So much effort goes into management of the spectrum."

Here's how it works. If I'm in my office in the shed behind my house and I'm too lazy to walk 30 feet to talk to my wife, June, I pick up my mobile phone and call our landline—okay, our VOIP line—and June picks up and tells me I'm an idiot, and then we're done. I know that the call turned into bits on the Internet and traveled down fiber from the Time Warner headend, through our hub and then our node, where it turned into bits carried on radio frequency signals on the coaxial cable to our house, where the VOIP modem turned those into a signal that made the phone ring and June pick up. But how did it get to the POTS, from which it made its way to that Durham headend? How do mobile phones work?

Jones explained. My call from the cell phone gets picked up by a local antenna—atop a church, atop a water tower, inside a fake tree, on a purpose-built tower for cell phone transmitters, maybe even on that somnolent Time Warner tower I can see from my window. One of these transceivers, which are constantly on the lookout for signals from phones like mine, catches the call when my phone casts it. Processing equipment at the base of the tower forwards that call to its mobile telephone switching office (MTSO), the equivalent of the telephone company's central office or the cable headend. "It's right here in the same building," said Jones of the AT&T MTSO. The signals from the antenna base stations generally get to the MTSO on fiber lines, though they still sometimes come via microwave relay if that's cheaper and easier. But again, Jones stresses that the only piece of the wireless network that's wireless is between my telephone and the antenna. It's no more complicated than my cordless phone, or the Wi-Fi network I set up in my house—or that every coffee shop sets up to allow its users access to the Internet.

What complicates wireless communications is that we don't keep still. We move around, and increasingly, while we're moving we're talking on mobile telephones. And, though every single one of us wants to be on the phone at all times, the spectrum available for cellular calls is limited. The cellular system solves both problems—it's a kind of geographical multiplexing.

Each company serving a region has access to fewer than 1,000 frequencies for use in cellular calls, and to make a call a user has to be within a few miles of one of its antennas. The way the companies "multiplex" those few frequencies is by dividing frequencies among several geographical "cells," making the antennas directional so that different cells do not interfere with each other, and reusing frequencies as soon as they're not in danger of interference. That is, if AT&T has access to frequencies A, B, and C, it assigns frequency A to cell 1, which borders cell 2, which uses frequency B, and so on. By the time you get to cell 4, you're far enough away from cell 1 that AT&T can assign frequency A to your call without interfering with whoever's on frequency A back in cell 1. Each cell has hundreds of frequencies, and each cell borders six others—the optimal pattern looks like the hexagonal cells in a beehive, hence the nomenclature. Hence, too, those familiar triangular arrays of antennas: The most effective use of a tower is to place it not in the center of a cell but at a border point, and in a hexagonal grid every border point lies at the intersection of three cells.

Companies increase capacity by increasing the number of cells: Twice as many cells means half as much area for each cell to cover, and so on until the number of subscriber calls in the cell doesn't exceed the number of available channels. Engineers can shape the coverage area, too, by controlling direction and power to the antenna. "Think of a sprinkler,"

Jones said. You can set it to water a long, narrow path—as antenna engineers do along highways—or a circular area, as they do in cities. As cells multiply, antenna power must diminish, as must antenna height, to prevent interference: hence tall towers with high power out along the highways, and nice low antennas—say, in church steeples—in towns, where there are lots and lots of cells.

The equipment at the base stations constantly listens for pings from subscriber phones from their networks so they can forward incoming calls, and the base stations ping back and forth among themselves, letting one another know when, say, I'm on the phone and my car nears a boundary, so the new cell can be ready to assign me to a new frequency pair and the old one knows when it can reuse the frequency it drops me from. The first generation—1G—of cell phones were analog, functioning almost exactly like early radios; 2G shifted to digital; and 3G offered digital transmission at speeds that support not just text messages, which take up a lot less bandwidth than a phone call, but photographs and video-conferencing and television shows. Next comes 4G, which will probably enable you to instantly download everything but donor organs. Dr. Martin Cooper of Motorola made the first handheld cell phone call in 1973, and even compared with broadcast, cable, fiber, and Internet evolution, cell phone technology has progressed from nonexistent to essential in a staggeringly short time.

BUT THE QUESTION REMAINS, OF COURSE: Do we really have so much to say? When Gilbert Millstein reviewed Jack Kerouac's *On the Road* in 1957 for the *New York Times,* he worried about living in "an age in which the attention is fragmented and the sensibilities are blunted by the superlatives of fashion (multiplied a millionfold by the speed and pound of communications)." Keep in mind that in 1957 our attention was fragmented by three television networks and whatever we heard on the radio, and even so Millstein hardly blazed a trail. In 1854, when the transatlantic cable was nothing more than excited speculation, Henry David Thoreau wondered in *Walden* whether "perchance the first news that will leak through into the broad, flapping American ear will be that the Princess Adelaide has the whooping cough," a prediction as accurate as the *Times'* predictions about morning news radio and multiple stations.

Technology may change, but human nature does not. We're a gossipy species. We like—need—to talk, and as fast as capacity expands, we think of new things to say to fill it up. So as much fun as it is to side with Thoreau about the great flapping ear, I think the data—the billions of bytes of it available to you every second—support another conclusion. It's fun, with Thoreau, to laugh at Twitter and *Survivor* and BabyFirstTV and whatever new, even-more-instant communications essential shows up 5 minutes from now.

But Pat Hourigan doesn't doubt the value of his work. "We call it entertainment," he told me, "but is it? I always point to 9/11; I watched the towers go down on TV." Yes, our attention spans are poor, and we drift from our work and even our play, always looking for the next ring, download, or tweet (and by the time you read this, talking about tweets may be as current as talking about a carburetor). However we're getting our constant messages by the time you read this, the ability to get them is no longer optional. Cable, wire, wireless—it's the communication of our species, and we can't live without it.

"It's news," Hourigan told me. "It's information. It's the way we understand our world."

CHAPTER 9

ANNIHILATING BOTH TIME AND SPACE

On Getting Around, Effectively or Not

I CAN GET ON A BUS RIGHT AT THE STREET CORNER near my house. That might not sound like a big deal to you, but in Raleigh, it's practically unheard of. And though the bus stop lacks a roof, it has an actual wooden bench on which I can wait; of Raleigh's 1,500 bus stops, only about 5 percent have shelter, and another 20 percent have a bench—meaning that the vast majority of Raleigh bus stops comprise nothing more than a sign on a pole. So I'm thankful for what I've got.

The bus heading away from downtown comes to my stop once an hour, every half-hour during rush hour; the downtown bus stops 2 blocks away, just as often. Which means that if I were to take the bus downtown in the middle of the day to meet someone to talk about transit, I'd probably end up waiting half an hour or more for my bus back home, illustrating some of the obstacles Raleigh transit faces. Just the same, to attract riders Raleigh occasionally offers a free-service day on the buses, and for additional incentive provides free ice cream at the downtown transit station. So on one such day I sat on the bench and waited for my free bus, which finally ground up the hill 20 minutes late because of the jump in ridership. I've lived in Raleigh for 17 years and this was the first time I'd ever gotten on the bus. I could tell the regular riders—they were the ones shocked by the crowd and surprised by the free fare.

I found the free ice cream easily enough, and I wandered around the Moore Square Transit Station while I enjoyed it. With brick sidewalks, tin roofs along the sidewalk waiting areas, cast-iron lampposts, and concrete bollards with thick, black chains separating pedestrians from moving buses, the open-air station had a nice downtown feel. A pretty brick kiosk sells tickets and keeps passengers abreast of coming buses with an LED sign, and the posted schedules easily informed me of where and when to catch the bus home. Unfortunately, when it was time to go home I was engaged in a brief conversation with a friend—and so missed my bus. Rather than wait an hour, I took a different route and walked home from a more distant stop. Transit planners generally figure that if people can't get transit within about a quarter-mile they won't take it. My plan B required me to walk a mile. Raleigh transit has a long way to go.

TRANSPORTATION MAY NOT SEEM LIKE INFRASTRUCTURE—it rides on infrastructure, to be sure, but is it infrastructure itself? It felt like it to me: Getting stuff and people around is a fundamental part of human life. But the trains that I hear squealing all night long, the airport that gets me hither and yon, and the buses that sort of enable me to get around if I have absolutely no other options seemed like the last systems to investigate. For example, when the local nuclear plant is turned off, my electricity probably comes from nearby coal plants whose fuel trundles through the railyard near my house, and my Thanksgiving turkey is probably fed by grain that moves by rail too. The bus running downtown might not be a big part of my life, but it's a big part for the people who depend on it. And considering how large a role shoehorning kids, carry-ons, and bags of overpriced snacks into cruelly undersized aircraft plays in my life, how could the air travel system not be infrastructure?

I started with that bus. Raleigh's transit history represents the American norm almost perfectly. Omnibuses—multipassenger carriages pulled by horses—were introduced in Paris in 1819, spread throughout Europe, and showed up in major US cities by 1831. Railroads were spreading across the United States during this same period, but because steam engines made such a noisy, smoky mess, citizens of many cities preferred that horses draw passenger cars over the tracks into the city. Railroads complied, and a lightbulb went off over somebody's head: The smooth ride on rails represented a huge improvement over the omnibus jostle through mud or cobblestones. So on Christmas Day 1886, when Raleighans took their first public transit ride, they rode down Fayetteville Street, Raleigh's main street, on mule-drawn trolleys. (Horses soon replaced the mules, who had the habit of sitting down in the middle of the street and refusing to move.) By 1890, the trolleys switched to electric power—and as happened in many cities, the company that supplied that power eventually grew into the local electric utility. Raleigh's trolley company even offered for rent a special streetcar decked out with lights, and so known as the Electric Diamond, for parties, as well as charters to Bloomsbury Park, an amusement park well past the city limits, which the company had built to give people a reason to ride the trolley. By 1902 Americans got around their cities on 22,000 miles of electric trolley tracks; horses still pulled the cars on only 250 miles.

Larger cities introduced cable cars and subway trains in the third quarter of the 19th century, but Raleigh stuck with the trolley. And then came the gasoline engine, and between loss of ridership to automobiles and improvements in bus technology, the Raleigh trolley company finally discontinued the electric trolley in 1933 and replaced the service with buses. Trees now tower over Glenwood Avenue, Raleigh's gateway road to the northwest, from the median that once carried the trolley tracks.

The shift away from trolleys, of course, happened all over the country. According to the American Public Works Association, a third of transit companies were bankrupt by the end of World War I. Buses were the new thing—they rode on nice smooth tires and stopped at the side of the road, not the middle. When Raleigh's streetcars were discontinued in 1933, they were replaced by six bus routes serving Raleigh's population of less than 40,000 people. The power company sold out completely in 1950, and as ridership declined the city itself purchased the struggling Raleigh City Coach Lines in 1975. Nationwide, total transit ridership had plummeted to 6.6 billion in 1973 from a peak of 23 billion in 1945. Raleigh was not the only city that had to acquire its transportation system and run it as a public utility; without subsidies, transit couldn't run itself any more than roads could build themselves. Today, as nationwide transit ridership has risen again to 12 billion, Raleigh serves its nearly 400,000 people with 1,500 bus stops along 26 routes, including a free circulator route around downtown.

RALEIGH TRANSIT ADMINISTRATOR DAVID EATMAN runs Capital Area Transit (CAT), and he knows he's got a long way to go: "We're building processes from the ground up, because they haven't existed before," he says. With its meandering, car-centered development, Raleigh offers an object lesson for how to discourage transit use. In a sprawling city in a sprawling region with choked roads, CAT offers only bus transit, which gets stuck in the same traffic that might send frustrated drivers its way; in a region with countless work and living hubs it offers very few crosstown buses, focusing instead on radial lines into and out of a central hub. "We're like an airport—you have to change in Atlanta," Eatman says. And with limited funding, it offers few amenities and frustratingly long headways—times between buses. "It has certainly been viewed as a mode of need instead of a mode of choice."

But things are changing now. The recently introduced free downtown circulator bus that runs every 12 minutes throughout the day connects several entertainment, shopping, and business districts from early morning until late at night. It's been highly successful, and Eatman expects it will introduce the system to transit Raleighans who are used to nothing but car travel. And "introduce" is the right word: "We hold Lunch and Learns," he says. "Like, 'Okay, I have a fare card: What do I do now?'" They show people how to pay; how to read a bus schedule; how to let the driver know you want to get off. When you've spent more than half a century discouraging people from using transit, they need basic instruction—and you'd like them to have that instruction before you ask them for money to fund a train system.

Yep: trains. "Transit is easy in Charlotte," 3 hours to the west, Eatman says. Like Raleigh, it has a radial system, with a hub and spokes, but unlike Raleigh, the Charlotte region centers on a single downtown surrounded by suburbs, so the radial system works. Raleigh, on the other hand, is part of a three-city region, with three downtowns, an enormous work center in the middle, and other emerging suburban and exurban employment and population centers. Its transportation prescription changes from month to month. Regional rail seemed a key solution, but a decades-long effort to create it died in 2006 when the region failed to meet changing federal density requirements and lost funding. Some sort of regional transit is clearly required: Each day at least 180,000 Triangle residents cross county borders to go to work (and that number is from 2000 so surely by now it's much higher). In 2009, the buses run by Triangle Transit carried 4,100 passengers per day, which means that of more than 180,000 people crossing borders to go to work, at most 2,000 of them relied on transit. Regional transportation needs to follow the same model as the electrical grid—with local distribution hubs and longer-distance transmission elements. CAT works more on the model of the water system: It has one "plant," the hub of downtown Raleigh, and Eatman focuses on improving and extending its spokes.

Making things better is a long process. For decades Raleigh's hundred or so buses have been wedged into a garage meant to house half that many. With federal stimulus money covering half its cost, the city broke ground on a new operations center; it's still seeking grant money for most of the rest—when it's done, the city expects to have put up less than 10 percent of the cost, though that's unusual now, Eatman says. "The burden more than ever is on local funding."

To get the funds for an ambitious plan involving expanded bus service, the rail service that city and regional planners have been trying to get started for 2 decades, and the kind of headway and facilities that will draw new riders, the counties in the Raleigh area plan to ask voters to institute a dedicated half-cent sales tax. Charlotte did the same a decade ago, and Charlotte now has a well-regarded 9-mile light-rail system. "It took Charlotte 10 years to go 9 miles," Eatman says, and Charlotte may still have to raise its transportation tax. "North Raleigh to Cary," the first leg of Raleigh's proposed light-rail system, "is 17 miles." A good average per-mile cost for light rail is $50 million, putting just the light-rail component of the hoped-for new system at close to $1 billion. Eatman knows he'll have a hard sell in explaining to a population that needs to be coached about how to ride a bus the ways in which $1 billion worth of light rail will improve their lives. The tough economic times don't help. But he has hopes: "*If* we educate, and *if* we time it correctly," he says, hesitating, "then yes, [the tax] can pass."

UNTIL THEN, EVEN EASY STUFF IS HARD. The system is building new shelters and benches, for example. "Most major stops are in the NCDOT right-of-way," Eatman says. And as I learned from the transportation engineers, NCDOT doesn't always like structures in its right-of-way. "And what if there's not enough space? Then we have to go to the home owner. That's not a real, real quick process." Eatman needs to consider things like the Title VI laws in the Civil Rights Act of 1964; until the 1960s, systems routinely reserved their best services for wealthy white passengers, and he can't buy a bus without running the purchase by the city, an advisory board, and a regional planning organization that might see more value in spending $350,000 for road improvements than for a new bus.

The news isn't all bad. On main lines the system runs a very reasonable headway of 15 minutes during rush hour, and Eatman plans to improve headway on other routes; my own route will soon run with half-hour headway all day long, which may increase my willingness to use it. The system's first real-time passenger information signs—updating actual bus positions and waiting times—are already being installed, though Eatman points out that at stops shaded by trees the signs, which get their information from GPS satellites, won't perform well. And above all, Eatman has time on his side. Every transit and traffic planner I spoke with agreed that only high gas prices and unendurable congestion will push people out of cars. Congestion in Raleigh continues to increase. In fiscal 2009, a high-gas-price year, CAT ridership increased by 10 percent, hitting 5 million; in the early months of fiscal 2010, even with gas prices lower, ridership still increased by another 12 percent.

"To me that shows that a lot of people that made that switch are saying, 'That wasn't as bad as I thought,'" Eatman says. He's right—and if that's not the highest praise a transit system ever received, at least it's a start.

BUT I STILL COULDN'T TAKE A BUS TO THE AIRPORT. Which explains, perhaps, my inordinate thrill when Mike McElvaney, deputy airport director for Raleigh-Durham International Airport (RDU), drove me to visit Terminal 2, the brand-new $570 million terminal serving most of the 10 million or so passengers traveling through RDU every year. Just before the terminal, McElvaney pulled up to the curb—*and we got out of the car and walked away.* His car had a tag identifying it as belonging to airport management, so we were safe. I consider blithely leaving a car parked in front of an airport terminal one of the high points of my life.

The new terminal has terrazzo floors, maple wall coverings, and granite counters; a clerestory fills the space with diffuse light, all beneath an undulating, arced roof meant to echo the rolling Piedmont terrain that surrounds it. It's shockingly airy and pleasant, like a place you might conceivably choose to go on purpose. To be sure, it's not one of those 19th-century train stations that's a monument to human engineering; nor is it even an iconic airport building like Eero Saarinen's TWA terminal at JFK International Airport in New York. But neither is it a late-20th-century beetling box, like the terminal it replaced, little more than long square tubes funneling passengers into low, grim waiting units. RDU Terminal 2 feels, actually, like a shopping mall.

McElvaney nods at the comparison: That's it exactly. People spend time at the airport, whether they like it or not. And the Raleigh-Durham Airport Authority, which runs the place, wants them to like it and to spend money in its shops, whether for newspapers and candy or barbecue sauce and sweatshirts. It thinks of travelers as customers because they are the source of its revenue. "We don't use any tax money," he says. "We solely rely on revenues." The revenues are generated largely by that passenger facilities charge that passengers pay on every ticket that routes them through just about every airport in the United States. But it also comes from parking, contracts with merchants and car rental agencies, and fees paid by airlines for the use of airport gates. The airport is a business—it looks like a mall because it *is* a mall. I once noted from the train platform at Reagan National Airport in Washington, DC, that, with its multiple domes, the terminal looks almost exactly like the Grand Bazaar in Istanbul. The more I learned about airport function, the truer that comparison rang.

RDU is like a tiny city, an infrastructure microcosm: It has its own firefighting and police units; it builds and maintains roads and sidewalks (though it's unfriendly to pedestrians and impossible to reach save by car); it provides power, water, and sewer systems (extensions of the systems of the surrounding cities); it provides telecommunications services. Before someone lays down the first dollop of asphalt, an airport will already have a stormwater system: Those acres of cleared and paved land produce a mighty torrent of runoff. That's why you'll never land at an airport that doesn't have a nearby lake, reservoir, or large river.

Airports are relatively new as infrastructure. At the dawn of commercial aviation, in the 1920s, any flat field was an airport. Before president Calvin Coolidge signed the Air Commerce Act in 1926, airplanes traveled with no rules or regulations at all; pilots were not even licensed. Under the provisions of the act, the federal government spent hundreds of millions of dollars supporting air travel: building airfields, providing weather services, and regulating airplanes for safety as air travel exploded into existence. Several aviation acts later, the federal government still pays for about 75 percent of most projects related to actual air safety: runway maintenance, airfield lighting, control systems. Airports themselves, though, are entirely local infrastructure. From the start, the federal government has treated them like city docks along a waterway: The feds will dredge the harbor, but the town builds its own docks.

RDU is Raleigh's dock. In 1940, former fighter pilot and Eastern Airlines chief Eddie Rickenbacker ran an ad in central North Carolina newspapers urging Raleigh and Durham to forswear "civic jealousies or selfish motives" and build a single airport to serve the region. He was late to the party—Wake and Durham Counties and the cities of Raleigh and Durham had agreed in 1939 to create the airport authority, which still by charter receives $12,500 from each entity (a $50,000 total that now constitutes 1/20th of 1 percent of its $87 million operating budget). Terminals have grown larger, jet bridges have replaced stairways on the tarmac, and security has become a much bigger pain, but RDU airport is still a regional system for sorting and distributing passengers—and selling them some coffee while they're around.

THE OPEN SPACE OF THE NEW LOBBY expresses Terminal 2's design as "a common-use building," McElvaney says. Instead of a long row of counters, each staffed by specific airlines, the lobby opens out onto two central blocks, where overhead screens announce which airline is using each particular station, which changes throughout the day. This improves both ticketing efficiency and dropoff—every passenger can walk into any door, instead of having to creep along looking for the name of his or her airline. The gates work the same way, allowing RDU to allocate them as the airlines need them. This approach constitutes a complete change in airline function since the Airline Deregulation Act in 1978. Before then, the federal government treated the airways as public space much like the radio frequency spectrum, assigning different routes to different carriers and regulating prices on those routes. Carriers then negotiated gate leases with airports—and basically owned those gates for the duration of the leases, with gates consequently sitting empty for long stretches of each day; ticket counters followed a similar pattern. Carriers could negotiate individual gate-sharing agreements with airport approval, but the system did not encourage quick responses from carriers or airports. Each carrier used proprietary computer and telephone systems, making sharing complex or even impossible.

Deregulation encouraged airlines to compete for routes to any market, and since then the physical infrastructure of airports has been trying to keep up. "Delta may need 10 gates this morning but only 5 this afternoon," McElvaney says. "The old way, that limited the use of the building," leaving five gates empty all afternoon. The new terminal provides backbone information technology systems, with airlines layering their own software on top, enabling any airline to use any gate or counter terminal by just logging on to different systems. It also encourages experimentation: "Say I'm a new airline and want to test the waters at Raleigh," McElvaney says. Instead of having to invest in loads of terminals, signage, and equipment just to try the market, "they can come in, set up, and try us with minimum cost up front. We even own the telephone system."

The Federal Aviation Administration characterizes airports according to size; the biggest are called hubs and come in small, medium, and large. As of 2008, the 29 large hubs each account for at least 1 percent of the 700 million–plus people who get on airplanes each year; together they account for 68 percent of passengers (the three biggest airports, Atlanta, Dallas/Fort Worth, and Chicago's O'Hare, account for more than 14 percent of boardings all by themselves). RDU is one of 37 medium hubs, which together account for another 20 percent of enplanements. After the 72 small hubs (8 percent of boardings) come the 244 tiny non-hub airports, each with fewer than 10,000 boardings per year. Note, though, that what the FAA means by "hub airport" is not what you or I would mean. That is, RDU isn't a hub for any airline.

After deregulation, airlines found that, like power or communications systems, people could be best moved around through a hub-and-spoke model, being sorted once or twice along the route. Just as an e-mail is processed and sorted numerous times along its journey, airlines found they could efficiently sort their passengers the same way. Suppose I need to get to Cleveland from RDU. Direct flight? Great. If not, I'll take a flight with, say, US Airways—they'll fly me to one of their hubs (Pittsburgh, for example), where I'll change planes and get on a plane to Cleveland. We route ourselves by the most convenient available path, like sentient e-mails. Our baggage—usually—makes the same journey, beneath rather than on the concourse.

Airport terminals show their function by their design. The new RDU Terminal 2 replaced a terminal built as a hub for American Airlines in 1987. When American discontinued its hub a decade later, the terminal it left behind was designed for hub traffic: It served few originating passengers, so it had limited counter, security, and baggage-handling capacity in the ticketing area. That made it all wrong for RDU's flow, 95 percent of which now is origin and destination traffic. An airport like Hartsfield-Jackson Atlanta International, the world's largest hub, is designed primarily to move passengers already within the airport from one terminal to another: hence the profusion of underground tramways and so forth. RDU, on the other hand, is designed to get people easily from their cars to their gates—hence the common-use system that improves car traffic in front of the ticketing area, and hence the 12,000 parking spaces in garages right next to the terminals. (And the 10,000 more in park-and-ride lots—passengers are willing to take the shuttles from satellite parking, which seem to be the only buses Raleighans ride comfortably.) No automatic trains talking in disembodied monotone female voices at RDU—the only way to get from Terminal 1 to Terminal 2 without driving is to walk through the parking garage.

RDU, in a way, is like a broadcast antenna or a cell phone tower: It's a piece of stand-alone infrastructure that sends things back and forth through the air. It's a distribution node, connected through the large planes that would be the equivalent of trunk lines in the telephone system, moving large volumes of passengers at once to hubs like Atlanta or Chicago, which are the telephone equivalents of central offices. Its flights to Nashville and Cleveland and Indianapolis are distribution lines that send smaller volumes to their destinations.

WE PASS THROUGH A FEW SECURITY DOORS to the ramp tower, a room with huge windows overlooking the taxiways, ramps, and runway on one side of the terminal, where a team assigns and manages the ticket counters, gates, ramps (the parking areas near the gates), and baggage belts. It's sort of the nerve center of the common-use system. Above the windows, three television screens show camera shots from gates not visible from the windows, and three guys keep one eye on reality out on the concrete and another on the scheduling system in front of them. When the planes leave the ramps for the taxiways, the ramp managers hand pilots over to the FAA employees who work in the air traffic control tower. The ramp managers not only communicate with aircraft but instantly send any changes to the FIDS—the flight information display system whose screens throughout the airport let passengers know where their planes will board or their baggage will arrive.

Speaking of baggage, beneath the terminal McElvaney shows me the unified automated baggage handling system: It looks a little like a long roller coaster in a parking garage, with open chutes snaking around above our heads, dropping bags down slides. Instead of each airline having its own system—and several of those enormous explosives-detection systems—in the ticketing area, the common-use system enables each airline to slap a bar code on a bag and fling it onto the single belt. The system sniffs for explosives out of sight and periodically scans bags to keep track of them, and its SCADA system flashes in red any segments that appear to be clogging or misbehaving. Down below it kicks each bag to an area for a particular airline (employees sort each airline's bags for particular flights). McElvaney sees the common-use system saving time and injuries among baggage handlers and preventing trouble for RDU passengers by improving the chances their bags will go where they're supposed to.

When we drive out onto the commercial taxiway, I learn the answer to the questions that have probably plagued everyone who has ever looked out the window of a landing aircraft. The numbers on the runways stand for compass headings, without the final zero. Thus a runway angled at 230 degrees says 23, though there will be two: 23L, on the left of the terminal for approaching aircraft, and 23R on the right. If you approach the same runways from the other direction the heading will be 50, so they will say 5R and 5L, with the R and L reversed, of course. Runways are designed for standard winds—aircraft take off and land better when they face into the wind. Most of Raleigh's winds come from the southeast, and 230 is 5 degrees off due southeast. The pretty blue lights you see at night outline the taxiway; the lead-in and main runway lights are white, shifting to amber 2,000 feet from the end. Four red lights mark the end of the runway. Green "in-pavement" lights, flush with the runway surface, mark turnoffs between runway and taxiway. (RDU used stimulus funds to replace almost all of its runway lights with LEDs, which last 10 times longer and save energy.) The big yellow letters on the black signs indicate specific taxiways.

Runways for modern planes must be at least 150 feet wide—roughly 13 lanes of highway traffic—and at least 7,000 feet long; RDU's are 7,500, with the exception of a single 10,000-foot runway capable of taking a fully loaded 747 or cargo plane, like the UPS flights that leave RDU every day. A runway has a reinforced concrete base at least 2 feet thick, and though runways may be covered in asphalt, the ramps won't be— spilled jet fuel eats asphalt, as do spills of oil and hydraulic fluid or de-icers. Workers inspect runways three times each day.

The great big thing in the grass to the side of the runway that looks like a giant bowling pin is a VOR indicator—a beacon for visual omni-directional range (VOR) navigation. Planes are focused onto the signals the VOR stations emit and basically follow from beacon to beacon until they reach their destinations.

THE REST OF THE AIRPORT'S AIR TRAFFIC CONTROL system, operating from a 200-foot tower, has been off-limits since 9/11. But the system is easy to understand. An aircraft, like a passenger, is not unlike a packet on the Internet. Just as I write an e-mail to my mom in Cleveland and my e-mail program slices it into packets, giving each one a header filled with information about the packet's origin, destination, content, order, and route, when the ramp controller at RDU hands a flight off to the FAA controller in the tower, the FAA controller generates information about the flight—its origin, destination, type of plane, route, and so forth. With e-mail packets, routers test the multiple redundant connections leading in the general direction the packet wants to go and send by what-ever route looks fastest, with the packet going from router to router until it reaches its destination.

Air traffic controllers are routers themselves, keeping track of planes by radar and radio contact. Each plane will have a planned route, and the flight will be handed from air traffic control center to control center along its path. Obviously controllers have many fewer options with planes than computer routers do with packets, but they maintain mini-mum distances between planes and reroute if necessary. The FAA esti-mates that at any average daytime moment, 7,000 aircraft are flying above the United States. The air traffic control system is making increas-ing use of GPS, but McElvaney is quick to point out that GPS will aug-ment, not replace, the current system. It will offer an easier, quicker, and more exact fix on aircraft position and may allow flights to move more directly from origin to destination—when the path from VOR beacon to beacon is circuitous, a flight may be able to fly more directly, its position still identified by GPS.

When McElvaney drops me off, I admit that of all the amazing things he showed me I might be most impressed by his parking in front of the terminal and leaving the car there; like everyone, I despise going to the airport to pick someone up and having to drive circles until they arrive. He tells me they've thought of that, too: The parking lot in front of the Airport Authority is available for what he calls "cell phone parking." You're allowed to park there, and when your pickup arrives and calls, you're seconds away. Air travel, roads, telecommunications. Everything fits together.

THE FINAL INFRASTRUCTURE I WANTED TO INVESTIGATE was, really, our very first modern infrastructure. From my bedroom at night and from my office during the day, I hear the clank and shudder of the Norfolk Southern railway yard, not half a mile away at the bottom of the slope of my neighborhood. Wheels squeal, horns sound, boxcars bang—it's like living in a country song. I love it, and so do my sons when we go visit. A little bent metal sign that sticks up by the side of one of the dozen or so parallel tracks of the yard says, simply, RALEIGH. How do the workers sort through cars and send them in all directions from here? How do these rails connect to all the other rails, and how long have they been around? And above all, those horn sounds seem to follow patterns. What are they saying?

I started by taking a closer look at my bird's-eye-view map of Raleigh in 1872. The map shows not a single utility pole, though Raleigh by then had had telegraphy for decades. Telephones were several years away, electricity was still more than a decade off; the water tower south of the capitol building and the pipes to feed it weren't even a gleam in an engineer's eye, and don't even think about sewer pipes. The stormwater made its way to the creeks without any help from Raleigh's 8,000 or so residents, who each still had to spend a few days every year maintaining the packed-clay roads. I had thought there were no bridges, either, but when I looked very closely at the map, I found a couple of little things that might be bridges over storm drainages. More important, I found one indisputable bridge.

It goes over railroad tracks.

In 1872, before any of those other infrastructure systems had been planned, much less implemented, Raleigh had three railroad lines—and had had railroad lines for more than 30 years. Raleigh's first railroad, called the Experimental Line, was built in 1833 to run from a quarry a mile or so southeast of the city: Horses pulled cars filled with granite blocks along tracks to Union Square, for the use of workers building a new capitol to replace the original, which had been destroyed by fire. The line ran so well that tourists visited Raleigh for weekend railroad pleasure trips. At the same time a line running from Weldon, North Carolina, near the Virginia border, to Petersburg, Virginia, just south of Richmond, first linked the state to growing rail networks in the northern states.

The Experimental functioned so well that the Raleigh and Gaston Railroad opened in 1840, connecting Raleigh with Gaston, a tiny town on the Roanoke River 86 miles away. It opened a month behind the Wilmington and Raleigh Railroad, which at 161 miles may have been the longest railroad in the world at the time, and it was certainly the most confusingly named: It didn't go to Raleigh at all, but rather ended in Weldon, a couple of miles from Gaston (in 1855 its name was changed to the Wilmington and Weldon Railroad).

Both Raleigh and Wilmington had the same idea: The railroad would "add essentially to the prosperity of the adjoining country," wrote the editor of the *Raleigh Register.* Attempts to render either the Neuse River or long-distance roads navigable had failed, so the railroad represented a vital link with the rest of the world. With connecting service one could travel the 338 miles between Raleigh and Baltimore in the astonishing time of 32 hours: "This seems," said a merchant quoted in the *Register,* "like annihilating both time and space." When the Tornado— one of the engines that ran on the line—regularly ran at the insane speed of 15 miles per hour, the railroad's chief engineer lobbied for a 12 mph speed limit.

The rest of the nation was experiencing the same sudden change. Though short, mule-drawn railroads had been in use in mines and for other industrial applications for decades, a railway in England first used a steam engine on rails to draw passengers and freight according to scheduled departures in 1825. The technology and system spread instantly. The state of Maryland chartered the first American commercial railroad, the Baltimore and Ohio (B&O) Railroad Company, in 1827. States and other government agencies originally considered the rails to be a public amenity, like public roads—and expected different companies to schedule different services along them—but the model of a modern railroad was sorted out extremely quickly. By the time the Raleigh and Gaston sent its first shipment of 20 cotton bales to Petersburg, though the locomotive itself was primitive—no roof for the driver, for instance—the railroad in most ways would have looked familiar to modern passengers: scheduled departures and arrivals; a single company owning both the rails and the rolling stock; the use of a gravel bed, wooden ties, T-shaped rails, standard railroad switches, and a 4-foot-8½-inch gauge, all still standard today. A cowcatcher protected the locomotive from cows and other obstacles, flinging them to the side rather than allowing them to fall under the wheels and risk the train's derailment; a sandbox dispensed its contents to improve traction on slippery rails. The Raleigh and Gaston was already only one of hundreds of railroads working or under development in the United States. In 1869, the Central Pacific and Union Pacific railroads joined in Utah, connecting the Atlantic and Pacific coasts with railroad ties.

That's fast, but they had help. The Army Corps of Engineers had been providing free surveys to railroads since 1824, and the federal government, recognizing railroads as a tool for economic growth, started giving land to railroad companies in 1833; the total land grants to the railroads eventually totalled some 130 million acres—about 7 percent of the land in the contiguous United States. The railroad companies had the additional economic benefit of slave labor, and the labor of immigrants who were virtual slaves. That's not to diminish the magnitude of the project: You don't get from "that sounds like a good idea" to "entire continent knit together by rails" in 40 years without lots of people involved, including the government, in a big way. By the 1920s, railroads transported a quarter of the passenger traffic and three-quarters of all the freight traffic in the nation.

BUT THEY DON'T ANYMORE. The freight cars banging around the local Norfolk Southern (NS) switching yard represent an industry that carries only about 4 percent of the nation's freight when measured by value, 12 percent when measured by weight. In the yard I see hopper cars full of grain, tankers of corn oil, gondola cars of scrap metal, and of course car after car filled with coal. Coal, mostly going to power plants, constitutes 45 percent of all rail shipments. Norfolk Southern sends two 100-car trains of coal each week to a Progress Energy plant in Greensboro.

Kraig Barner, operations manager at the yard, doesn't much care what's in them; to his crews, a train is like a UPS truck, with each car a package. "We don't even look inside," he said. "It's kind of like public transportation for freight." He explains his system, but he almost doesn't have to: By now, I know how it works. Local systems moving material in one direction—water, wastewater, solid waste—are like trees, with twigs and branches and trunks; big national or worldwide systems moving materials in all directions are like wheels, with hubs and spokes. Barner's small yard is the equivalent of a final distribution node. Long trains come in, and his crews break them down and pull them together for local distribution runs, bringing rolls of newsprint to a newspaper or sand to a cement yard; NS rails run right to the loading docks of those companies. "All the traffic we get here is classified in a hump yard in Linwood," Barner says. A hump yard is a fan of dozens of tracks, all spreading from a source track at the top of a hump; locomotives push a train up the hump, and at the top cars are released, one by one, to different tracks, forming trains going in different directions. "Then we will classify it again for our customers."

Delivery crews bring back the empties, or bring full cars back from producers: Raleigh gets a lot of lumber and grain moving through. Wherever the cars are going, full or empty, they first go to Linwood. "They'll call and say, 'Hey, Kraig, I got a car we need to move to San Diego.' What we do [is], we have a computer system for the best route," and Barner sends the car on the first leg of that route. It's impossible not to compare it to an enormous, slow-moving Internet. Norfolk Southern is one of seven Class I railways, with operating revenues of at least $401 million, in the United States. Like fiber-optic backbone lines, they all interconnect, shipping one another's cars to destinations through reciprocal agreements. Each car has a tracking transponder that enables companies to keep track of where it is, and each company has routing computers and traffic management systems run by dispatchers. NS has 11 dispatch centers, with the closest one to Raleigh in Greenville, South Carolina. "The track is energized," Barner says, "and when a car rolls over it, it completes a circuit. That dispatcher, he'll have a screen, and he can see the track energize." Signals along the track are controlled electronically; each signal-to-signal space is called a block, and the dispatchers manage the traffic on their lines exactly like air traffic controllers—or Cisco Systems routers on the Internet. The system as a whole handles about 2 billion tons of freight per year along its 140,000 miles of railroad (94,000 of which are run by Class I railways; 22,000 miles of that belong to NS), and it has the expected bottlenecks (40 percent of all freight passes through Chicago at some point; it can take 2 days to get through the tangle) and other complexities.

"Grade crossings are the root of all evil," Barner says of crossings where rail and road meet on the same level, with the resulting possibility of collision. A locomotive weighs 125 tons, a loaded car weighs 60 tons or more, and even local NS trains usually haul at least 10 cars: close to 1.5 million pounds of steel and cargo, moving up to 50 mph through Raleigh—and then someone in a minivan decides to try to beat a signal to cross a track. He doesn't even like to think about it.

THOSE GRADE CROSSINGS WORRY Patrick Simmons, too—he's the director of the NCDOT rail division, and he has just spent months finishing North Carolina's proposal for its share of the $8 billion that the 2009 stimulus package included for high-speed rail. Six passenger trains per day stop in Raleigh's tiny Amtrak station, a quarter-mile from that original bridge over the train tracks. Three trains go southwest: Two end in Charlotte and the third goes to Miami; heading northeast, one train from Charlotte ends in Raleigh and two others go on to New York. That means that to travel by train to Raleigh's nearest natural business partners, Charlotte and Richmond, you have two choices per day, and both take longer than driving would.

Nothing surprising there: Passenger rail has suffered even worse than freight railroads. Although it had already been losing passengers to cars and airplanes for decades, trains in 1950 still carried passengers for 33 billion miles (that was 6.5 percent of total intercity travel). In 1972 that number had declined to 9 billion—a drop of 80 percent since 1920, down to 0.7 percent of total intercity travel. Railroads were in such dire straits that in 1970 Congress passed a law allowing them to transfer money-losing passenger service to the federally run Amtrak, which began service in 1971 and promptly took over almost all passenger service in the country. Amtrak served 16 million passengers in 1972.

But Simmons has reason for cheer. For one thing, recent years have been kinder to rail travel—annual ridership on Amtrak in 2009 hit 27 million. For another, in 1992 the US Department of Transportation designated the Washington, DC–Raleigh–Charlotte Southeast Rail Corridor as one of five future high-speed rail corridors for passenger trains. Since then North Carolina has been working on improving its crossings, sometimes with the help of federal funds, and the route between Raleigh and Charlotte is well on its way to becoming a sealed corridor, within which every crossing has automatic gates, lights, and alarms. Simmons has become an expert on grade crossings.

"They're a big subject for us," he says. "Railroads were built early, and then communities grew around them," leaving the state with an awful lot of roads crossing the rails. National policy, he says, is to "close them where we can and grade-separate the others," but of course that's expensive and not always possible. NCDOT has done video studies of grade crossings that show vehicles of all sorts—"police cars, school buses, tanker trucks"—crossing tracks in defiance of all the lights and barriers. They've found that putting bars across all four lanes of traffic instead of across just the lanes waiting to cross improved compliance from 48 to 98 percent. "We built a better mousetrap," Simmons says. That's good as far as safety is concerned, but it creates other problems. He mentions a grade crossing in west Raleigh that he calls the most complex in the state—a six-lane road crosses the railroad, which lies between a four-lane and a three-lane road. Twelve freight trains and four to six passenger trains go through that crossing every day. Unless an expensive bridge or tunnel is built at that intersection, additional trains, whether from proposed regional rail service or high-speed rail traffic, will make the grade crossing a permanent traffic nightmare.

Just the same, Simmons sees rail traffic—both freight and passenger—only increasing in Raleigh's future. He's very hopeful about high-speed rail: Apart from the improvements the state has already made between Raleigh and Charlotte, "we've designed a completely grade-separated railroad from Raleigh to Richmond." The state owns its own railroad line—the North Carolina Railroad Company—that it leases to Norfolk Southern, and the state's third major carrier, CSX, also has tracks running through downtown, so there are several options for a high-speed rail route through the city. Track improvements have cut 75 minutes from the journey between Raleigh and Charlotte, and between that and rising gas prices, ridership on the now-3-hour trip has leapt by 34 percent since 2007. Like Raleigh's transit riders, its intercity passengers loudly wish for better headway—more than three daily departures from Raleigh's tiny Amtrak station. But the high-speed rail that might come through Raleigh excites modern North Carolinians for the same reason the Raleigh and Gaston line excited their ancestors: It will truly connect Raleigh with the vast rail networks of the Northeast. Half a dozen departures each day in each direction, knitting Raleigh's fortunes with those of Charlotte to the south and the entire northeastern megalopolis to the north? Business and political leaders quiver in anticipation of the reduced traffic congestion and the greater choice for travelers.

Taxpayers still resist rail and transit, though Simmons believes the resistance is mistaken. "If rail is wrong, why does it work elsewhere? The rest of the world has observed us," but they're not emulating us. "Transportation doesn't pay for itself," he goes on. "Trucks pay for a whole lot less of the road they use than people think. It's going to take a greater level of investment from all levels—federal, state, regional, and local." Trucks account for 58 percent of cargo transport, but changes in shipping and improvements in efficiency might change that. "The Panama Canal widening will be done in 2015, so there will be a larger flow of goods from East Coast ports. Freight railroads are getting ready for that." A gallon of fuel moves a ton of freight 436 miles by rail, he says, three times as far as the same gallon gets the same ton by truck. According to the Federal Railroad Administration, on even a 300-mile cargo trip, travel by rail rather than truck saves 115 gallons of fuel; a cross-country trip of 2,000 miles or more will save a thousand gallons of fuel, with the attending benefits to pocketbook and atmosphere.

"The era of building the interstate system is over. Highways as the only thing we do—that's over. Transit and intercity and high-speed rail make sense. They make a hell of a lot of sense."

IMPROVED RAIL TRAFFIC and public transportation would definitely increase mobility and help unchoke Raleigh's streets and interstates, and might even give us a few more nice bridges. The original bridge I found on that 1872 map has been replaced, but the street still crosses the railroad. Now a brew pub sits at one end of the bridge, affording a lovely view of the Raleigh skyline and also overlooking more switching yards. You can nurse a stout or a pale ale and listen to the clangs and the bashes and the sounding of the horns. Which Barner explained: "Two long, one short, one long," he said, "that's before a grade crossing. Three short? That's backing up." And two beeps, strong and simple?

"He's going ahead."

So may we all.

THE VIRTUE OF NECESSITY

Regarding Engineers, Taxes,
and Getting What You Pay For

EARLY IN MY EXPLORATION OF INFRASTRUCTURE, I took a side tunnel off the main culvert channeling the Pigeon House Branch beneath central Raleigh. Bent low in a 5-foot concrete tunnel, I splashed my way upstream in the trickly flow until I saw something odd—daylight. I quickly reached what turned out to be a hole of some kind, with dirt, broken pipe, and pieces of asphalt jumbled together where the culvert had collapsed. I crept forward and stuck my head out for a better look only to hear the *beep* . . . *beep* of a reversing piece of heavy equipment and find myself staring at an approaching backhoe. I scuttled back, and in a moment I heard the backhoe engine stop. I slowly stuck my head out again and shouted, "Don't dig me!" The engineer, backhoe driver, and other workers presented satisfactorily openmouthed expressions as I popped up in their construction site like a Whac-a-Mole.

What had happened, I learned, was that a track hoe sent to excavate a patch of sinking pavement a few days before had itself caused further collapse and fallen into the hole. The track hoe had been fished out, and the current crew, watched by a city engineer, was using a lighter back-hoe, picking its way into the collapse to investigate. Since I came from underground, the engineer asked if I would mind going back down and shooting a couple of pictures inside the culvert, especially of a crossing water main under which I had ducked to get to the hole. That afternoon gave me my first sense of how truly intertwined all these systems are. The engineer asked me to take pictures because, GIS or no, maps and records or no, he wasn't at all sure what lay under that collapsing street. And the next city engineer I spoke with, Veronica High, explained what the city would have to move in order to fix the hole.

"For this one?" she said. "I think telephone, cable, electricity, fiber optics, gas, water, and sewer." A blithe smile. "And even moving a pole isn't simple, because you have to wait to find out who owns it, and then for everybody to do their work." Whoever owned the pole (the electric or telephone company) would have to work with the city to choose a place for the new pole, then install it. Then one by one the utilities would have to reroute their lines; that could be a week right there. "At least," High said.

And the systems aren't complex just because they hang from the same poles or lie in buried conduits next to each other, or because they require one another's assistance to work (try generating electricity without water to cool the generator, or treating water without electric pumps; try doing either without fiber-optic communications). No, they're becoming more complex every day just in what they do. And what they do, we can no longer do without. Everybody knows somebody who's proudly going "off the grid," right? With wind generator plans downloaded from the Internet and building supplies delivered by trucks over paved roads and a pipe bought at Home Depot to channel water that's potable because of modern upstream sewage treatment and stormwater management. You can't go off the grid anymore; we're all on the grid. We *are* the grid. And it's marvelous—it's miraculous. It's the eighth wonder of the modern world. Maybe it's the first seven, too.

That also presents a problem. Raleigh sewer collection superintendent Gene Stanley, who grew up on a farm, sees something scary in the way people depend on an infrastructure they don't understand and don't know how to live without. "You go to the grocery store," he says, "and they can't even count the change," much less grow tomatoes and corn or shoot a squirrel ("You put him over rice, you got you a good meal"). But cut off the electricity or wreck the trucking routes and the processed food goes with them, along with the fuel we use to cook. Striking closer to his job, every year his family used to dig a new hole, move the outhouse, and use the dirt from the fresh hole to cover the old one. He doubts that one family in a hundred would know to do as much if the system he maintains failed. "It'll be the downfall of America," he told me.

I couldn't shoot a squirrel to save my life, and I utterly depend on my freshwater and electricity and sewage treatment as much as anybody else. And now that I've spent a lot of time with those systems, I still only just understand them. I naively hoped that by the end of this project I'd be able to walk down the street and answer any question about any wire hanging above my head, about any mysterious iron disk in the pavement, about every road and rail design. Of course, I can do nothing of the sort, and I've decided that's just fine. With systems this complex, this intertwined, this miraculous, you could spend all day every day thinking about them and you'd still be behind—unless you work for a utility company or one of the relevant government agencies, you just can't worry full-time about power, or water, or sewage, or cable, or trash, or roads. But that's okay: You deal with enough of the people who unclog your sewer pipes and clean your water, who interrupt their vacations to call power companies when they notice something that looks funny, and you develop a sort of awe for them.

On the other hand, you do have to know a little, because as a citizen you have decisions to make: How much to allocate in taxes? Which projects to support? Which rate increases are reasonable? You can't just ignore the infrastructure; you can't not know a thing about it. Ignorance is irresponsible, even indecent. Something that important, that central, requires your awareness and your conscious assessment. You have to have an opinion about the infrastructure.

Now I do. In fact, I have three opinions.

MY FIRST OPINION IS, THANK GOD FOR ENGINEERS. Whenever anyone claims that they yearn to live in some pre-20th-century Good Olde Days,

I have always had an easy answer. "Two things," I say. "Antibiotics and modern dentistry." People who pretend they would be just as happy without them are fools.

But to those two essentials I now add every stream of infrastructure I traced for these pages and the people who make them go. I have drunk water probably 5 or 10 times per day every day of my life—call it 150,000 drinks of water and you're in the neighborhood. And the next time I get some sort of waterborne illness from my drinking water will be the first. That's nothing short of a miracle, especially when you consider that at least a sixth of the world's population lacks access to safe drinking water. This is an unimaginable luxury, worth—well, ask one of those people without access what they'd pay to get clean water for their kids. Yet we not only take it for granted but actively complain about it, especially if the people managing the water systems wish to charge us for that life-giving, lifesaving service. We'll protest the cost of our freshwater going from a third of a penny to a half-penny per gallon—all the while sucking like infants from the dollar-a-pint plastic bottles of water we seemingly can no longer leave our houses without.

On and on. I don't go over the river and through the woods to get to Grandmother's house for Thanksgiving. I get in my car, which is in my driveway, and climb out in a parking lot 15 steps from her door, three states away, without ever having to do anything more onerous than change radio channels or pee in a public restroom whose cleanliness may not reach my lofty standards. If I'm in a hurry, I can jump on an airplane and get to Grandmother's house in a couple of hours. Either way I go, chances are I'll complain pretty much full-time about the high cost of fuel, or the capacity or quality of the roadways, or the capacity or quality of the waiting area, or the capacity or quality of the aircraft. If you think that's complaining, though, ask me for tax money to improve any of it—then you'll hear some complaining.

Nietzsche called architecture "triumph over gravitation," but really it's the engineers who fight not only gravity but all the forces of the physical world—the reality that heavy trucks destroy roads, that steel stresses, that lines sag, that water and sewage flow downhill. In our fresh-from-the-dryer, central-heated, smooth-paved, bright-lit, 10-gigabyte-per-second lives, we never need spend a moment thinking about the trouble those physical forces will cause if we're not on guard every second. We have engineers to do that for us, and planners and guys with 16-foot-long shovels and guys who throw rubber blankets over energized power lines and guys who push around spewing water and sewer pipes in the middle of the night with mist freezing on their eyelashes. I've talked to a lot of those people, and I've decided I trust them.

Mind you, nobody wants to blindly trust engineers, or industry, or regulators, or government, or anybody else (including environmentalists, or me). I liked seeing the guards at my nuclear plant carrying machine guns; local publications, however, have run stories about lax security and propped-open fire doors. In 2007 disgruntled employees of the Peach Bottom plant in Pennsylvania leaked video of guards sleeping on the job. Most observers painted the Nuclear Regulatory Commission itself as dangerously complicit in the problems that caused the 1979 partial core meltdown at Three Mile Island, and whether utilities begin building new plants or not, the current plants are aging and will require significant oversight as utilities determine whether and how to extend their lives. I hate mountaintop removal coal mining as much as the next guy, and I holler about it and want it stopped. Just the same, like most people, I leave my computer and my lights on all day and enjoy a nice hot shower. The real way to make change in energy policy is to change energy use. We could stop mountaintop removal mining in a minute if we were willing to get along on the power generated by nuclear, hydro, and gas and oil plants. And if that means rolling blackouts, maybe rolling blackouts are good for the soul.

The point isn't that I know the solution to safe and responsible power generation; I manifestly do not. The point is that we bring the problems to the engineers and the engineers solve those problems: We say we want abundant power available to every customer every minute of every day, and we appear to place a higher value on that than on our West Virginia mountaintops, and so we end up with what we've got now. I trust my energy company to try to do well by its investors and its customers and the environment, but I trust it a whole lot more if regulators and utility commissions and the EPA are on the job. There are only so many hours in the day for worry, and worrying doesn't solve problems. I'm deciding to trust the engineers. I may blame us for demanding too much, but I don't blame the engineers for bringing us the infrastructure we demand.

Every industry faces the same issues. As I write, the Raleigh wastewater treatment-plant is fighting a fine levied on it for groundwater contamination. Local environmental groups actually support the plant's request for a diminished fine, but you probably don't want to ignore it when a government agency has made a mistake—and this mistake was caused not by incompetence but by actual malfeasance. We need journalists to dig and regulators to poke around opening folders and locked cabinets.

But first we need engineers. And what the engineers need is citizens who understand the basics of what they do. Do you know the difference between an amp and a volt, between a kilowatt and a kilowatt-hour? Do your teenage kids? We should. Should you be using your garbage disposal? Should water cost more than it does now? How safe is the soil treatment products the wastewater plant makes from your poop? Where does your water come from, and where does your trash go? We need to know these things—our kids need to know these things. We need these issues on our minds because in the next years and decades engineers are certainly going to present us with scary trade-offs, and we're going to have to make very tough choices. What happens to the planet if we keep burning coal? If we create more piles of nuclear waste? If we cover entire deserts with solar cells? Neither Ayn Rand laissez-faire true belief nor touch-nothing environmental idealism answers the questions.

AND SO MY SECOND OPINION IS, GET OUT YOUR WALLET—and be glad for the opportunity. "Infrastructure is destiny" is the catchphrase of the moment among the infrastructurati, but I got to using instead the phrase "our infrastructure, ourselves," which I think comes closer to the point. Since the end of the Roman Empire, allowing your infrastructure to rot has been a fine way to speed societal collapse. Nothing new there, yet we've chosen that road and seem to be sticking to it. Back in 1981, the authors of *America in Ruins,* which suddenly got everybody talking about infrastructure, estimated that we were behind in our infrastructure investment by about $842 billion, and they figured *that* put us in crisis. Every couple of years the American Society of Civil Engineers (ASCE) puts out another report card, and we get another spate of Ds. In 2009, recall, they said it would take $2.2 trillion to get us back up to speed. In 2008 the Urban Land Institute estimated that we run an annual infrastructure funding deficit of at least $170 billion.

People actually can take action to shore up the infrastructure. Atlanta, which was losing 20 percent of its drinking water to leaky pipes and fouling its rivers and creeks with combined sewer overflows, in 2001 elected mayor Shirley Franklin, who passed a 1¢ sales tax increase and an increase in water rates; she called herself the sewer mayor. "If we don't protect water, we will be without water," she told the ASCE. "It's a question of who's going to pay, how much are you going to be willing to pay in order to insure that your children live the kind of life that we as Americans have promised them?" Atlanta has so far been willing to pay $4 billion. But most of us, like indulgent parents of lazy children, shake our heads at those Ds and exact a promise to try harder next time, or maybe we even start another study or another plan. Then we wipe our hands and move on.

And by "we" I don't mean "you"—I mean me, too. The original ham-handed Raleigh pogrom against garbage disposals, poorly managed though it was, had genuine value, and we all know that small steps add up: Raleigh has a fabulously low sanitary sewer overflow rate because it simply flushes its sewer pipes according to a schedule. So the very least I could do would be to stop using our garbage disposal—but I haven't. We have a baby, and he loves to go spelunking in the garbage, so our kitchen trash can is near the back door, on the other side of a baby gate. Leaning over the gate, trying to use an elbow to push open the spring-loaded can lid and somehow scrape food scraps into the trash? When I can just stand over the sink and stuff it all into the magic hole before I toss the plate in the dishwasher? Garbage disposal 1, best and well-informed intentions 0. I mean to do better, I honestly do, but . . . I'll just keep my fingers crossed that regular pipe maintenance will keep my zucchini fragments from clogging our neighborhood sewers, and that the treatment plant keeps on scooping them out.

No matter how often someone reminds us that these systems are important and need our attention, we don't change. China spends 9 percent of its gross domestic product on infrastructure; Europe spends 5 percent; the United States spends about 2.4 percent, and that's *down* from 3 percent 50 years ago. Vehicle miles traveled in the United States have doubled since 1980, but we've built just 4 percent more roads to handle the extra traffic. The Federal Highway Trust Fund is running out of money, but the 18.4¢-per-gallon tax that funds it hasn't gone up since the 1980s. Meanwhile, your tires—and the tires of the trucks carrying new iPhones to malls—are shaking the highways to pieces. So the North Carolina Turnpike Authority wants to put a toll on new highways it plans to construct in Wake County, and instead of saying, "Gosh, a nice new road—and for once at least we know how it will be paid for," people start brandishing pitchforks. If you still haven't had your fill of outrage, ask people for tax money for public transportation.

The Urban Land Institute advises the increased use of direct user fees for roads using wireless transponders that will do everything from automatically paying tolls to actually tracking road use mile by mile, making it possible to charge drivers far more specifically for actual road use. People balk, of course—as they balk at the tiered Internet fees some service providers talk about instituting. Then again, the water and telephone systems mostly started with simple hookup fees and unlimited use; now you have to pay for what you get. And right here in Raleigh the Public Utilities Department plans to institute tiered rates for water use (the more you use, the more each unit costs). Drought or no drought, citizens don't like it.

David Mohler, chief technology officer of Duke Energy, described the complex position of an investor-owned utility: obligated by regulation to provide power to every customer in its territory as cheaply as possible, but obligated as a business to satisfy investors. Now that utilities, which make their living selling power, are supposed to encourage conservation, he said, the problem becomes almost unsolvable. He told me he measures whether people are paying what power ought to cost by the furious calls his company gets when a storm knocks out power. "When the power goes out," he said, "the meter stops turning." So people don't have power, but they're also not paying for it, which would seem like a break-even situation, but it obviously is not. "What that tells me," he said, "is that people value it much more than they pay for it."

Nobody likes to pay taxes; nobody's looking for more taxes to pay. But everything costs money, from paving roads to regulating power and telephone systems to cleaning and delivering water. I've seen people doing those things, and I like the results of their work. I say let's pay for it.

MY THIRD OPINION IS, LET'S LEARN TO LOVE OUR INFRASTRUCTURE. Beyond knowing just enough to help the engineers maintain it, and beyond digging out the funds to pay for it, we should appreciate it. Pliny and Herodotus called the sewers and aqueducts the crowning achievements of Greece and Rome; the 4th Dynasty Egyptians in 2700 BC left behind a sculpture of an official bearing the title "Superintendent of Works," and the 5th Dynasty did them one better, actually building a monument tomb for someone named Ti (or Tih) who held the same title under the pharaohs Neferirkare Kakai and Nyuserre Ini. By comparison, the I ♥ PUBLIC WORKS sticker on the office door of Raleigh's public works director lacks a certain multimillennial permanence.

But I don't suggest celebrating public administrators—I suggest celebrating the works themselves. One day I visited an electrical transmission line of 500 kilovolts—three long, drooping parallel arcs of wire held up by steel latticework pylons thousands of feet apart along a 100-foot-wide right-of-way that, mowed only often enough to keep trees from interfering with service, had reverted to meadow. In 15 minutes out there I saw five different species of butterfly and uncounted types of bug and fly. The thunderlike snap of the current overhead, caused by static as the air in the huge current around the wire ionizes and recombines, harmonized with the whirring and clicking of hoppers, bees, and beetles in the underbrush. The solemn march of those giant towers away from me in either direction struck me as almost indescribably beautiful: They're like the Cyclopes in Greek mythology, giants who did the enormous tasks for which mankind lacked the strength.

And as much as I was awed by the power lines they carried, I was absolutely taken by the pylons themselves: four skeletal legs narrowing to a waist, atop which a sort of skirt spread, holding double strands of insulators that supported and stabilized two of the wires. Above that was an almost lyrical steel hexagon encircling the angle of insulators holding the final wire. The pylons reminded me of ballet dancers spinning, arms above their heads, and I couldn't help wondering: If the Eiffel Tower is beautiful, how on earth is this not beautiful? Why are we not laying trails along the right-of-way so that we can ride our bicycles beneath these pylons? Why do we not hire artists to paint them in celebratory colors? Festoon them with colored lights and garlands? I look at transmission pylons wherever I travel now. The pylons along the road leading into Raleigh from the west have three gently arching limbs on each side, growing smaller as they climb—I can never decide whether these pylons look like the masts of square-riggers under full sail or like a row of Southern belles hitching up their skirts and flouncing into town. When we drove across the country when I was a kid, my brother was reading *The War of the Worlds* and, developed a complex taxonomy of the different types of transmission pylons based on the machines the Martians created. Somehow, since then I—we—have forgotten to even see these things, much less appreciate them.

Clevelanders love the panoply of bridges across the Cuyahoga River; Philadelphians have no less love for the Ben Franklin Bridge and San Franciscans for the Golden Gate. Places like Raleigh, newer to city status, missed out on much of that burly industrial construction. But we've got poles and tubes, pipes and wires, and people need to begin seeing that those too merit celebration.

Creative types sometimes take over Raleigh's abandoned old water plant; its rotting innards have provided the perfect setting for an art installation about water and a moody backdrop for posy band portraits. But nobody takes pictures of the new plant. In downtown Raleigh, Randy Clifton, my guide to the electrical distribution system, pointed out the powerhouse, built in 1910, that had once held Raleigh's original coal-fired steam turbines and has since held a series of failed restaurants, but across the street from that he also pointed out one of Raleigh's few industrial thrills: the nondescript downtown substation. Thanks to Clifton and a few of his co-workers, the transformers, switches, and the crisscrossing steel and aluminum framework of the substation are surrounded by evergreen plantings and lit at night by pale purple spotlights, in plain celebration of this little piece of infrastructure that the burgeoning entertainment district couldn't move out of its way. "We decided to do it just for the area," Clifton told me. "Just to enhance." He and his fellow linemen, that is, saw past the necessity to the virtue. They should do the same thing with the cooling tower at the nuclear plant.

The taxpayers see less clearly. In the median of one of the main roads into downtown stands a public sculpture, installed in 1995, that I think of as Raleigh's first piece of infrastructure art. Called the Light + Time Tower, the 40-foot galvanized steel tower is covered by glass panels backed by diffraction grating. Hit by the sun from different angles at different times, the panels glow in colors from a fluorescent orange to brilliant purple, changing as drivers throttle past at 45 mph. Whoever decided that drivers slogging their way through traffic during rush hour deserve a piece of artwork to look at should get an infrastructure medal, but instead critics immediately attacked it as looking like a broadcast antenna or cell phone tower. *Precisely.* Could there be any more perfect response to those fatuous cell phone towers dressed up to look like a tree drawn by a young child who has never seen a tree? I claim we need to start loving our infrastructure and celebrating it. Dale Eldred, the artist of the Light + Time Tower, agreed. Although in 1995 the people of Raleigh disagreed profoundly, I hope they'll eventually come around.

"MONEY AND POLITICAL WILL," transportation engineer Eric Lamb told me, are the two ingredients defining every roads question. In system after system, person after person told me the same thing: The technical problems the systems face aren't even close to unsolvable. Smart grid? A few hurdles, but we'll get there; it probably won't be cheap, though. get the bridges back up to snuff? We've had that technology since the 19th century. Stop pouring freshwater out through leaks, start shoring up the pipes, plus build new aqueducts and reservoirs where we need them? Sure, we can do that. All we have to do is pony up. People persist in believing that these systems will somehow maintain themselves, expand themselves, improve themselves without anybody having to put anything in. But we can keep this remarkable infrastructure, this eighth wonder of the world, only if we're willing to work together for it. It's that simple.

When I'm out riding the streets with a highway engineer or running pipes with a sewer guy or inspecting conductors with a lineman, I can be an optimist and an epicure of industrial magic, but once I'm at home watching the news or reading the newspaper I lose hope. I haven't seen much in my infrastructure-rich neighborhood that makes me believe taxpayers are suddenly going to start asking to fund the projects that will keep our systems from falling down on our heads. I feel like a late-empire Roman, just hoping things hold out long enough for my kids to stay relatively safe. I'm left with the melancholy belief that we're going to stand around bickering while the pipes clog and the wires fall and the roads crumble. And it doesn't help that once again it's stopped raining—when last I checked, Raleigh's rainfall was 8 inches low for the year, and our reservoir, Falls Lake, was 4 feet low already. Isn't this where I came in?

And then, finally, I got a mailing from a candidate for the City Council who was campaigning to "reward households for their conservation and not punish them with water rate increases for doing what was asked of them." Atlanta raised its taxes twice to address its water problems, and in Raleigh we still think our rates are too high because in the middle of a drought we had to stop watering our lawns. Shortly before the election, the Raleigh region won another best-of accolade: The Web site The Daily Beast called us America's Smartest City. Maybe, but the cheap-water candidate won. During the campaign, everyone who went to his Web site and registered was entered in a drawing. The grand prize?

A new garbage disposal.

BIBLIOGRAPHY

I have organized my sources for this project into sections, beginning with general sources on infrastructure and engineering, both modern and historical, then continuing to the main sources for the history and function of each of the systems discussed, organized by chapter. I list books that are especially rich in detail or otherwise worth your while in **boldface type**.

Truly Indispensable Resources

The books and Web sites listed here were resources of first resort, filled with detail and context. I consulted them during the research and writing of every chapter of this book. If my information proves erroneous, unclear, or unsatisfactory, these are the first places to which I would refer or send any reader for clarification or further information:

Books

Ascher, Kate. *The Works: Anatomy of a City*. New York: Penguin Press, 2005. Diagrams of systems based on New York City

Dreicer, Gregory K. *Me, Myself and Infrastructure: Private Lives and Public Works in America*. Reston, VA: American Society of Civil Engineers, 2002. Factoids, pictures, and connections, based on a traveling exhibition mounted by the American Society of Civil Engineers.

Hayes, Brian. *Infrastructure: A Field Guide to the Industrial Landscape*. New York: Norton, 2005. Sort of a Peterson Field Guide to the infrastructure of the modern world, this enormous book filled with color photographs often answered questions that people actually doing jobs couldn't.

Melosi, Martin V. *The Sanitary City: Environmental Services in Urban America from Colonial Times to the Present.* Pittsburgh: University of Pittsburgh Press, 2008. This book provides foundational information on freshwater, wastewater, and solid waste infrastructure and I used it heavily not only for all three chapters but for understanding all infrastructure systems.

Web Sites

The site www.infrastructurist.com is a constantly updated treasure trove of trustworthy, newsworthy, and reliable information on everything related to infrastructure.

The American Society of Civil Engineers—at www.asce.org—provides links to plenty of engineering resources and, especially, the regular Report Card for America's Infrastructure.

General Engineering and History

American Public Works Association. *History of Public Works in the United States, 1776–1976.* Chicago: American Public Works Association, 1976. This vital book contains thorough histories of the development of every infrastructure stream we now take for granted.

Armytage, W.H.G. *A Social History of Engineering.* Cambridge, MA: The M.I.T. Press, 1966.

Barker, Michael, ed. *Rebuilding America's Infrastructure: An Agenda for the 1980s.* Durham, NC: Duke University Press, 1984. (N.B.: Part I of this book comprises *America in Ruins: The Decaying Infrastructure,* the study by Pat Choate and Susan Walter, published in 1981 by the Council of State Planning Agencies.)

Cardwell, Donald. *The Norton History of Technology.* New York: Norton, 1995.

Chant, Colin, ed. *The Pre-Industrial Cities and Technology Reader.* London: Routledge, 1999.

Chiles, James. *Inviting Disaster: Lessons from the Edge of Technology.* New York: HarperBusiness, 2001.

Committee on History and Heritage of American Civil Engineering. *The Civil Engineer: His Origins.* New York: American Society of Civil Engineers, 1970.

DeCamp, L. Sprague. *The Ancient Engineers.* Cambridge, MA: MIT Press, 1970.

Flynn, Stephen. *The Edge of Disaster: Rebuilding a Resilient Nation.* New York: Random House, 2007.

Guyer, J. Paul, ed. *Infrastructure for Urban Growth: Proceedings of the Specialty Conference.* New York: American Society of Civil Engineers, 1985.

Hanson, Royce, ed. *Perspectives on Urban Infrastructure.* Washington, DC: National Academy Press, 1984.

Hibbert, Christopher. *Cities and Civilizations.* New York: Welcome Rain, 1996.

Hill, Donald. *A History of Engineering in Classical and Medieval Times.* London: Routledge, 1996.

Hindle, Brooke. *Technology in Early America.* Chapel Hill: University of North Carolina Press, 1966.

Hoy, Suellen M., and Michael C. Robinson, eds. *Public Works History in the United States: A Guide to the Literature.* Nashville: American Association for State and Local History, 1982.

Humphrey, John W., John P. Oleson, and Andrew N. Sherwood. *Greek and Roman Technology: Annotated Translations of Greek and Latin Texts and Documents.* London: Routledge, 1998.

Hughes, Thomas P. *The Human-Built World: How to Think About Technology and Culture.* Chicago: University of Chicago Press, 2004.

Ierley, Merritt. *Wondrous Contrivances: Technology at the Threshold.* New York: Clarkson Potter, 2002.

Jackson, Kenneth T. *Crabgrass Frontier: The Suburbanization of the United States.* New York: Oxford University Press, 1985.

Landels, J.G. *Engineering in the Ancient World.* London: Chatto and Windus, 1978.

Levy, Matthys, and Richard Panchyk. *Engineering the City: How Infrastructure Works.* Chicago: Chicago Review Press, 2000.

Maddex, Diane, ed. *Built in the U.S.A.: American Buildings from Airports to Zoos.* Washington DC: Preservation Press, 1985.

Pierce, Neal R., and Curtis W. Johnson, with Farley M. Peters. *Century of the City: No Time to Lose.* New York: Rockefeller Foundation, 2008.

Regional Plan Institute. *America 2050: An Infrastructure Vision for 21st Century America.* New York: Regional Plan Association, 2008.

Rybczynski, Witold. *Last Harvest: How a Cornfield Became New Daleville.* New York: Scribner, 2007.

Rybczynski, Witold. *Looking Around.* New York: Viking, 1993.

Sobey, Ed. *A Field Guide to Roadside Technology.* Chicago: Chicago Review Press, 2006.

Stilgoe, John R. *Outside Lies Magic: Regaining History and Awareness in Everyday Places.* New York: Walker, 1998.

Tainter, Joseph A. *The Collapse of Complex Societies.* New York: Cambridge University Press, 1988.

Trefil, James. *A Scientist in the City*. New York: Doubleday, 1994.

ULI–The Urban Land Institute and Ernst and Young. *Infrastructure 2008: A Competitive Advantage*. Washington, DC: ULI–The Urban Land Institute, 2008.

ULI–The Urban Land Institute and Ernst & Young. *Infrastructure 2007: A Global Perspective*. Washington DC: ULI–The Urban Land Institute, 2007.

Weisman, Alan. *The World Without Us*. New York: Thomas Dunne Books, 2007.

Chapter 1: Land and Surveying, and Raleigh

Cumming, W. P. *North Carolina in Maps*. Raleigh: State Department of Archives and History, 1966.

Godfrey, Michael A. *Field Guide to the Piedmont: The Natural Habitats of America's Most Lived-in Region, from New York City to Montgomery, Alabama*. Chapel Hill: University of North Carolina Press, 1997.

Holmes, Hannah. *Suburban Safari: A Year on the Lawn*. New York: Bloomsbury, 2005.

Linklater, Andro. *Measuring America: How an Untamed Wilderness Shaped the United States and Fulfilled the Promise of Democracy*. New York: Walker, 2002.

Murray, Elizabeth Reed. *Wake: Capital County of North Carolina*. Raleigh, NC: Capital County Publishing. Vol. I, 1983; Vol. II, with K. Todd Johnson, 2008.

Raleigh City Council. *Early Raleigh Neighborhoods and Buildings*. Raleigh, NC: City of Raleigh, 1983.

Raleigh Planning Department. *Raleigh Neighborhoods*. Raleigh, NC: City of Raleigh, undated.

Reeves, R. B., et al. *Raleigh, 1792-1992: A Bicentennial Celebration of North Carolina's Capital City*. Raleigh, NC: Bicentennial Committee, 1992.

Stewart, Kevin G., and Mary-Russell Roberson. *Exploring the Geology of the Carolinas*. Chapel Hill: University of North Carolina Press, 2007.

Stolpen, Steven. *Raleigh: A Pictorial History*. Norfolk, VA: Doning, 1977.

Waugh, Elizabeth Culbertson. *North Carolina's Capital City, Raleigh*. Raleigh, NC: Junior League of Raleigh, 1991.

Vickers, James. *Raleigh, City of Oaks: An Illustrated History*. Woodland Hills, CA: Windsor Publications, 1982.

Chapter 2: Stormwater

Bartlett, Ronald E. *Surface Water Sewerage, 2nd ed*. New York: Halsted Press, 1981.

Butler, David, and John W. Davies. *Urban Drainage*. New York: E&FN Spon, 2000.

Carr, Donald E. *Death of the Sweet Waters*. New York: Norton, 1966.

Ellis J., Bryan, ed. *Impacts of Urban Growth on Surface Water and Groundwater Quality*. Wallingford, UK: IAHS Publishers, 1999.

Ferguson, Bruce K. *Introduction to Stormwater: Concept, Purpose, Design*. New York: Wiley, 1998.

Heath, Ralph. *Basic Ground-Water Hydrology: US Geological Survey Water-Supply Paper 2220*. Washington, DC: US Geological Survey, 1983.

LeGrand, Harry. *A Master Conceptual Model for Hydrogeological Site Characterization in the Piedmont and Mountain Region of North Carolina*. Raleigh, NC: NC Department of Environment and Natural Resources, 2004.

Lenat, David, and Kenneth Eagles. *Ecological Effects of Urban Runoff on North Carolina Streams*. Raleigh: North Carolina Department of Natural Resources and Community Development, 1981.

City of Raleigh. *Stormwater Management Design Manual*. Raleigh, NC: City of Raleigh, 2002.

Stephenson, David. *Stormwater Hydrology and Drainage*. New York: Elsevier, 1981.

County of Wake. *Wake County Stormwater Design Manual—Draft*. Raleigh, NC: Wake County Government, 2006.

Chapter 3: Freshwater

Blake, Nelson. *Water for the Cities: A History of the Urban Water Supply Problem in the United States*. Syracuse, NY: Syracuse University Press, 1956.

Bratby, John. *Coagulation and Flocculation in Water and Wastewater Treatment, 2nd ed*. London: IW, 2006.

Didion, Joan. "Holy Water," in *We Tell Ourselves Stories in Order to Live: Collected Nonfiction*. New York: Alfred A. Knopf, 2006.

Faust, S.D., and Osman M. Aly. *Chemistry of Water Treatment*. Boca Raton, FL: CRC, 1996.

Jennings, C.A. "Uses and Accomplishments of Chlorine Compounds in Water and Sewage Purification." *The American City* 19: October 1918.

Kenny, J.F., N.L. Barber, S.S. Hutson, K.S. Linsey, J.K. Lovelace, and M.A. Mupin. *Estimated use of water in the United States in 2005*. Washington, DC: US Geological Survey, 2009. Distilled in Fact Sheet 2009-3098, October 2009.

Melosi, Martin V. *The Sanitary City: Environmental Services in Urban America from Colonial Times to the Present*. Pittsburgh: University of Pittsburgh Press, 2000.

Chapter 4: Wastewater

Cosgrove, Joseph J. *History of Sanitation.* Pittsburgh: Standard Sanitary Manufacturing, 1909.

George, Rose. *The Big Necessity: The Unmentionable World of Human Waste and Why It Matters.* New York: Metroolitan Books, 2008.

Office of Water Programs, College of Engineering and Computer Science, California State University, Sacramento. *Operation and Maintenance of Wastewater Collection Systems, 6th ed.* Sacramento, CA.: California State University, Sacramento Foundation, 2004.

Praeger, Dave. *Poop Culture: How America Is Shaped by Its Grossest National Product.* Port Townsend, WA: Feral House, 2007.

Read, Geoffrey and, eds Ian Vickeridge F. *Sewers: Rehabilitation and New Construction—Repair and Renovation.* New York: Arnold, 1995.

Schladweiler, Jon. Sewer History. www.sewerhistory.org.

Webster, Cedric. The Sewers of Mohenjo-Daro. *Journal (Water Pollution Control Federation)* 34 (1962) : 116–23.

Chapter 5: Roads

American Association of State Highway and Transportation Officials. *Rough Roads Ahead: Fix Them Now or Pay for It Later.* Washington, DC: AASHTO, 2009. http://roughroads.transportation.org/RoughRoads_FullReport.pdf.

Hoete, Anthony, ed. *Reader on the Aesthetics of Mobility.* London: Black Dog, 2003.

Kay, Jane Holtz. *Asphalt Nation: How the Automobile Took Over America, and How We Can Take It Back.* Berkeley, CA: University of California Press, 1998.

Lay, M. G. *Ways of the World: A History of the World's Roads and of the Vehicles That Used Them.* New Brunswick, NJ: Rutgers University Press, 1992.

U.S. Department of Transportation. *Manual on Uniform Traffic Control Devices.* Washington, DC: US DOT, 2003. http://mutcd.fhwa.dot.gov/kno_2003r1r2.htm.

Vanderbilt, Tom. *Traffic: Why We Drive the Way We Do (and What It Says About Us).* New York: Knopf, 2008.

Chapter 6: Power

Friedlander, Amy. *Power and Light: Electricity in the U.S. Energy Infrastructure, 1870–1940*. Reston, VA: Corporation for National Resarch Initiatives, 1996.

Harrison, J. A. *An Introduction to Electric Power Systems*. New York: Longman, 1980.

Hughes, Thomas Parke. *Networks of Power: Electrification in Western Society, 1880–1930*. Baltimore: Johns Hopkins University Press, 1983.

McNichol, Tom. *AC/DC: The Savage Tale of the First Standards War*. San Francisco: Jossey-Bass, 2006.

US Department of Energy. *National Transmission Grid Study*. Washington, DC: US Department of Energy, 2002. http://www.ferc.gov/industries/electric/gen-info/transmission-grid.pdf.

Wasik, John F. *The Merchant of Power: Samuel Insull, Thomas Edison, and the Creation of the Modern Metropolis*. New York: Palgrave Macmillan, 2006.

Chapter 7: Solid Waste

Cozic, Charles P., ed. *Garbage and Waste*. San Diego: Greenhaven Press, 1997.

O'Brien, Martin. *A Crisis of Waste? Understanding the Rubbish Society*. New York: Routledge, 2007.

Raleigh Department of Public Works. *Refuse Disposal: Evaluation of Alternatives*. Raleigh, NC: City of Raleigh, 1969.

Rathje, William, and Cullen Murphy. *Rubbish! The Archaeology of Garbage*. New York: HarperCollins, 1992.

Royte, Elizabeth. *Garbage Land: On the Secret Trail of Trash*. New York: Little, Brown, 2005.

Strasser, Susan. *Waste and Want: A Social History of Trash*. New York: Metropolitan Books, 1999.

Chapter 8: Telecommunications

DeFleur, Melvin L., and Everette Dennis. *Understanding Mass Communication*. Boston: Houghton Mifflin, 1988.

Douglas, Susan J. *Listening In: Radio and the American Imagination*. New York: Times Books, 1999.

Edgerton, Gary R., and Jeffrey P. Jones. *The Essential HBO Reader*. Lexington, KY: University Press of Kentucky, 2008.

Friedlander, Amy. *Natural Monopoly and Universal Service: Telephones and Telegraphs in the U.S. Communications Infrastructure, 1837–1940*. Reston, VA: Corporation for National Research Initiatives, 1995.

Gordon, John Steele. *A Thread Across the Ocean: The Heroic Story of the Transatlantic Cable*. New York: Perennial, 2002.

Holzmann, Gerard J., and Björn Pehrson. *The Early History of Data Networks*. New York: Wiley-IEEE Computer Society Press, 1994.

Lewis, Tom. *Empire of the Air: The Men Who Made Radio*. New York: Edward Burlingame Books, 1991.

Chapter 9: Transportation

Federal Railroad Administration. *Preliminary National Rail Plan*. Washington, DC, Federal Railroad Administration, October 2009 http://www.fra.dot.gov/Downloads/RailPlanPrelim10-15.pdf.

Friedlander, Amy. *Emerging Infrastructure: The Growth of Railroads*. Reston, VA: Corporation for National Research Initiatives, 1995.

National Surface Transportation Policy and Revenue Study Commission. *Transportation for Tomorrow: Report of the National Surface Transportation Policy and Revenue Study Commission*. Washington, DC: 2007.

Petzinger, Thomas Jr. *Hard Landing: The Epic Contest for Power and Profits That Plunged the Airlines into Chaos*. New York: Times Business, 1995.

Post, Robert C. *Urban Mass Transit: The Life Story of a Technology*. Westport, CT: Greenwood Press, 2007.

ACKNOWLEDGMENTS

Everyone quoted in this book gave generously of his or her time while at the same time trying to keep the water or electricity flowing or the pavement from buckling, and I extend my deepest gratitude to all those who did so. In addition, many people whose names didn't make it into these pages explained historical or background elements in great detail; I provide only a short list of some of those whose names you will not have encountered here:

Raleigh city manager Russell Allen, planning manger Mitch Silver, public utilities director Dale Crisp, and public works director Carl Dawson all spoke with me at length about managing the many systems that keep a city running. Julia Milstead, Mike Hughes, and Becky Daniel helped me find my way through the world of electric power generation, and Melissa Buscher, Amy Bristle, and Herb Crenshaw did much the same with elements of the telecommunications systems.

So many people in so many departments of the city of Raleigh answered so many questions that it wasn't until very late in the game that I noticed that nobody ever told me not to ask or even wondered why I was asking. If I wanted to know how deep the asphalt went or how the sewer pipe laser worked, somebody just found out and told me. If you're looking to borrow a cup of "not my job," drive past Raleigh; they're fresh out.

I'm not an engineer, and not always a very good student, so trying to distill years of history and complexity into 20 or so pages per system struck me as a good way to end up saying something preposterous: that water flows uphill, say, or that radio waves reach their receivers on the backs of tiny flying mice. So I asked people who should know better to read most of the chapters of this book in order to try to limit at least the most humiliating errors. Of course, any errors in this book are my own, but I am grateful to have had as early readers Sherrill Styers, Kris Bass, John Garland, Jon Schladweiler, Eric Lamb, Becky Daniel, Tom Knox, David Kushner, and my beloved friend David Clemens.

A residence at the Weymouth Center for the Arts and Humanities helped galvanize this book. Colin Dickerman and Gena Smith at Rodale provided the kind of editing writers dream of, and Greg Villepique added an enormously helpful line- and copy-edit. Nancy Bailey and Nancy Elgin provided additional fine editing farther down the line. My agent, Michelle Tessler, did an especially fine job shepherding this project from concept to publisher. During completion of this book, the attendees of Souper Night somehow adopted this project and kept it progressing and me functioning, and I thank them all, though I reserve special gratitude to Kirsten Bachmann for conversations and to Jeff Langenderfer for conversations and early readings that helped me find my way. As ever, I am grateful for the support of my fabulous wife, June, and for young Louie and Augustus, who forwent many weekend adventures because Daddy was busy. Additional catering by Leigh Menconi.

INDEX

Boston *(cont.)*
  streets and roads in, 78
  trash management system in, 155
  water supply system in, 66
Bridges, 114–15, 224
British Public Health Act (1848), 79
Brogden, Andy, 67–70
Brooklyn (New York), 79
Brown, Harold, 132
Bureau of Land Management, 19
Bureau of Public Roads (now Federal
    Highway Administration),
    111
Burke, James, 7
Burning trash, 162–63
Buses, 193–98

C

Cadastral surveying, 12, 19
Caesar, Julius, 115–16
California's trash management
    system, 147
"Call before you dig" lines, 26
Cameron Village (Raleigh), 37
Capital Area Transit (CAT), 196–98
Capital Boulevard (Raleigh), 33,
    39–40
CAT, 196–98
Caterpillar Landfill Compactors,
    158–59
C.C. Mangum (infrastructure
    company), 17
Cecil soil, 15
Cell phone, 189–90
Center Road (Raleigh), 100
Central Pacific Railroad, 170
Channelization, 38
Chappe, Claude, 169, 179, 188
Charles River (Boston), 80
Charlotte (North Carolina), 196–98,
    211
Check dams, 43
Chicago
  electrical system in, 133
  sewage system in, 79–80, 92

trash management system in, 155
  water supply system in, 56
Chiffoniers, 154
Chlorination, 58–59
Cholera epidemic (1854), 58–59
Civil Right Act (1964), 198
Clarification tanks, 89–90
Clean Water Act (1972), 29, 39
Clean Water Act (1987), 41
Cleveland, 224
Clifton, Randy, 121, 123–26,
    224–25
Cloaca Maxima (sewer), 35, 78
Coaxial cable, 177, 180
Colton, Mitch, 180, 182–83
Combined sewage overflow (CSO),
    81
Community antennas, 177
Conductors (electrical wires), 123
Congestion pricing, 114–15
Continuously Operating Reference
    Stations (CORs), 23, 27
Coolidge, Calvin, 200
Cooper, Martin, 191
CORs, 23, 27
Crabtree Creek (Raleigh), 34, 37–38,
    40–41, 50, 80
Crabtree Valley Mall (Raleigh), 37
Crisp, Dale, 63, 82
CSO, 81
Cumberland Road (first funded
    interstate), 111

D

Dams, 43, 50, 52–54, 81
Danielson, John F., 37
Dave (engineer and inspector), 87
Daylighting, 45
DC electricity, 132
Decomposition, 89
Degeneration process, 161–62
Dempster, George, 47
Denver, 108
Department of Transportation
    (DOT), 104

P

"Packet sway," 176
Panama Canal, 212
Paper mills and pulping, 152
Paper, recycling, 150, 152–53
Paris (France), 77–78, 105
Passenger rail service, 211–12
Paving streets and roads, 95–98
Peel, John, 121, 125
PET, 150
Philadelphia
  design of, 14
  sewage system in, 45, 78
  stormwater management system in, 45
  streets and roads in, 78
  trash management system in, 152, 155, 165
  water supply system in, 56, 66–67
Philip II (French king), 77
Philip VI (French king), 77
"the Pig." *See* Pigeon House creek branch
Pigeon House creek branch (Raleigh), 33, 35–41, 44, 46–50, 81, 215
Pigs and trash management system, 153–54
Plain old telephone system (POTS), 185–86, 189
Planes and airports, 199–206
Polyethylene terephthalate (PET), 150
Portland (Oregon), 44–45
POTS, 185–86, 189
Power outages, 129–31
Power usage, 138–40, 144–45
Progress Energy (North Carolina power company), 118–21, 123–24, 128, 130, 138–40

R

Radio, 173–75
Rag pickers, 154
Railroads, 181, 194–95, 206–13

Rain gardens, 44
Raleigh (North Carolina)
  as best place to live, 2–3
  design of, 14
  drought in, 4–6
  electrical system in, 121–28, 131–32
  GIS and, 25
  growth of, 1–3
  infrastructure in early, 206
  railroads in, 207–13
  sewage system in, 74–75, 80–92
  soil of, 15–16
  stormwater management system in, 29–30, 35–37, 41–44, 46–50
  streets and roads in, 98–105, 107–8, 113–15
  telecommunications system in, 170–75
  telephone in, 171–73
  television in, 175–80
  terrain of, 14–15
  transportation system in, 193–98, 207
  trash management system in, 148–53, 156–61
  Tropical Storm Hanna in, 50
  water supply system in, 4–6, 50–60, 63–64, 226
  water usage in, 54–55, 70–71
Raleigh and Gaston Railroad, 207
Raleigh-Durham International Airport (RDU), 199–200, 202–6
Raleigh Solid Waste Services Department, 147, 156
Rare-earth magnets, 150
RAS, 90
Rathje, William, 161
RDU, 199–200, 202–6
Reagan National Airport, 199
Reagan, Ronald, 22
Real estate development, 2–3, 13, 102–3
Real Time Kinematic (RTK) networks, 23, 27